THE MUSIC OF JOHANN SEBASTIAN
BACH
THE CHORAL WORKS
STEPHEN DAW

Rutherford • Madison • Teaneck
Fairleigh Dickinson University Press

Associated University Presses, Inc.
4 Cornwall Drive
East Brunswick, N.J. 08816

Associated University Presses Ltd
69 Fleet Street
London EC4Y 1EU, England

Associated University Presses
Toronto M5E 1A7, Canada

Library of Congress Cataloging in Publication Data

Daw, Stephen.
   The music of Johann Sebastian Bach, the choral works.

   Bibliography: p.
   Includes index.
   1. Bach, Johann Sebastian, 1685–1750. Choral music.
I. Title.
ML410.B1D27   784.1′0092′4   78-68624
ISBN 0-8386-1682-8   AACR2

Cover design by Mike Carney

Printed in the United States of America

This book is dedicated to my wife
GILLIAN
and to all others who concern themselves
in performance with the essence of great music

Contents

Acknowledgements

The author acknowledges the work of many individuals and the various institutions responsible for much of the material presented here. The world of Bach scholarship would today be quite different (and out-of-date and mistaken) were it not for the prodigious industry and the clear-sighted wisdom of a few individuals. Without the work of Alfred Dürr, Georg von Dadelsen, Werner Neumann, Christoph Wolff, Hans-Joachim Schulze, Arthur Mendel, Walter Blankenburg and their many colleagues in the production of the "Neue Bach-Ausgabe," this book would have added little to a general impression of Bach's choral music already present in England by 1950; as it is, so much information has since come to light that there is now an urgent need for an up-to-date book on the subject in the English language.

Music has more to it than historical fact and critical discussion: our picture of Bach and his time would also be quite contrasted without the expert and devoted work of specialist musicians: the inspiration of performers of the calibre of Alice and Nikolaus Harnoncourt, Gustav and Marie Leonhardt, the Kuijken family, Frans Brüggen and Concerto Amsterdam remains an influence that ought to be recorded. Among those in close contact with the author, whose counsel has always proved stimulating and reliable, Jaap Schroeder and Peter Williams deserve a special mention here: their performances have made a lasting impression.

Insofar as the book is inadequate or inaccurate, responsibility clearly rests with the author: many of the remaining original materials must be attributed to his remarkable good fortune in being surrounded by an encouraging family, in being trained by a number of outstanding teachers, and in enjoying, both as a student and as a lecturer, the privilege of working with excellent colleagues and students.

For assistance with the discography, special thanks are due to David Naylor and a number of record companies who supplied information and even recordings on request: the British representatives of

Telefunken and Deutsche Grammophon, and the small British firm Peerless Records, were especially helpful. For advice regarding the text, to Robin Leaver and my father, Leslie Thomas Daw. For services in reading and checking, to my brother, John Richard Daw, and my wife—also my dedicatee. The illustrations include a coloured one specially supplied with permission by the Museum der Geschichte der Stadt Leipzig; the specially commissioned impression of Bach, sketched from preserved portraits by Barbara Money, also deserves mention.

Finally, thanks are due to the publishers, and most particularly to the series editor Derek Elley, for patience, practical assistance and co-operation throughout this project.

Editorial Preface

This series is specifically designed to explore the sound of each composer as his most distinctive feature, and, to this end, recognises the equally important role that recordings now play in musical life. Footnotes throughout the main text contain critical references to such recordings when it is felt that they clarify or highlight the composer's intentions. In the Appendix, these and other recommended recordings are re-grouped in a purely factual listing of catalogue numbers, performance details and any divergencies from the composer's expressed wishes.

Since the aim of the series is to clarify each composer's sound, particularly for the non-specialist, this approach should prove doubly rewarding: treating concert music as a living rather than an academic entity and showing the virtues and faults of its reflection through Twentieth-century ears.

Introduction

The extremely practical nature of Bach's music must command the
respect and admiration of anybody who has taken the trouble to consider
it in appropriate contexts. In discussing it, any writer must constantly
face the fact that he cannot do justice to it; Bach's own ability to
fashion his material expressively, yet without losing either coherence
or unity, is remarkable, and such peaks are beyond the sight of so-called
creative criticism. Writers who have contemplated Bach have therefore
usually avoided extended general accounts of his choral music, restricting
themselves in scope so as to avoid the accusation that their work
"lacks the commanding rightness of the subject it treats."

This book is quite a short introductory study to a larger range of
music than is usually discussed between two covers. To treat *all* the
choral music (instead of, say, the cantatas alone) is rare outside general
studies of Bach's whole output, yet it has been kept as a priority here
that no important music for voices composed by him should be omitted
from consideration. The treatment is chronological, but uneven. The
unevenness is the result of two factors: the first is the inadequate
knowledge of Bach's own compositional activities, which results in
there being far more precise information about some periods of his life
than others; the second is my decision to try to stress the progress of
Bach's personal creative development in the light of recent researches
which have quite revolutionised our impressions. Emphasis has been
placed, therefore, upon the earlier, rather than the later, works which
display any particular characteristic, with the result that, for example,
the years 1726/27 are given far less extensive treatment than they
might have been accorded in a study designed to select its materials
more "evenly."

Bach's practicality was, of course, incomprehensible to those
generations between his time and our own who had little notion of the
musical practices of his day. Although his music has sturdy qualities

that enable it to retain power or grace despite all manner of distortion, this was, in a sense, to its grave disadvantage. When Bach's choral compositions were otherwise barely known, his four-voice chorales were suffering emaciating "corrections" at the hand of the patronising Carl Maria von Weber, who removed from them "crudities" which might offend the taste of a "superior" age. It is partly because of our increasing awareness today of the real sounds Bach expected to hear, and of their significance, that his choral music peculiarly suits this series of books devoted to the sound-worlds of the great composers. Because Bach was so comprehensive and thorough in his art, our reward is so much the greater. Until after 1950, only a few far-sighted organists and even fewer imaginative students of instrumental history had more than a scant notion of his skill in the manipulation of sound-colours. Bach, once considered as "master of the organ and polyphony," is, indeed, a master of far more, and as we discover more about his contemporaries, his surroundings and his personal history, our respect for his creative vision, as well as his created achievement, must grow.

Ironically, we really know very little of Bach himself. Our impressions depend heavily upon limited materials, many of which demand thorough investigation themselves. Two examples illustrate the problem. Bach's appearance is most familiar as portrayed in Haussmann's late portrait of 1746: there are two versions of this portrait, the better-known of which is on view to the public in the important Leipzig Museum für Geschichte der Stadt. That museum displays in its galleries a considerable number of other Haussmann portraits—mainly portraits of the city's Burgomasters whose elections were celebrated in Bach's *Ratswahl* compositions. Haussmann's style is well represented by the Bach portrait; but the austerity of the pose, the actual physical build, the height of the forehead, the character within the eyes are no more —or little more—Bach's own than they are those of Haussmann's other subjects. When we recall that the wig also obscures much of the composer's appearance, and that Haussmann's manner of portraying the lips, in an age of dental and hygienic ignorance, is but a tidier version of his English contemporary Hogarth's, we begin to wonder how far Bach is represented at all. No doubt he is; but how, and how far, are subjects for consideration and debate: little can be taken for granted.

Closer to the choral works and their history is the well-known account of Bach's short temper during a cantata rehearsal: Bach flung his own wig at the "organist of the Thomaskirche," who, though in general competent, on this occasion had made such a serious mistake that Bach also shouted to him that he should have been a cobbler. This report dates from 1850 and C. L. Hilgenfeldt's disorganised and generally untrustworthy book on Bach; through its date, it cannot be first-hand. We have a first-hand report from Bach's pupil Johann Christian Kittel that Bach's continuo accompaniments were played by "one of his most capable pupils" rather than the organist of the Thomaskirche, a view that is accepted today. Hilgenfeldt was apparently imprecise in his knowledge, which casts doubt on his sources: he has also either invented or accepted a factual error, and his report must be taken as unreliable. Quite how far it is fictional may never be known, yet it has been printed in English translation among much more reliable reports, and without a detailed source-reference.

Bach's contemporaries seem to have had as little notion of Bach's remarkable creative abilities as he expressed himself. They did vary in their opinions regarding his significance, but even as a brilliant keyboard virtuoso he commanded respectful admiration rather than enthusiastic adulation or extravagant material reward. Nineteenth-century historians expressed much surprise regarding this treatment, which they saw as an undervaluation of genius, but their opinion was itself limited by the subjective considerations of the period which they represented. As for Bach's own times, they were dominated by a tradition of feudal service, in which each individual, like each instrumental line within a section of music for "broken consort," was seen to have a particular "place": this place was still determined partly by birth, partly by economic prosperity, partly by personal good fortune in education and in simply being in the right place at the right time. Opportunism was at least as much the key to professional success then as it is today: professional skill, dedication and finesse were admired in a master-craftsman but such admiration did not extend beyond the limits considered as appropriate. Nobody asked Bach for his opinions regarding politics or religion, but questions of many kinds are recorded regarding Bach's methods of approaching specific musical problems—especially problems regarding performance. The theory that Bach gradually became more of a middle-class, bourgeois townsman as his life progressed, that he planned to publish his music more and more extensively so as to gain fame and fortune in the latter part of his life, does not conform readily to the pattern of philosophy usual in efficient and industrious individuals who have a successful record by the standards of family tradition. Neither does the theory stand very firm in the face of the evidence, which indicates that, if Bach was not actually more conservative as a composer towards the close of his life, he was nevertheless at least as varied in stylistic output as he had been in earlier periods: his published output from 1739 consists mainly of highly effective applications of traditional techniques.

*

A few terms require clarification. Bach himself did not often use the word "cantata" (*Kantate*); to his generation, the word *Kirchenstück* (plural: *Kirchenstücke*) indicated the kind of music we associate with the word "cantata," both in general and in particular. Further, it might be used also as a general term for Passion music, oratorios, Magnificat or Mass compositions. To Bach, the word "cantata" would imply Italianate operatic connotations which are only occasionally appropriate, and an attempt has been made here to indicate where that is the case.

The reader is expected to know the meanings of terms such as "recitative," *arioso*, "chorale" and "motet," although to understand their associations for Bach himself may require some reflection or study: conventional opera of Bach's time, for example, with its dramatic set-pieces, its cultivation of the *confidante* in solo song and duet, its heroes of youthful contralto register (falsetto, castrato, even treble), was something that is quite remote from our experience today. Words with special German significances—"pietism," "orthodox Lutheranism"—the chorales and the social order of Bach's times are well introduced by Spitta, Bruford, Terry and Geiringer, all mentioned at the end under Recommended Books. To a German scholar, "madrigalian texts" are those especially cultivated in the Seventeenth to Eighteenth centuries in which imagery and symbolism are so deployed within rhymed or metrical verse as to become its principle distinguishing feature: the "death-wish" so frequently attributed to Bach himself was a fashionable development in such poetry. This species of verse dominates those arias, recitatives and even occasional choruses where direct biblical quotations and established chorale texts are absent from Bach's libretti. Obviously, chorales whose stanzas date from the Seventeenth century or later often themselves display the influences of madrigalian verse.

The reader should perhaps be warned that Bach's music will sometimes puzzle him, provoke him, demand responses from him. To expect music written for other purposes to soothe us is misguided but, in any case, response to any art so far removed from that of our own times almost inevitably results in our being confronted with questions, some of which cannot be answered at all. In the case of Bach, we can only count ourselves fortunate that so much has been preserved, so much rediscovered, and so much disseminated to enrich our experience. Bach would have been amazed and shocked to see the reverence with which he and his work are regarded throughout the world today, and if he had been able to forecast this, he might well have ceased to compose, have composed differently, or have died younger. The universal quality of his creative output recalls outstanding artists of other fields —Shakespeare, Michelangelo—who have also developed their arts along personal paths to penetrate the consciences and the consciousness of our civilisation. Yet we know enough of the man himself to share in his bourgeois existence, to understand to some degree why he quarelled with his colleagues or made a lasting impression upon his more able students. His expressive language reminds us that we have a common heritage, and his impressive faith inspires and invites us to dwell upon the great mysteries. One could hardly expect of anybody a better sense of proportion than one encounters, in many manifestations, throughout Bach's choral music. It is because of that sense of interrelationship that the personal, the universal, the local and the infinite fit together so perfectly. The English Eighteenth-century musician Sir John Hawkins wrote that musical enjoyment was equivalent to the aesthetic pleasure derived from the observation of the sphere, the cube or the cone. He has been much ridiculed on account of the observation. The proportions, relationships, dimensions and perfection of Bach's music—from the same century—might teach us that Hawkins, who had the good fortune to see special qualities in that music at a remarkably early date, was trying to express something that is, in fact, profoundly true.

Bach the Man

Bach was born on March 21, 1685, the son of Ambrosius Bach, musician, of Eisenach in Thuringia, an area of Lutheran South-Western Saxony noted for its provincial character (there are no large towns) and its musical traditions, which are alike bound up with traditions of organ-building and -playing and the history of the almost ubiquitous Bach family; in some places, it is reported that the very word "Bach" was understood to mean "musician." Johann Sebastian's mother died when he was only nine years old, his father less than a year later, so that he was adopted by his eldest brother Johann Christoph (1671–1721), who took him to live in his own home in Ohrdruf. There the young Sebastian began to excel academically and musically as a professionally successful treble singer: he also commenced his musical studies on keyboard and possibly also stringed instruments.

At the age of nearly fifteen, Sebastian and one of his Ohrdruf schoolmates, Georg Erdmann, were accepted as specialist singing scholars of the famous Mettenchor (Matins-Choir) attached to the Michaeliskirche in Lüneburg. Lüneburg is over two hundred miles north of Ohrdruf, so that this marked the beginning of Sebastian's sturdy independence, a characteristic which he inherited from his forbears. The move also formed a logical continuation of his musical and general education: the Lüneburg choir library is known to have contained large quantities of good Lutheran church music of all previous periods and types. The school's training in literature (Greek, Latin and the vernacular) and theology was thoroughly orthodox in its adherence to Luther's teaching. Perhaps more striking were the influences of neighbouring musical establishments. The brilliant and refined organist composer Georg Böhm, himself resident in Lüneburg since 1698, was organist of the Johanniskirche; Böhm himself, whilst probably of Bohemian extraction, had been born near Ohrdruf in 1661, and may well have been in touch with Johann Christoph Bach and his family in the 1690s. Slightly further away, but certainly visited during this period by the youthful Sebastian, was the distinctly Frenchified court at Celle, where highly-refined performance practices and an artistically sympathetic cultural climate fascinated the impressionable youth. Better still, his ability on the violin was recognised there, and he gained occasional freelance employment for the first (recorded) time as an instrumentalist. By Easter 1702 Sebastian had completed his studies at Lüneburg's Michaelisschule, and the loss of his treble voice (around 1701/2) led him to terminate his scholarship in the Mettenchor. His precise activities for the next year-and-a-half are still obscure but, after a very brief period of service for the Weimar Archduke Johann Ernst (1664–1707), on August 14, 1703, he took up his first post of independent distinction: that of organist of the Arnstadt New Church. His musical apprenticeship was now at an end.

Arnstadt was a pleasant, up-to-date town of quite some distinction. Its situation as the local capital of a rambling rural area, with a ruling archduke of good taste and more than usual perspicacity, produced a pleasant environment in which Bach began to follow what had for years appeared to be his inevitable professional vocation. However, his talents resulted in minor criticisms of his personal behaviour and even of his organ-playing. During the winter of 1705/6, Bach arranged for his deputy to perform his duties during his absence, and travelled to Lübeck in order to hear the famous composer Buxtehude: it is extremely likely that during this visit Bach heard both organ and choral music by Buxtehude, including also the notable *Abend-Musiken* (evening concerts of sacred music performed during Advent) organised by the master in Lübeck's imposing Marienkirche; he overstayed his permitted leave by a substantial period—usually taken as indication of a prolonged stay in Lübeck, but possibly evidence of visits to other northern towns *en route*.

In late October 1707 Bach became organist of the Blasiuskirche in Mühlhausen: this was a reasonable promotion for the twenty-two-year-old musician, who had just married his cousin Maria Barbara (1684–

1720). Mühlhausen afforded Bach the opportunity of composing church choral music for purposes other than weddings and funerals (!), and his brief period of service was well recognised locally. When he left in 1708 to take up a Court Chapel post, this was again recognised as a logical progression.

The Court Chapel Organist's post was in Weimar, in the palace of the brother of his former employer there, the Archduke Wilhelm Ernst. This employer was somewhat conservative and eccentric in disposition, but he was interested in both theology and all aspects of worship, including the musical ones. Bach's appointment at a young age to this post marked him as a notable performer on the organ, whose reputation was now spreading further afield than his immediate locality: similar impressions are gained through a study of his apparently contemporary organ compositions, and through his increasingly being consulted—again at rather an early age—regarding both proposed and executed organ construction. By 1713 a young musician sent to study in Weimar could write:

> Until Whitsun the organ in the Castle here will be in optimum condition . . . Also, especially after the new Weimar organ is ready, Herr Bach will play incomparable things upon it; thus I shall be able to see, hear and get copies of a great deal . . .

During this period, Bach apparenty commenced the collection and composition of his own works especially with a view to their assembly in groups: this applies especially to the organ chorale settings (partitas and the *Orgelbüchlein*), but it seems probable that certain chamber works (especially trio-sonatas for two violins and bass which have barely survived in that form) and keyboard pieces (early suites, toccatas) may also have been considered for collective presentation. It appears from the preserved Weimar organ music of the period by Bach, Walther, and others whose music their pupils and admirers copied, that two sorts of chorale settings were especially required in the town. One was the standard type of the day—a fairly expansive treatment of any structural type, in a rather improvisatory style, but written down so as to facilitate a more intricate kind of contrapuntal organisation. These pieces had grown out of the *expressive* type of organ-setting, in which the organist preluded in the place where a chorale would otherwise have been sung by the congregation. The more specifically local type was far shorter in duration and—most especially in the hands of Bach—of extremely dense and intensive structure and character: although such settings may have grown out of the chorale-praeambula played by German organists before the congregation began to sing, this does not appear to have been their function in Weimar. In the Schlosscapelle where Bach worked there would hardly have been a "congregation" in the usually accepted sense. Although Bach's *Orgelbüchlein* preludes obviously serve as master-examples of motivic manipulation, of improvisatory embellishment beneath or around a chorale line and of mood- and word-painting after the manner of the day, their precise applications in church services are unknown, and it is better to admit this than to pretend that we do know.

On March 2, 1714, Bach was promoted in Weimar to the post of Concertmeister—a position that effectively increased both his status and his salary. His twenty-ninth birthday was approaching, and even though he had probably hoped for promotion to an even more responsible appointment in the preceding months, the creation of the new post for him was itself an honour. The new appointment necessitated, besides its titular function of leading the court orchestra (presumably from the first violin desk), that of composing monthly a piece of sacred vocal music for the archduke's chapel. Bach probably tried to arrange things in such a way that he would, within four years or so, have completed a year-cycle (Jahrgang) of such pieces: the idea of fulfilling a larger purpose by assembling the parts came gradually, as much from the Lutheran concept of the Works of the Spirit as it did from Bach's own ambition, which was probably kindled by a growing acquaintance with foreign models by such composers as De Grigny and Vivaldi. It seems probable that contact between Bach and J. G. Walther—a distant cousin of Maria Barbara and hence also of Bach himself—widened Bach's local and international awareness of repertoire and even performance practice.

During this period Bach's musicianship resulted in his increasing recognition locally and elsewhere. There was some degree of competition between those seeking him as a teacher. He was becoming recognised as an authority on the organ. By the end of 1717 his services were even sought in the final "proving" of the largely-rebuilt Scheibe instrument of the Paulinerkirche, Leipzig—the town's most ambitious instrument to date, and one that required an assessor whose expertise was both mechanically and tastefully aware, but also up-to-date in matters of style, for it had been commissioned by Leipzig's fashion-conscious university, and was, indeed, of "progressive" design. In the preceding autumn, Bach had apparently been put forward as a local representative in a harpsichord-playing competition with the distinguished Frenchman Louis Marchand. As an organist, he was in 1717 simply referred to as "dem berühmten Organisten zu Weimar Hrn. Joh. Sebastian Bach" ("the distinguished Organist of Weimar . . .") by Mattheson, who was writing in Hamburg where he had been in frequent contact with Handel: both Mattheson and Handel were regarded as outstanding organists. These external approbations probably impressed Bach but little: his attention was always focused on immediate musical problems, and the results of this professionalism mark all of the surviving complete compositions. That feeling of controlled rhythmic and expansive power which was appearing in his music then would be retained, and would distinguish his music from that of even his most admired contemporaries until fatal infirmity interrupted his final creative schemes.

The new retrospective attitudes to music which Bach seems to have adopted and embraced at Weimar led him away from its esoteric but conservative court to the employ of Prince Leopold I of Anhalt-Cöthen. In the course of this transfer of allegiance, Bach fell foul of the Weimar authorities, nominally for "too stubbornly forcing the issue of his dismissal," on November 6 (after not being allowed to leave the Weimar employment within the first three months of his nomination to a clear promotion at Cöthen!). He was henceforth in official disgrace at Weimar, and was only freed after four weeks' confinement; but he was compensated at Cöthen by a special allowance of 50 thalers (the Capellmeister's salary for a month-and-a-half over and above the normal rate, or about double payment for the period of his arrest). Such detention was at that time regarded as unfair, but not particularly exceptional.

At Cöthen, Bach experienced positive appreciation by his music-loving and apparently musically-talented employer. He directed and composed music for a highly capable chamber ensemble—the only one of semi-international calibre that he was ever to control. From September 1720 the prince also employed a family of French singers at quite high wages: they continued in his employment until the following season (the mother probably died but there were two daughters) when they moved on towards Berlin, where Mattheson heard them in July 1722. They were probably then temporarily replaced by Anna Magdalena —possibly with her two sisters (all were singers) and her trumpet-playing father. The Wilken sisters certainly remained in Cöthen for more than a short visit, and Anna Magdalena later became Bach's second wife.

Cöthen's patron Leopold was a Calvinist, but his mother had been a staunch enough Lutheran to persuade his father to build a church for those of her own persuasion: the main town church of Bach's time, the Jacobikirche, and the palace's chapel were, therefore, Calvinistic; the Agnuskirche, the newer building referred to above, was the region's centre of Lutheran orthodoxy, and the place of worship of Bach, his two successive wives, and several of his colleagues. Bach's post contrasted with his previous and succeeding positions in that it did not necessitate the composition of elaborate—or, indeed, any—church music. However, it was one of his tasks to celebrate his employer's birthday and to flatter him at New Year by furnishing suitable odes of homage. A few other occasions presented Bach with opportunities to compose choral and vocal music, but some of the Cöthen pieces in this *genre* were not to survive.

Writing to a youthful friend in 1730, Bach was later to state that he was so happy working for a prince who "both loves and understands music" that he "expects to end *his* days there." Only the short-lived first marriage of Leopold to an unmusical wife resulted in his agreeing "to become a Cantor after serving as a Capellmeister." In fact, the years after 1720 will have been ones in which Bach's two elder sons first began to show academic promise. Probably because Leopold had spoken of his earlier friendship with the Dresden musician Heinichen, Bach had been led to seek wider artistic horizons for his own music; possibly both he and his new wife Anna Magdalena* were anxious to increase the educational opportunities open to his children.

Bach was appointed to the joint post of Cantor (Tertius) in the Thomasschule and Director Chori Musici in the town of Leipzig at the age of thirty-eight. With impressive industry and even more astonishing versatility he immediately started to attend to his basic responsibility: that of providing the town's First Choir with a weekly piece of dramatic religious music designed either to frame or to precede the sermon at the *Hauptgottesdienst*—the main Sunday morning service. Responsible for the musical standards of four churches, only one of which did not require a trained body of part-singers, he was allowed only one full rehearsal with the instrumentalists, and the First Choir occupied most of the allotted one-hour rehearsal on four days of every week. The soloists were probably trained privately in his home; the provision of essential extra instrumentalists was also his responsibility. Astonishingly, Leipzig's professional musicians numbered only eight—the number also available in the provincial town of Mühlhausen.

The striking thing about Bach's work in those first Leipzig years is his output: a tally of nearly ninety new *Kirchenstücke* within two years was none too remarkable in that age of musical craftsmanship —it is only with familiarity that the measure of Bach's achievement becomes apparent. Even so, Bach found time to continue his activities as a composer of keyboard music (especially the Partitas for harpsichord and the Sonatas for organ) and of orchestral chamber music: the *Ouvertüren* (often referred to as Orchestral Suites) are probably products of this stage of Bach's life.

The publication of harpsichord music (the Partitas which eventually became the *Clavierübung*, part I) indicated both that Bach had decided that his keyboard music was worthy of the attention of the rich connoisseurs who could afford such luxuries, and that he had come to realise that other forms of music that he had assembled so far—the

---

* Maria Barbara Bach died whilst Bach and Leopold were in Carlsbad on July 7, 1720. Bach married Anna Magdalena, previously employed as a court singer, on December 3, 1721, after what would then be considered an entirely appropriate interval.

Brandenburg Concerti, the first Cantata Cycles, certain organ music and the unaccompanied solos—were less likely to prosper commercially than domestic keyboard music. Even so, Bach was probably not sufficiently aware of commercial needs, or sufficiently influenced by them, to choose to publish easier suites first (such as the "French" suites, which remained unpublished in his lifetime). In Leipzig, Bach's associations with the Thomasschule, the Nicolaikirche (which had its own day-school) and the university resulted in his being ever more pressingly sought as a teacher and writer of testimonials. His great activity was mainly musical and creative: but the same energies and a forceful argumentativeness characterised the defence of his apparent rights when he considered that these were in danger.

The previous four periods have all started with a clear change of employment for Bach. The next is less clearly defined, and its character is, whilst no less dependent on the composer's activities, more the result of his pursuit of his own inclinations than had apparently been possible hitherto.

The gradual easing off from the composition of the so-called Cantata Cycles became possible largely because Bach had by then prepared suitable musical pieces for most of the obvious biblical interpretations that were likely to arise in sermons at Leipzig's two main churches. His position did not demand continuous original composition so much as a regular furnishing of appropriate pieces: their suitability was the criterion by which they would be judged.

Bach was thus able to turn his attention to new activities—the improvement of his choirs and their accompanists, the greater involvement of skilled students in church music, the drawing of the attention of the authorities to the hindrances he encountered. He was in a position to concentrate his energies as a composer on new, and in many respects original, extensions of his previous activities. The relationship between the *Johannespassion* and the *Matthäuspassion* is an example of his expansion of structure in one kind of piece. The larger forces required to accompany his newly-composed choral music of between 1727 and 1740, together with a new lightness of texture which is now written into many of his scores, became something rarely encountered in his whole output: almost a chronologically related stylistic trait. New activities included his assumption of the direction of one of the two Collegia from Easter 1729. The new involvement in university music-making was particularly relevant to the studies of his two sons Friedemann and Emanuel* and, after each had left Leipzig and the University,†

---

* Friedemann (born November 22, 1710) matriculated on March 5, 1729; Emanuel (born March 8, 1714) on October 1. 1731.

† Friedemann for Dresden in late June 1733; Emanuel for Frankfurt-on-the-Oder in late August or early September 1734.

he lodged a student (often a youth of the Bach family) in their places: the most important of these from the biographical point-of-view is Elias Bach of Schweinfurt, who served also as Bach's private secretary between early (by April) 1737 and November 1742. Many students of the university approached Bach for musical tuition and examination in order to obtain testimonials for future musical employment. The mature and respected musician found his organ-playing acclaimed in Dresden and Cassel. In 1735 the publication of the second volume of the *Clavier-übung* was probably inspired by and intended as a homage to the internationally-conscious François Couperin (who had died in 1733)—a grand gesture which would have gone completely unnoticed earlier in his career: like the Partitas, it probably did not gain much recognition because of its technical difficulty and through mere bad fortune. Bach's position in an important trading and travelling centre which was already becoming famous for its book trade resulted in his being cited as a selling agent for various works including J. G. Walther's "Musicalisches Lexicon" of 1732, a reference-book which tells much about Bach's environment but rather less about him personally and musically than we might wish, partly because of the continuing necessity for caution in discussion of him in its town of origin, Weimar.

During the 1730s, Bach began to seek for musical recognition from the Royal Electoral House of Dresden: this he eventually obtained in the form of an honorary composer's position which was non-residential, but which enabled him to refer to himself as Royal Polish and Electoral Court Composer from November 19, 1736, onwards. The period ends with a fine occasional publication in the form of *Clavierübung III*, a magnificent set of chorale-based pieces for organ, composed to celebrate the two hundredth anniversary of the adoption of Reformation theology and philosophy in Leipzig. The varied treatments accorded to the chorales within the collection—those associated in particular with the large and small Catechisms of Luther himself—naturally compare most interestingly with those of the same chorales in the choral works.

Bach's last ten years saw him particularly active in the composition, collection and even the dissemination of his music. Partly this tendency was the result of a fashion followed by others: a composer was then expected to publish more than had been the case in Bach's youth, and his published music to be discussed in the new critical press. In Leipzig, Lorenz Mizler began to give lectures in music at the university; in Berlin, Emanuel Bach's house was frequented by the poets Lessing, Rammler and Gleim; in Halle, Friedemann published harpsichord sonatas and advertised them there and in Leipzig; critics squabbled—as they probably will never cease to do—over Bach's compositional methods, the appeal or otherwise of his music, the "academicism" of his counterpoint and the meticulous ornamentation written out in some of his scores.

As the "age of reason" gained its hold on the German towns, Bach could not avoid being affected, but, like Goethe, he showed little evidence of real involvement, more an inclination to observe and bear witness. Bearing witness is a recurring feature of his work: yet it would be foolish to assume that Bach's attitude was principally that of a representative of conservatism, as many writers have done. In his later years, the composer seems to have been very much concerned with two aims: first, to create overwhelmingly masterly examples for those who have the ear and the heart to notice; second, to try, in the same music, to demonstrate the unnecessary nature of the barrier which earlier and contemporary critics had tried to erect between Music of Demonstration (*Musica Accademica*) and Music of Expression (*Musica Prattica*). The first of these aims was generous, slightly intimate and affectionate in nature; the second was the result of deep thought about the nature and function of music as it had usually been understood in European civilisation.

Bach died, after an illness of uncertain but considerable duration, on July 28, 1750. He had enjoyed good health and reasonably good fortune by the standards of his profession and time, and there was no reason for the public that failed to recognise the riches within his scores to mourn him with more than the customary tokens of respect and regret at his passing. His unhappy widow and her luckless dependants were to be homeless and poverty-stricken now that the mainspring of their existence and prosperity was gone. The family's shortage of the practical human essentials is all the more pitiable when we consider Bach's own scrupulously practical nature, and the wholesome and considerate humanity of his output. Accounts of his life usually draw attention to details including the careers of his children, his various wranglings with the Leipzig authorities, his extremely interesting preserved instructions and recommendations regarding certain musical matters. In fact, his outward life was generally fairly conventional, more than usually successful for a musician of his background and family. Comparatively few factual details form the foundations for the amazingly diversified but complex superstructures which have been constructed by historians: the connotations of the French word *histoire* have much to commend themselves with regard to the *story* of Bach's life. Although the questions that we shall find posed by the music are also many, at least there is a sounder degree of communication here than there is in the apparatus of the conventional historians.

1: Youthful Choral Works

Bach was promoted to the position of Concertmeister on March 2, 1714. Thenceforth, until his death, his terms of employment constantly involved him in the provision of regular or occasional vocal pieces, so that he became a professional composer of *Stücke*: previously, his output had been occasional and generally to commission. However, the idea that Bach's lack of experience left him deficient in expressive power does not hold water with regard to these so-called early works. At the age of twenty-two, Bach wrote two cantatas of peculiarly expressive and polished character, and there are also few, if any, signs of immature or unfinished technique in the remaining completed works.

CANTATA NO. 131, *Aus der Tiefen* (Out of the deeps), was written at the request of the Mühlhausen pastor Georg Christian Eilmar, who officiated in the Marienkirche there during Bach's period as organist of the Kirche Divi Blasii. The text, which Eilmar himself may well have selected, is taken from Psalm 130 and Bartholomäus Ringwaldt's chorale of appeal to Christ, "Herr Jesu Christ, du hochstes Gut" (1588). The work has certain characteristics that remind us of the continuous madrigalian philosophical works of Buxtehude: partly, the text dictates this, but partly Bach seems to have revelled in the chance to employ such a style.* Structurally, the mainsprings of the work are juxtaposition of pregnant and plastic motives and contrasts of texture; materials are drawn from Italian instrumental sonata styles and more motet-like, even rhetorical chorus-work. The cantata is in outline symmetrical:

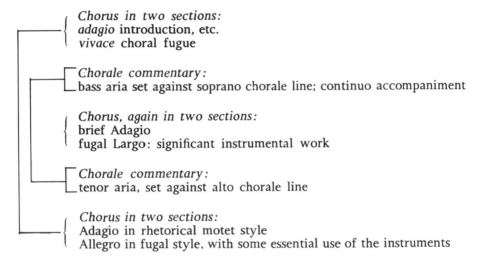

Chorus in two sections:
adagio introduction, etc.
vivace choral fugue

Chorale commentary:
bass aria set against soprano chorale line; continuo accompaniment

Chorus, again in two sections:
brief Adagio
fugal Largo: significant instrumental work

Chorale commentary:
tenor aria, set against alto chorale line

Chorus in two sections:
Adagio in rhetorical motet style
Allegro in fugal style, with some essential use of the instruments

Bach almost certainly designed the work in this balanced way quite deliberately. It was considered at the time natural and reasonable for music, as architecture, to be constructed in such simple symmetrical patterns. One effect of such a structure is that it forces the attention of the composer and the listener who is provided—as was customary— with a text-sheet to the inner movements: again, a parallel may be drawn with late Seventeenth-century classical architecture. Here, we encounter the two chorale commentaries† and the central choral prelude and slow fugue which separates them.

The first commentary is a study in contrasting sensations: the bass aria of anxiety is answered by a reassuring verse from the chorale. The

---

* Bach had travelled to Lübeck in the winter of 1705/6, and had outstayed his leave to hear Buxtehude, and probably also to associate with him. A good idea of Buxtehude's personal fluid style in setting Psalm-texts may be gained from records: *Mein Herz ist bereit* is given a spirited, if slightly unpolished performance under Hans Thamm; *Herr, wenn ich nur dich habe* is tidily presented under Hans-Martin Linde. These two works (BuxWV 73 and 39 respectively) make an interesting comparison generally with Bach's earliest cantatas.
† The free part usually comments upon sentiments mentioned in or represented by the chorale in this type of movement, but occasionally the relationship of the two voices may be reversed: in either case, the term "chorale commentary," which is this author's invention to describe such movements, seems appropriate.

delicately poignant oboe obbligato exploits the sighing semitone *appoggiature* and the delicate arabesques that we associate with sadness and uncertainty, but the firm, mostly stepwise and purposeful bass-line has contrasting purposes—particularly since the harmonies it supports are largely straightforward and diatonic: it serves the musical purpose of keeping together the otherwise rather broken lines of the bass voice and oboe, and through this the dramatic one of providing a link between the perplexed Psalmist, the Christian consolation through the chorale, and the witnessing listener: "This," it seems to say, "is how things happen." Bach's magnificent and often highly characterised bass-lines are frequently as essential to his expression as are the more apparently conspicuous upper voices. The second commentary is for the tenor an aria of impatient witness, for the chorale alto one of repentance: as the aria proceeds, the former gains some apparent consolation during the intermediate passage of time. The time of waiting concludes at the ensuing chorus; the chorale refers directly to salvation through Christ's Blood. Both of these movements—and the many like them throughout Bach's works—raise an interesting problem in performance to which no clear solution has yet been presented: should the chorale be sung solo or chorally, and, in either case, should it be sung expressively (in volume, timing, phrasing, even ornamentation) in the manner of an aria, or should it be sung in a more strict and dogmatic manner? There is hardly any written evidence concerning performance traditions in this respect, and one must conclude that the best course in the Twentieth century is to judge each alternative method of presentation on its merits.

The chorus "Ich harre des Herrn" starts rhetorically, and establishes identity between congregation and text by emphasising the diverse interpretation of the word "I"; then follows a fine and dignified accompanied motet-styled chorus on the words "meine Seele harret und ich hoffe auf sein Wort." The yearning and waiting elements are expressed through the sighing vocal suspensions in prolonged chains of chords of the seventh; the delicate patterns of the accompanying oboe and violin lines emphasise the passage of time, partly because their figures are designed on an altogether quicker time-scale (2/4 or 1/4, effectively, as opposed to the vocal 4/4), partly because the steady rocking figures which they weave so attractively* are probably written to sound like the mechanism of a clock: if this is so, it is the first of a number of instances of clock-effects within Bach's music. The whole chorus has the pathetic connotations that Bach seems to have associated with F minor (compare BWV 106, 2d; BWV 12, 2; BWV 21, 5—all in that key), and it would have formed an excellent separate movement to

---

* Unfortunately these are none too clearly audible in the Steinitz recording.

introduce the sermon in a less elaborate service than that heard at Mühlhausen on this occasion.

Together with *Aus der Tiefen* belong the fine funeral cantata *Gottes Zeit* and, in all probability, the chorale-variation cantata *Christ lag in Todes Banden*. At a memorial service, the congregation is placed in a highly impressionable position; Bach's response to this situation in a family setting is one of the most impressive early examples of his sense of appropriate music for any context. CANTATA NO. 106, *Gottes Zeit* (God's time is the best of all), has been much discussed from its structural point-of-view: possibly too much emphasis has been placed on the distinctive instrumentation, which is quite conventional in its use of gambas and recorders at this period. Our consideration will therefore be focused on the estimated effect which the music must have had for those receptive and experienced musicians who were, no doubt, present.*

The work starts with a highly evocative sinfonia. To write music that combines tragedy with dignity was possibly easier in the late Baroque than it has been at any other time in musical history, but even so, the listeners must surely have noticed the command with which the lower gamba is used in the opening trio harmonies,

the intense simplicity of the sighing beaked flutes,

---

* There are two good recordings, under Jürgens and Gottsche. The former is rather smoother and tidier, with the positive advantages of good organ continuo playing from Leonhardt and well-balanced choral treatment of the alto chorale—features lacking in Gottsche's performance. However, the latter has a particularly attractive intimate freshness, and its consequent spontaneity compensates for its slightly less tidy choral ensemble and rather less suave sound qualities.

and the expressive use of discordant intervals:

The opening chorus starts immediately, and continues with a fine ensemble fugue for the full ensemble: the text "In Him we live, move and have our being" is illustrated generally by constant energetic activity, and by the long soprano held note at bars 31–34 on the words "so lange." The third section, marked *adagio assai*, brings us back to the anguish of death and the rightness of God's timing of it. Even an audience familiar with the intense possibilities of Seventeenth-century harmonic colouring would find this passage striking:

In the ensuing tenor aria of agitation a sense of rhetoric and responsibility is communicated through the effective use of the tenor voice, which is clearly invited by the chains of falling thirds to apply *appoggiature*,* through the precise adaptation to the text of the standard operatic pattern and by the highly effective self-developing nature of the quartet accompaniment for six performers. To add to the effect of the tenor solo, it is followed by an even more active and considerably more vigorous bass exhortation to put one's house in order. This short but effective movement might strike us as "modern" for 1708, especially if we pay attention to the recorder flourishes, but it has a considerable resemblance to the "Wachet auf, meine Stimme" section of Buxtehude's *Mein Herz ist bereit*.

As Arnold Schering pointed out in 1927, the magnificent *andante* quartet (always sung as a chorus, but surely possibly for four soloists), with accompaniment including a chorale, is central alike to the cantata's musical structure, to its message of faith and consolation, and to its possible liturgical function. This is a particularly notable piece, striking in its dramatic use of small resources, its effective application of contrasting texts and styles within itself, and highly original in its conclusion, where, contrary to all musical tradition, the upper treble part, the voice of the New Testament and hope, concludes alone with those two essential words: "Herr Jesu." The disciplined fugue of the lower voices is the first preserved example that we can date with any certainty of the chromatic, withdrawn style that Bach used quite frequently to present Old Testament—sometimes even Lutheran—laws and principles in direct statement. There is always a grand inevitability about it, but here this is wonderfully transformed through the addition of the soothing material representing Christ and his church. Well performed, this can be one of Bach's most romantically affective movements. The two following solos—the first for alto the second for bass with an accompanying alto chorale-line—may be said to balance the tenor and bass solos which precede the great F minor chorus. The first, a fine song of trust and hope, is, as we shall later often find in Bach's work, given to a boy alto; the age of eighteen was considered an age full of expectancy: many young men would start work at almost exactly the age at which their voices reached maturity, and it seems highly probable that this particular association was respected alike by Bach and his contemporaries. In the second we encounter another hymn-melody of Thuringian origins: while the aria quotes Christ's promise to the penitent malefactor (St. Luke XXIII, 43: ". . . today shalt thou be with me in Paradise"), the chorale comments, "With peace and joy

---

* A careful study of *appoggiature* indicates that they were particularly favoured in songs expressing emotional purpose: their apparently arbitrary application and/or omission in many of our performances is regrettable.

*1: View westwards from Leipzig in 1740 by
Alexander Thiele*
(Historical Museum, Leipzig)

2: *Stadtpfeiffer Gottfried Reiche holding a coiled clarino* **trumpet,** *by E. G. Haussmann, c. 1730*
(Historical Museum, Leipzig)

I pass away, as God wishes"—a paraphrase of the "Nunc dimittis." The uncle for whose funeral Bach is thought to have composed the *actus tragicus*, Tobias Lämmerhirt (1639–1707), was in all probability a fine and devout old man, so that the parallel with the biblical Simeon would be all the more telling. The final movement, a setting of the doxology verse of the chorale "In dich hab' ich gehoffet, Herr," is interesting in that the instruments are made to enter conspicuously into the expression of the text in a strikingly direct, somewhat rhetorical way: it is also notable that the last lines of the text ("May God-given power . . . Amen.") stress again the main theme of the cantata—the difference between the Old and New Covenants results in our cause for joy when confronted by death, through Christ's salvation. The final "Amen" drives this point home the more emphatically through its extension into fugal treatment. To treat words such as "Hallelujah" and "Amen" polyphonically was quite conventional long before Bach was born; but there can be little doubt that its elaboration in this instance is for expressive, as well as conventional, reasons. It is in *Gottes Zeit* that the great dramatic power, the skill in the characterisation of texts, the absolute ensemble of solo voices, choral voices and instruments, and the treatment of fundamental Christian truths unite for the first time in Bach's preserved music. This is the same Bach who will write the Passion settings and the B minor Mass.

CANTATA NO. 4, *Christ lag in Todes Banden* (Christ lay in death's bondage), is somewhat conservative in its essential structure, since it is designed on the so-called chorale variation principle: each verse, including even the brief but telling Sinfonia, is effectively a variation movement built on the magnificent Easter melody. From verse 1 to verse 7 (all movements except the Sinfonia), the voices sing through Luther's complete text (1524). It is not clear whether the verses for one and for two vocal lines are intended to be taken by soloists, or by the choral *ripieno* of the specified voice—either works well in material of this type. However the music was performed, it is clear that these movements were designed to balance one another outwards:

(Sinfonia)
Versus 1: SATB: chorale fantasia: *cantus firmus* in soprano
Versus 2: SA: imitative duet over pattern bass
Versus 3: T: aria treatment with fiery string accompaniment
Versus 4: SATB: motet treatment with continuo: *cantus firmus* in alto
Versus 5: B: *lamentoso* expanded aria treatment with essential string ensemble work
Versus 6: ST: imitative duet accompanied by essential upbeat "Halleluja" and celebratory *motifs* in the continuo line
Versus 7: SATB: direct four-part harmonisation, but with colouristic harmonies, particularly effective at the final, ritually significant "Halleluja."

It is interesting to compare Bach's scheme with that employed by Johann Pachelbel in his own chorale-variation cantata on the same melody and, essentially, the same text. There is no certainty that Bach was aware of its existence, even though it was certainly composed earlier. Pachelbel does not employ the melody in every verse, although it would not be difficult to trace allusions to it (falling and rising semi-tones, leaps of a third, the harmonic or melodic interval of a diminished fourth—all these are features of the melody's character). His scheme does compare most interestingly with Bach's, however:

(No Sinfonia: however, instrumental prelude of twelve bars, leading up to:)

Versus 1: SATB: chorale fantasia, with *cantus firmus* in soprano

Versus 2: ST: imitative duet, with continuo

Versus 3: B: bass *arioso*, over which the two violin parts play the chorale as a *cantus firmus*

Versus 4: first section: tenor declamation with fierce string battle-effects in illustration of text

second section: tenor, later alto *arioso* with continuo, for the more discursive material of the text and the "Halleluja"

Versus 5: SATB: a motet-styled setting, with instrumental support in sympathetic style to the vocal material, and with the chorale as a tenor *cantus firmus*

Versus 6: ST: musically identical with Versus 2

Versus 7: SATB: free and largely declamatory choral setting with contrapuntal implications

It will be noticed immediately that verse 1 of the text is similarly treated, that Pachelbel's verse 5 is roughly equivalent to Bach's verse 4, and that, although Pachelbel actually uses the same music for verses 2 and 6, both are set as duet movements by the two composers as a foil for the outer movements in more formal styles. The presence of the chorale in Pachelbel's settings of verses 3 and 5 adds to the symmetrical strength of his whole, but the treatment of the central portions of the text (verses 3–5) by the two composers are different, and Bach's preference throughout to sharpen the seventh note of the Dorian mode (usually D sharp) adds a punch to his harmonies that is less prevalent in Pachelbel's. Less directly dramatic is Bach's motet-setting of the description of the conflict between life and death in verse 4: here, he almost seems to have withdrawn into the restrained world of the Classical Unities, where reported action is at its most dispassionate—or seemingly so—when the actions reported are most violent. Pachelbel, on the other hand, not only reports the dramatic and weird conflict with shimmering strings and jagged vocal contours; at the words of scriptural commentary, the commotion of the battle retires, and the alto's final Hallelujas are adorned with the most elaborate melodic embellishments in the work. Verse 5, in which Luther discusses Christ's role as the

Easter Lamb in symbolic allusions, is very effective in Pachelbel's motet setting, but here Bach produces a rather less formal, more personal response in his fine bass lament, with its shuddering references to the murderous intentions of the devil, its effective string accompaniment in a kind of wordless dialogue with the voice, and its flowing sense of progress: the inevitability of Easter is, indeed, conveyed as effectively by Bach's elaborations as it is by the chorale that inspires them.

Some features of Bach's version—the basic structure, which could be traced back through Tunder (1614–67) and Praetorius (1571–1621) to the Sixteenth century; the ostinato- and pattern-accompaniments, which are used in an operatic way; the strict adherence to *cantus firmus* processes without recitative or even *arioso* of the Buxtehude type—these are traditional. Nevertheless, the composition points forwards also. Strict adherence to a chorale text without paraphrase or additional elaboration is, for Bach himself, something that will not return to favour until 1725 (in Cantata No. 137, *Lobe den Herrn*, where, interestingly, the melody of the chorale appears in each verse). Preference throughout the composition for the sharpened leading-note could be claimed as a modern, rather than a traditional, effect. Finally, despite the inclusion of two viola parts (certainly a traditional feature), Bach's music includes technical elements for both violins and continuo cello that are derived from Italian bowing techniques:

These contrast strongly with the far less idiomatic and more functional instrumental parts of Pachelbel's work—even though Pachelbel himself displays his mastery of Italian idioms in his instrumental music.

Our consideration of *Christ lag in Todes Banden* should not end without reference to its evocative Sinfonia, a masterly miniature which, in its way, is no less effective than many of the short chorale preludes for organ which also speak a language deep in associations, and which come to us from Bach and his contemporaries. Whether we try to read into this short introduction an illustration of the Resurrection, a development of material from the first and last lines of the chorale melody simply as music, or an evocative opening invitation to share in the musical experience that is to follow, we ought not to be disappointed.*

Bach's HOCHZEITS-QUODLIBET (BWV 524), a fragment, is of somewhat obscure origin: it was apparently designed for a family or intimate social occasion, the customary celebrations on the nuptial eve at the bride's house. The music is fast-moving, but full of happy, if short-lived, ideas: we admire the fluidity of Bach's simple continuo accompaniment, which anticipates late Weimar and even Leipzig techniques; we smile at the caricatures of academic counterpoint and the Lament essential to any secular cantata of the time. It is sad that the music and text are not all present, but happy that we have even this brief glimpse of the gayer side of Bach's personality at (then) undergraduate age: much of the early choral music is, probably by coincidence, on the sombre side.†

CANTATA NO. 71, *Gott ist mein König* (God is my King of old), was composed for the annual festivities connected with the celebration of civic power at the annual elections. It was composed to commission, and—uniquely among Bach's preserved vocal compositions—was subsequently published (by the council at its own expense). Bach referred to the work as a "Gratulatory Motetto." Its text combines various more or less appropriate Old Testament passages in praise of the Establishment, Just Government and even nostalgia for one's birthplace, with a less literary verse that refers directly to the Emperor Joseph I.

---

* The Concentus Musicus/Chorus Viennensis/Vienna Sängerknaben performance with soloists under Nikolaus Harnoncourt is a pleasantly direct performance, with interesting attempts to recreate the string articulation of Bach's time, but a certain softness in the vocal *timbres* which detracts from the tonal directness of the larger choral movements. Karl Richter's Munich Bach Choir and Orchestra are too large and aggressive to prove effective in this intensely sensitive work, but there is a fine, rather dignified reading under Wilhelm Ehmann which includes the doubling parts for a cornetto and trombones which Bach added temporarily to the work in Leipzig—and most effective they sound, too.

† The *Quodlibet* is attractively and affectionately performed by the Leonhardt Consort. Terry's article in "Music and Letters," January 1933, includes an English attempt to translate the rather nonsensical text.

The opening chorus is notable in that it shows Bach in control of a full festive orchestra for the first time. There are, as the contemporary chronicler reported, trumpets and drums in the ensemble: this fact was not inserted in his report out of mere casual interest—it was significant. The governors of the Free Imperial City were entitled to be acclaimed with a full choir of trumpets—instruments which, at least in numbers of more than two, were reserved for royalty and their immediate representatives through a long-standing monopoly negotiated over a century earlier by the Trumpeters' Guild and the Emperor Maximilian I. Even in Leipzig, where he was in a position of some authority, Bach was seldom to use three trumpets unless he was writing for a church or civic festival, when the council would be in official attendance. *Gott ist mein König* also requires eight skilled wind-players (a less skilled performer would probably play the drums—possibly an apprentice): we know that there were eight professional musical employees (*Stadtpfeifer*) in the town, and these probably played the instruments concerned.

The work is the only one from the first group of preserved sacred pieces to plunge straight into its text without any instrumental prelude. The way in which the various ensembles within the whole are used in rhetorical dialogue—the so-called "concerto style"—is so colourful and dazzling in its effect that it has been described as the *"alfresco* style" —words we associate rather with mature works like the *Magnificat*, and Handel's chorus-work at its most dazzling. The instruments, however, soon fade into the background: after the long, held notes illustrating the words "von altersher," the good fortune of all in receiving God's bounty (through the city council, of course!) is stressed by a motet-like polyphonic setting which makes use of sequences, such as we have already encountered in *Gottes Zeit*, to convey quantity. After the fine chorale commentary on old age, the earnest chorus "Dein Alter sei wie deine Jugend" rounds off the first section. The bass solo introducing the second main idea is a song of praise to the Creator, particularly to the creator of the stars, night and day and the countries of the Earth. Only after we have been impressed by the majesty of the piece do we wonder how it is achieved: the answer is to be found largely in the ponderous, striding bass-line of the accompaniment, which seems to swing on its axis like the heavenly bodies, and which, in its shadings of expression through harmony, gives a sense of evolution from shade to light and back again (see example on next page). This aria might be said to be the musical high point of the cantata.* Its *da capo* form is probably

---

* Particularly when it is sung as well as is the case in the old Leipzig recording by Theo Adam. The performance is otherwise a trifle colourless: the accompaniment to the second movement requires more plasticity of line, that to the fifth greater rhythmic drive and the authentic tone of natural trumpets.

intended to stress the alteration of night and day : it is the first preserved aria to conform simply and directly to this pattern.

The alto battle-aria, No. 5, back in the trumpets' key of C major, is another first preserved example of a later standard type : it is interesting that Bach has chosen the voice of youth and promise (the alto) for this particular purpose. It is followed by a short aria for the choir—that is, a chorus in homophonic style, and in which the soprano dominates the choral writing, whilst there is a distinct figured accompaniment. The final chorus is a particularly interesting movement from the point-of-view of structure and originality of language. Much of the music discussed in this chapter sounds like that of Bach's great predecessors in some respect—and it is none the worse for that. However, the only music that this final chorus is "like" is later Bach.

Less certain in origin is CANTATA NO. 150, *Nach dir, Herr, verlanget mich* (Unto Thee, O Lord, do I lift up my soul); it is believed to come from early in the Weimar period.* It is Bach's earliest extended work in B minor and contains some of the composer's most traditionally rooted music, but also, in the choruses "Leite mich in deiner Wahrheit" and "Meine Augen sehen stets," passages prophetic of Nineteenth-century choral expression. Indeed, the latter sounds so similar to some of Brahms's choral writing that one feels that it was probably through

---

* The recording by Helmuth Rilling and the Gächinger Kantorei/Bach-Collegium Stuttgart makes a valiant attempt to give point and shape to a work that is probably incomplete instrumentally and, as a result, not easy to project: generally, the faster movements and sections sound better than the slower ones (the "Leite mich" intro-duction is surprisingly feeble). In claiming that the work is a study in Baroque *lamento* style, Manfred Schreier's notes adopt a curious argument: the yearning, which is indeed a characteristic of the cantata, is one for enlightenment, godliness and strength—there is no real lament in the music, and no call for it.

his attention being drawn to it that he stumbled upon the *Ciacona* theme of the seventh movement: as is well known, it was this latter motive that Brahms adapted chromatically to form the basis of his Fourth Symphony's Finale.

The "Hunting Cantata," CANTATA NO. 208, *Was mir behagt, ist nur die muntre Jagd* (My chief delight is in the *sporting* [lit.: lively, gay] chase), has an extended and conventionally flowery text by the Weimar Consistorial Administrator Salomo Franck: it would be unjust to judge him solely on this, his first known collaboration with Bach. We have no reason to suppose that Bach had previous experience as a composer of homage-cantatas, although the Mühlhausen *Hochzeits-Quodlibet* had displayed his mastery of secular over-demonstrative conventions in a different, but no less significant way. The circumstances of performance at Weissenfels are none too clear: on the morning of the Duke's thirty-first birthday (February 23) a serenade would have been performed by his Capelle; the composer of this music would probably be his resident Capellmeister Johann Philipp Krieger, whose own sixty-fourth birthday was to follow three days later, and who had been in Christian's service since before Bach's birth. The afternoon would in all probability have been passed in actual hunting, and the evening would have seen, during or after a festive banquet on the spoils of the hunt, the first performance of Bach's allegorical *Tafelmusik* (table music).

The work requires two sopranos, a tenor and bass, and a mixed four-part chorus; usually, in his Leipzig years, Bach would have employed a five-part (SSATB) chorus to support the two sopranos. The orchestra requires two horns, two recorders, two ordinary oboes, one taille (military alto, of straight construction and alto/tenor range), bassoon and continuo ensemble. These forces would not conveniently suit Bach's colleagues in the Weimar Capelle, and there is no preserved record of a wholesale visit by this ensemble to Weissenfels on the occasion. However, on the nearest date at which a record of Weissenfels musicians is available (1726) the performers appear to be highly suitable. There were no regular female singers in the Weimar Capelle: yet Bach's work demands two sopranos, the one a virtuoso coloratura singer representing Diana, the goddess of Hunting, the other a more lyrical voice for the music of Pales, the pastoral goddess and foil of Pan. However, there was no need, apparently, to import a *prima donna* to personify Diana: Christiana Paulina Kellnerin (alias Pauline Kellner), Soprano for many years at Weissenfels, was probably Bach's direct inspiration in writing that part.

The work is constructed in three episodes. 1: dialogue in clearly separated recitatives, arias and a duet, between Diana and the hunter Endymion: her aria praises hunting, his is a conventional love-song; their final recitative discussion and duet bring in Christian's birthday, which is about to be celebrated in pastoral style by Pan; the *scena* occupies Nos. 1–5. 2: Pan and his pastoral partner Pales introduce contrasting elements: his is a cheerful, dance-like aria, the perfect foil to Endymion's pleading love-strains; Pales introduces and, through her beautiful pastoral aria, transfigures the Good Shepherd parallel usual in such compositions (it is ironic that it is through this music alone that Duke Christian has become of any significance to posterity whatsoever); Diana and Endymion are reintroduced through her short introductory recitative to a chorus in praise of the duke, who, having already been twice mentioned as an "earthly Pan," is twice saluted as the "Sun of the Earth"—a particularly well-worn *cliché* of obvious French extraction; this scena comprises Nos. 6–11. 3: the four soloists congratulate Christian generally and wish him a long and prosperous life; Diana and Endymion's duet is an exercise in parallel horizontal movement—a device which Bach associates with unanimity of expression; the aria of Pales is another of great charm, much of which comes from the quasi-*ostinato* bass-line, a highly expressive representation of happy freedom. Pan's final aria, again dance-like, heralds in the final chorus, which, if it were shorter, might sound insincere at the end of Bach's longest preserved choral work to date, but if it were longer, might subject its text to too much repetition.

Bach returned to the material of this work repeatedly—in 1716, possibly around 1720, in 1725 (BWV 68), 1728/29 (BWV 149), 1740 (Neumann V) and 1740/42 (208a). It may possibly have been performed again at Weissenfels in or around 1729, and Bach wrote an interesting instrumental movement over the bass-line of Pales's second aria—his only preserved small ensemble work without voices for which the oboe is prescribed (BWV 1040). No other vocal composition to survive contains so much internal and external evidence of repeated performance by Bach.

The cantata is constructed on the basic operatic plan of alternating recitative and aria for the first ten of its fifteen movements. The last section, which introduces the chorus and eschews recitative altogether, is so distinguished because it is a performance within a performance: it adds to the musical effect by increasing the extent to which the listener's emotions are involved as the work proceeds. A very common weakness in occasional compositions is their lack of cumulative intensity through drama: Bach and Franck have managed to compensate musically and, by re-starting the *Tafelmusik* at the first chorus, to avoid the obvious danger of monotony. The chorus does not sing until ten numbers have passed. This may well have been due to a condition of the original performance, in which some of the chorus were probably required as servants elsewhere in the Weissenfels palace (service at table? washing up?). It is quite possible that here, as elsewhere in music written so consciously to meet practical requirements, Bach has again made a virtue of necessity.*

There remain several pieces whose dating is uncertain, yet which fall into the early period on stylistic or historical grounds. CANTATA NO. 143, *Lobe den Herrn, meine Seele* (Praise the Lord, O my soul), has a text assembled from Psalm 146 and the chorale "Du Friedefürst, Herr Jesu Christ." Dürr goes to some trouble to stress his feeling that the work belongs to the period 1708–14, rather than the Leipzig period, and after examination concludes that it was completed before 1714.

The main interest in the work, apart from the textual and historical aspects, lies in the musical qualities of the three chorale movements which are of such contrasted types. The soprano setting "Du Friedefürst" is a rather remote, awe-filled trio for unison violins, (surely) choral trebles and imitative trio-bass: it anticipates features of the great "Zion hört" chorale setting from Cantata No. 140, *Wachet auf*. The sixth movement, outlined above, is a rather warmer and more personal aria. The final chorus, striking through its introductory Hallelujas, has the elaborate structure of some of Bach's early concluding choruses, but also the strong internal thematic power of the accompanying figures that becomes common in opening movements of the Leipzig Chorale-Cantata Cycle (1724/25, see later). The *concertante* material for the two upper horns is their most challenging, but also their most rewarding, work in the composition.†

Cantata No. 63, *Christen, ätzet diesen Tag in Metall und Marmorsteine!*, and Cantata No. 21, *Ich hatte viel Bekümmernis*, are extended pieces of compound origin which seem to have been started during the early Weimar years, or possibly, in the case of Cantata No. 21, earlier. The later history of CANTATA NO. 63, *Christen, ätzet diesen Tag* (Christians, engrave this day on metal and on marble slabs!) is decidedly vague until the first Christmas that Bach spent in Leipzig (1723), when it was heard, possibly for the first time, in the form published in outline by Rust for Volume XVI of the Bach-Gesellschaft edition (Leipzig, 1868). It was heard later, around 1729. The complexities of its history between 1713, when Bach first had dealings with the Halle poet Heineccius, and 1723 involve doubtful associations with Bach's visit to Halle (December

---

* The best current recording, from Amsterdam under Rieu, gives a good overall impression. The instrumentalists are notably tidy and sweet-toned, and the singing well characterised if generally lacking in zest. The aria for which the work is today famous is played unusually fast, and it is a particularly regrettable fact that we presently lack an alternative, more peaceful version.

† The only section of the work on record is the second movement: Steinitz and the London Bach Society capture the spirit of the music well, although there are smudges of detail; the recording is rather distant, the rhythms a little lifeless.

12, 1713), Christmas in Weimar in that year, and the concurrent celebration of Duke Johann Ernst of Weimar's birthday (December 25). Later, the text was adapted for the Reformation Festival of 1717, which may have involved Bach's music. As Bach's surviving parts (his score or scores have not come down to us) display through the NBA edition, the work has a balanced structure, framed by two fine and extended choruses, in which the unusual luxury of four trumpets (two actually marked "clarini," and thus indicating special talent in the performers) is exploited in a style that is closest to that of *Ich hatte viel Bekümmernis*, strangely, of all the preserved works. There are no ordinary arias, but instead two fine duets; however, the work is most notable for its highly expressive recitatives, of which the instrumentally projected Nos. 2 and 6 are particularly striking. However, the first of these, the fine "O sel'ger Tag," does not strike the present writer as a clearly "early" movement at all: it has rather more of the character of late Weimar works—such as Cantatas Nos. 161 and 132—and might even have reached its final form only at Leipzig. Of the two outer movements, the last is by a small margin the more effective, mainly because the central section of its *da capo* structure has a fugue on two fine and expressive themes:

At first, the contour of the lower line reminds us of the Jewish Law chorus of the *Johannespassion*, but the material is really closer in essence to the thanksgiving/peace chorus of Cantata No. 29 and the B minor Mass. Its essential contours are similar, its cumulative, close entries are used to the same effect, and its employment of the accompanying instrumental ensemble is also comparable.

This chorus also has a similar structure to those from cantatas that we have already studied here. Is it not possible that this single movement was Bach's trial composition in 1713 at Halle, and that he wrote the remaining duets, some recitatives (not necessarily the surviving ones) and the opening for Duke Johann Ernst's birthday, possibly adding the third and fourth trumpet parts also to the final chorus at that stage?

Whether this version for Johann Ernst was designed for church or secular performance cannot be ascertained, but it is quite possible that it was, in fact, already essentially a Christmas piece. The recitatives, which might well be the work of a Weimar poet (Franck?), could have been added for yet another Weimar performance, in which, we may assume, the only one having an instrumental ensemble was the pen-ultimate movement. Finally, the work reached the form we know today at Leipzig, where it was performed three times in slightly different versions. Seen against this hypothetical background, the work becomes understandable and reasonable from historical, source-critical and stylistic points-of-view.*

The fine penitential CANTATA NO. 21, *Ich hatte viel Bekümmernis* (I was exceedingly sorrowful), has a rather less uncertain Weimar history: in short, two early works, both uncertain in purpose, were eventually united to form the eventual whole. One was a nine-movement piece, which became the first nine movements of the final work: it may have been composed after a fire at Mühlhausen in 1707, or it may have been written for its later stated season—Trinity + 3— around 1712. The other source was another large-scale piece, from which the chorus "Das Lamm, das erwürget ist" is derived, and was probably rather more festive in character: perhaps this was the lost Mühlhausen election piece for 1709? The work has clearly been put together with the Gospel and Epistle for Trinity + 3 very much in mind: the former relates the parables of The Good Shepherd and The Lost Coin (Luke, XV); the latter (1 Peter, V, 6–11) is summarised in the words ". . . the God of all grace, who hath called us unto his eternal glory by Christ Jesus, after that ye have suffered a while, make you perfect, stablish, strengthen, settle you." Indeed, the whole subject-matter of the cantata is the turning of deep spiritual suffering into joy through Christ.

Fine though the choruses are—especially the direct, madrigalian "Was betrübst du dich, meine Seele?"—it is for the arias and the introductory Sinfonia that the work is most remarkable. Here we meet

---

* Of the two recordings, under Rilling and Richter, Rilling's is the more pensive and romantic, with a slight lack of immediacy and rhythmic control, especially in the outer choruses; Richter's, however, is too roughly articulated in the outer choruses, and has some poorly-controlled soprano solo work in the first duet. Each has a fine alto, the Stuttgart performance Hildegard Laurich, the Munich Anna Reynolds. The Frankfurt Choir is at its best in lyrical moments like the quoted fugue from the Finale, but its approach to the opening of the same movement combines with instrumental awkwardness of articulation to break up the flow of the whole. The large Munich Bach Choir has a heavier accompaniment, but still plenty of grace, as we hear in its final account of the dance-duet "Ruft und fleht den Himmel an"; the choir itself is extremely tidy and well-disciplined, and its style is well suited to the homophonic openings of the great choruses: however, the shrill tone of the Munich trumpets and that one deficient soloist would persuade many purchasers to prefer Rilling.

an expressive intensity, an apparent involvement, that gives the music's poignancy an added immediacy. Trio textures predominate; the rhythms have a free, expansive quality that sounds right, whether the phrases are orthodox and even

or extended.

The Sinfonia, the oboe solo part of which has features in common with the obbligato of a duet from Cantata No. 63, is effectively a Bachian application of Corelli's trio-sonata style: this is a fact of some significance, if the work has original connections with the young Weimar Prince, Johann Ernst, whose expected return from Utrecht in 1713 prompted a musical youth then in Weimar to expect to hear "much fine Italian and French music." There is also the possibility that Bach's copy of Frescobaldi's *Fiori musicali* was a parting gift, or even a birthday present from the same prince. The exception to such trio-domination is the tenor's aria of anxiety and grief, "Bäche von gesalznen Zähren," which is a fine string-accompanied piece. The sobbing strings and the agonised runs as the poet is alarmed at being swamped by the tempest of his grief are both derived from the text. This aria has the clear thematic style of accompaniment, with extended ritornello patterns that Bach used freely throughout his mature works: the combination of expressive fluidity with structural control is already characteristic, however.*

Our impressions of Bach's early styles of composition have become clearer since 1951, when Alfred Dürr's initial foray into the pre-Leipzig cantatas clarified the situation so perceptively. Previously, many writers had fallen into the Nineteenth-century musical historians' error of regarding any music which appeared to them awkward, crude, short or unfinished as automatically "early." With regard to the choral music at least, that notion is inappropriate. Bach's mastery of so many musical styles, traditions and techniques is particularly secure, even in a lightweight piece like the *Hochzeits-Quodlibet*. The early music often has a great expressive warmth and even a slight exaggeration of the emotional element: whether we are safe in linking this characteristic with the slightly fiery and emotional character of Bach's recorded youthful behaviour is questionable: the "early" organ works, insofar as they are datable, also display a fine expressive rhetoric, and some of them are highly serious in intention. More fruitful would be a thorough investigation of the changing fashions in Bach's circles—Weimar, Lutheran music generally, Utrecht, the Saxon Courts, the contemporary Bach family, etc.—which might well result in the conclusion that the sometimes rather restrained and formal contrapuntal styles of the early Italian violin composers (Vitali, Corelli) were, indeed, being treated with increasingly romantic intensity and elaboration between about 1700 and about 1720. From around 1720 onwards, the same styles began to be treated almost as caricatures—for example, extremely rapid, rather lightweight contrapuntal fugues and *alla breve* pieces seem to have been composed with increasing frequency, the *affettuoso* mannerisms to have become more pronounced in instrumental music, and choral writing increasingly simple harmonically and rhythmically. These tendencies had some effect on Bach's music as his life progressed, and his music was to some extent written in a conscious desire to combine tradition with contemporary artistic developments.

---

* The recordings available include that of the Vienna Concentus Musicus under Harnoncourt, a performance under Rilling and a Munich one under Karl Richter, with Mathis, Haefliger and Fischer-Dieskau as soloists. The Concentus Musicus performance has some excellent oboe playing from Jürg Schaeftlein, good work from the soloists (especially the boy soprano, although Equiluz is in good form, too); however, this is not one of the most outstanding recordings of this highly-talented group, and it is marred by lack of rhythmic bite and rather slack editing: the pause at the *da capo* of the treble aria (No. 3) is, for example, disconcertingly long.

2: Weimar Concertmeister

The terms under which Bach was promoted to the post of Concertmeister on March 2, 1714, included the provision that he furnish "Monatlich neue Stücke" (new *church*-pieces monthly) with the Weimar Capelle. Recent commentators agree that the works composed during the remaining months of the Weimar period to October 1717 (a total of forty-four calendar months) were accumulated towards a complete "year-cycle" of music proper to the celebrations of the liturgical year : this Jahrgang might well be one of the five mentioned in Bach's obituary notice. The fact that some of the Weimar pieces were later absorbed into the first Leipzig-Jahrgang (1723/24) would not reduce the apparent—or indeed, the real—level of achievement in the eyes of his contemporaries; besides, the re-arrangement of performing materials from Weimar to Leipzig notation and practice would itself have involved some considerable creative effort on Bach's part.

For a long time, the Palm Sunday Cantata No. 182, *Himmelskönig, sei willkommen*, was considered to be Bach's first cantata to be performed in his new capacity. However, the identification of the author of CANTATA NO. 54, *Widerstehe doch der Sünde* (Beware sin, therefore), has revealed also that the text was intended for performance on Oculi Sunday. The idea that the work was incomplete, which had resulted from its brevity (two arias separated by a recitative), has also proved to be unfounded. The text's brevity may well have been a reason for Bach choosing to set it hurriedly for performance only two days after his promotion. In fact, the work is essentially a continuous monologue in three sections—as Dürr points out, it is a cantata in the word's true Italian sense of "operatic scenario"—not at all the kind of music that we associate with Bach's usual church pieces; and, if it were more lightly scored (for continuo and voice only, say), we might be tempted to assume that it was composed for chamber, rather than chapel performance.

What was almost certainly the first passage that Bach composed as Concertmeister is remarkably bold:

Indeed, the whole of the first aria is full of dramatic, anxious excitement, as Bach, probably composing with a speed inspired alike by involvement and practical necessity, draws an awe-inspiring picture of the perils of Satan's kingdom. The recitative, which expands into an *arioso* style to preface the succeeding aria, also illustrates the cankering effects of sin. The second aria is in motet style, with fugal imitations shared between the violins and violas and the alto voice, over a bass that starts independently and continues by sharing in the motivic dialogue. This little cantata is, most regrettably, little known and performed today: this is a pity, for it has much of the bitter-sweet quality that has attracted public attention to certain works of Purcell, Buxtehude and others of the mid-Baroque; Bach's contemporaries thought well of it, and it is possible that its opening movement was re-used at Leipzig in Bach's lost *Markuspassion*.*

* A fine recording of much historical and musical interest by Alfred Deller with Baroque strings under Gustav Leonhardt was recorded for Austrian Vanguard around 1955: magnificent singing, sensitive, if under-developed authentic accompaniments, and over-resonant monaural sound; a new performance of this cantata from the Leonhardt Consort as it now is, over twenty years later, with Paul Esswood makes a fascinating contrast.

Widerstehe doch der Sünde was performed so soon after Bach's appointment as Concertmeister that he would have had little time to plan it in detail, to rehearse it, and to set about his new task of directing church music. His next preserved cantata, performed less than a month later, would have been far more of a challenge, since he would have had ample time for preparation (by the standards of the day), and plenty of choice with regard to instrumentation, structure and expressive language. CANTATA NO. 182, *Himmelskönig, sei willkommen* (King of Heaven, be welcomed), does not immediately strike us as a work of special demonstration or creative effort, in the way that, for example, the first large-scale Leipzig cantata (No. 75), *Die Elenden sollen essen*, does. Only when we consider the original circumstances of performance of these two works does their relative significance fall into place. In Leipzig, Bach probably knew very well the unenthusiastic spirit with which he had been appointed; he would also have been aware that in Leipzig his work would be heard critically by men well versed in Theology, Rhetoric, Poetry, Philosophy, Music and Civic Pride, that his first church music would be reported in printed journals, and that, possibly above all these secular considerations, he was now vested with a new responsibility by the Almighty. In Weimar, on the other hand, Bach had been promoted because of his employer's enthusiasm and recognition of his promise. *Himmelskönig, sei willkommen* is a piece designed to salute Christ as God's representative on earth: as is clear, Wilhelm Ernst, Bach's employer, was all too conscious of his own parallel role—and, apparently, Bach was happy to accept this.

The work was presented twice at Weimar. On the first occasion, it took its present shape until the tenor aria "Jesu, lass durch Wohl und Weh," at the conclusion of which the opening chorus was repeated. The biblical bass recitative and the following three arias were thus framed by two presentations of the same chorus, and the sonata served as a preface. Later, however, it appears that the composer decided that this formal outline was imperfect: he therefore composed two further movements and added them to replace the repeat of the second chorus after the tenor aria. In this later form, the cantata is of the roughly symmetrical construction we have come to expect from Bach's earlier works. The opening sonata and chorus are balanced by the closing chorale and chorus: the bass recitative and aria balance the tenor aria to frame the alto solo, which, as an aria of committed devotion, is readily identifiable with the philosophies both of Bach and of his patron. The presence of three arias in tripartite structure, all expressing devotion to Christ, may represent the concluding words of the Gospel for the day: "And the multitudes that went before, and that followed, cried, saying, [1.] Hosanna to the son of David, [2.] Blessed is he that cometh in the name of the Lord, [3.] Hosanna in the highest." (Matt.

XXI, 9). Working outwards from the central aria, we encounter another way in which the work balances symmetrically:

alto aria 5

bass aria 4   tenor aria 6

biblical quotation 3   chorale projection 7

free chorus 2   free chorus 8

Here, the sonata is less involved in the plan of the whole, but the text is seen to be an important element in the work's structure. In fact, the sonata does seem to have been conceived from the outset as a part of the whole work, for its harmonic, melodic and expressive characteristics all combine to attach it to the remainder of the composition: indeed, the idea appears here of basing successive movements on recurrent, dominating *motifs*—an idea which is not new to Bach—*Christ lag in Todes Banden* is the obvious earlier example—but one which is to become a hallmark of his Weimar style. From 1714 his concern to intensify the expressive power of his music, whilst also increasing the internal organisation of its material through the use of *motifs*, is a feature of his work there.

In the first performance, the tenor aria ending in B minor was followed immediately by the repeated chorus *Himmelskönig, sei willkommen* in G major; in the later performance, still at Weimar, Bach added the fine chorale-fugue on the melody *Jesu Leiden, Pein und Tod*, also in G major, and a new concluding chorus to take the place of the repeated second movement. The chorale text, which points us forward to Passiontide, is set to a relentless melody: both show the necessity of Christ's Passion, and Bach sets it in a powerful, forward-moving *fugato* that emphasises this. Its effect in the new structure of the whole cantata is to counterbalance the Biblical recitative (No. 3): Christ's teaching is balanced with Lutheran interpretation, statement balanced with statement, dignified but expressive feeling with equivalent emotion. The main characteristic of the final chorus is its directness and homophonic simplicity. This is a feature of many of the Weimar choruses, and we are probably correct if we assume that some strong preference for this style in Weimar was responsible for Bach's frequent writing in this style. Possibly the Archduke himself let it be known that he particularly favoured this almost folk-song-like simplicity, or perhaps Bach's first wife Maria Barbara—who must certainly have had some musical preferences, and was, after all, a country girl—was responsible for it. In its latter version particularly, Cantata No. 182 is especially satisfying. It was incorporated into the first Leipzig Jahrgang in 1724, and it appears to have been heard again in Leipzig in about 1728; there were probably several other Leipzig performances, of which no trace survives in the preserved sources.*

Bach's April composition was the fine Jubilate piece, CANTATA NO. 12, *Weinen, Klagen, Sorgen, Zagen* (Weeping, lamentations, pity, hopelessness). The third Sunday after Easter takes its name from the Psalm proper to the day—Psalm 66—which, together with the Epistle (I Peter II, 11–20) and Gospel (John XVI, 16–23) stresses the need to trust in God in times of trouble. The mournful opening Sinfonia is a rather more grief-dominated version of the type established in Cantata No. 21, *Ich hatte viel Bekümmernis.* It prepares the listener most effectively for the succeeding chorus, and this preparation adds a dimension to that movement that its later adaptation, as the Crucifixus of the B minor Mass, lacks. This chorus, one of Bach's most memorable settings, has the quality of the great Passion paintings—a quality of static, contemplative involvement. This is achieved through the use of a dignified, conventional form—that of the chromatic ground bass—such as, for example, Purcell had used to great effect in Dido's famous static, contemplative and tragic aria; through the affective setting of the poetic madrigalian text, which leans heavily towards Pietism; through the effective restraint which is not immediately apparent—the tragedy lasts for just the right length of time, the instrumental accompaniment is contributing more than might at first appear to be the case, and so on. In view of prevailing performance practice, Dürr's view that the contrasting central section of the "Weinen, Klagen . . ." chorus should be accompanied *colla parte* by the strings should be reported here.

The remainder of the cantata is also particularly rich in contrasts —contrasts between the Jubilant and the penitent aspects expressed in the Psalm for the day. The final chorale, whose text summarises the Christian philosophy that God turns even the deepest suffering to good, is associated with Johann Pachelbel, one of Bach's great predecessors, and the teacher both of the stepbrother who had brought Bach up and the distant cousin Johann Gottfried Walther, who was apparently in close contact with him at this time in Weimar. This setting, which probably resounded in the triumphant key of C major at Weimar, has a striking descant over an expressive, yet rather an old-fashioned vocal setting: possibly the whole vocal arrangement was incorporated rather than freshly composed for Bach's *Stück*, and the descant added partly to "fill in" the "missing" thirds at two cadences.

---

*The fine recording under Leonhardt, with excellent and stylish playing from Frans Brüggen and the unnamed continuo player (Anner Bylsma?) and clear, direct singing, is one of the Amsterdam ensemble's best; the Deutsche Bachsolisten/Westfalische Kantorei recording under Ehmann is far less supple, less subtle and less well sung, but does give some idea of the work. On neither record is there banding to enable the listener to repeat the opening chorus to obtain the effect of the first performance.

Weinen, Klagen . . . has several features—notably the inclusion of the direct final chorale-setting to introduce the sermon—that might lead us to associate it with Leipzig rather than Weimar if we did not already have contrary evidence. The great dramatic chorus which opens the text, the neat and vital characterisation of the arias, the care with which the theological arguments of the text are represented in the music, all remind us of the early Leipzig cycles. In fact, Bach himself recognised this kinship when he incorporated the work, with less alteration than usual with the remaining Weimar compositions, into the first Leipzig *Jahrgang*, and performed it, more or less as it stood, on April 30, 1724.*

The third Weimar "monthly" cantata, CANTATA NO. 172, was the first composed there for a major feast—indeed, apart from the possible connection of the earliest versions of Cantata No. 63 with Christmas, Bach's first cantata associated with an important ecclesiastical festival. It was performed on Whitsunday 1714, and its text, *Erschallet, ihr Lieder* (Sound forth, O songs) makes reference to the coming of the Holy Spirit as companion, representative of the Trinity, the Comforter, as a lover and finally, through Communion, as an internal sustainer.

Its symmetrical design recalls both versions of Cantata No. 182: the opening chorus, with its festive trumpet fanfares and its lilting triple anacrusic rhythms, is repeated to conclude the work. The scriptural bass recitative balances the penultimate chorale setting. Between these two movements are arranged three arias, of which the last is a duet. The central aria, "O Seelen-Paradies," is a particularly striking hymn of praise for the earth's creation as a garden of Paradise for souls, since God is again present here, as at the Creation. Bach produces for this text a magnificent unison accompaniment for the four upper parts (two each of violins and violas): this melody seems to have the strength, the time-lessness and the inevitability of God the Creator, but also the warmth, the concern, the ardour of the Creator Spirit. The quality of the music here is matched by a fine poetic text. As this is something of a rarity in Bach's music, out of respect for its probable author, Salomo Franck, it is worth reproducing here:

> O Seelen-Paradies,
> das Gottes Geist durchwehet,
> der bei der Schöpfung blies,
> der Geist, der nie vergehet;
> auf, auf, bereite dich;
> der Tröster nahet sich.†

---

* The Vienna performance under Harnoncourt is very expressive and well coloured; the first chorus is taken at a rather fast speed, and loses some of its intensity as a result; also its connection with the Sinfonia is somehow less apparent as a result of this.
† O Paradise of Souls, that is inhabited by God's Spirit *again* as at the Creation, the Spirit that *will* never fail us: come, rise! prepare yourself: the Comforter approaches.

The remaining movements are good examples of more or less standard types that we have already encountered: the opening chorus has a similar *alfresco* design, with trumpet figures to illustrate the words "Erschallet" and "ihr Lieder" independently of the vocal parts, as we encounter much later in the first chorus of the Christmas Oratorio. The biblical recitative for bass (the bass voice is frequently used to represent Christ in the cantatas and passions) is of a rather lyrical *arioso* type, similar to its equivalent in Cantata No. 182: its gradually expansive nature, both textually and musically, leads effectively into the bass aria in praise of the Trinity. This has a martial quality: the presence of trumpets stresses the magnificence of God, the unity of three in one is stressed by the three instruments, which play partly in unison, partly contrapuntally, and the opening thematic figure of both the solo voice and the trumpet is built on one triad, a musical equivalent to the Trinity. The chorale-duet is also a highly effective love-duet: its text reminds us of the even more direct quotations from the "Song of Songs" in Cantata No. 140, *Wachet auf!*: the melody of "Komm Heiliger Geist, Herre Gott" is heard exquisitely decorated above the vocal duet—its seasonal appropriateness is obvious. Although the intended (wind?) instrument is not designated, an oboe would appear to be the only likely one in Weimar. Oboes may have doubled string lines elsewhere—for example, in the main chorus of the cantata, or in the descant to the chorale heard in the following movement. The cantata was performed, like the two preceding works, during Bach's first year at Leipzig, and again in 1731: the work contrasts effectively with later settings for the same festival, and its acceptance into the Leipzig repertoire indicates that Bach himself had a high opinion of it, and that he probably performed it quite a number of times there.*

CANTATA NO. 199, *Mein Herze schwimmt im Blut* (My *hands are stained with* blood*), is a second solo-cantata to a text by Georg Christian Lehms of Darmstadt, the author of the text of *Widerstehe doch der Sünde*. The text alternates soprano recitatives with arias (Nos. 2, 4 and 8) and a chorale setting (No. 6). The four paired recitatives and their associated philosophical soliloquies move from guilty despair through self-examination and repentance to discovery of salvation in Christ (the chorale movement) and consequent joy. The first aria includes another of those grief-stricken oboe accompaniments that we have noticed already in Cantatas Nos. 21 and 12: as in those, the melodic character of the instrumental line is such as inspires players well-practised in Eighteenth-century performing techniques to add notes and ornamental passages to the already highly poignant lines. The

---

*The literal "My heart swims in blood" does not convey the undertones of guilt in the German.

second aria, that of repentance, is highly expressive in both music and words: the English writer Alec Robertson, otherwise rather unreliable on Bach, has drawn attention to the emphasis placed on the word "Reue" (repentance) and the illustrative repeats of the word "Geduld" (patience) just before the *da capo*. The final aria, which has the character of a French *gigue* in B flat major, inevitably invites comparison with the Finale of the Sixth Brandenburg Concerto.

After three months (September to November), Bach's next preserved choral work is CANTATA NO. 61, his first setting of a text starting with the chorale *Nun komm der Heiden Heiland* (Come now, Saviour of the Gentiles). The text is by Erdmann Neumeister of Hamburg: it is taken from his "Geistliche Poesien" (Sacred Poems) published in Eisenach during the same year (1714). It is typical of Neumeister's whole approach that he incorporates diverse elements into his text to produce a unified, effective whole, and of Bach's assurance at the age of twenty-nine that he manages to add further diverse elements, yet retain the structural unity, the artistic balance.

The first movement combines the stylistic mannerisms of the French *ouverture* with a treble *cantus firmus* presentation of Luther's magnificent Advent text and its associated melody. As Karl Geiringer has pointed out, this is the first datable preserved example of the fusion by Bach of the French *ouverture* with other elements: he refers directly to Cantatas Nos. 20, 97 and 119 as later examples: to these might well be added the fine chorale prelude on *Wir glauben all'* (BWV 681) and the Sixteenth Variation of the "Goldberg" set. The use of an *ouverture* for a work that celebrates the start of the Church Year must have been deliberate: the tenor aria stresses this aspect of the prescribed Sunday, the First in Advent. Another important aspect of Bach's use of the form is the way in which the first two lines

> Nun komm, der Heiden Heiland,
> Der Jungfrauen Kind erkannt*

are set to expectant slow, dotted rhythms, whilst the faster and more jubilant music that follows illustrates, through its fugal and rhythmic aspects, the meaning of the two remaining lines:

> Des sich wundert alle Welt;
> Gott solch Geburt ihm bestellt.†

The tenor aria "Komm, Jesu" is full of the expectancy of Advent; the

---

* "Now come, Saviour of the Gentiles, known to be the son of a virgin."
† "The whole world marvels that God has ordained such a birth for Him."

apparent delay which results in our "awaiting" the coming of Christ is
clearly portrayed in the extended beauties of the unison upper strings'
accompaniment:

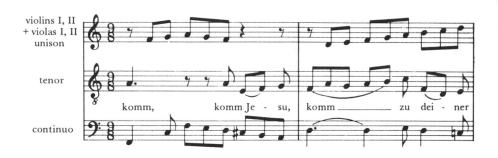

Recitative No. 4 is a setting of the words

> Behold, I stand at the door and knock.
> If any man hear my voice, and open the door,
> I will come in to him
> and will sup with him
> and he with me.
>
> (Revelation III, 20)

The expectant mood is maintained by the melodic line (for bass, as the
words are attributed here to Christ); the knocking on the door is
effectively represented by *pizzicato* strings (marked *senza l'arco* in the
preserved autograph full score); the effective impression of a long wait
is conveyed by the extended tonic pedal under unresolved discords at

the start of the movement—a parallel in recitative to the aria opening of
Widerstehe doch der Sünde:

This recitative is only ten bars long, yet its effect is considerable.
especially if the soloist takes some of the opportunities presented for
ornamentation according to the conventions implied by Bach's notation.
For the commenting soprano aria, an accompaniment of "violoncelli" is
required: the nimble part-writing is a fine testimonial to the skill of
Bach's players. The anticipation of the opening motive ("Öffne dich") in
the instrumental obbligato makes it clear that Bach intended the words
to be conveyed by the accompaniment as well as the voice. In this
respect, we must remember that it was customary for the text to be
made available on leaflets in Lutheran churches of the time; the texts
of Bach's Weimar cantatas very probably had to be approved personally
by the duke or one of his many attendant clergy in advance, and would
also have to be available at the service for his perusal. The final chorale
is interesting in that it follows Neumeister's text in making use of only
a part of the great Advent/Epiphany chorale "Wie schön leuchtet der
Morgenstern." The interesting features here include the expressive violin
descant, the festive spirit, with its ascending ending and, as some might
claim, a sign of Bach's identification of himself with the "Ich" of the
final line through his apparent extension of the movement to fourteen
bars' length (in number symbolism, B-A-C-H is represented by 14).*

---

* The two interpretations currently available on records provide some interesting
contrasts: that by soloists with the Munich Bach Choir and Orchestra under Karl Richter
has a rich and orchestral mellowness of tone, well-judged speeds and disciplined
control in rhythm and intonation; that by soloists with the Kantorei Barmen-Gemarke
and the Deutsche Bachsoloisten under Helmut Kahlhöfer has less polish and an infinitely
less satisfactory standard of recorded quality, but its sound as music is more Bach's
chamber-music kind of sound, and it has a quality of care and sincerity which will
for many listeners amply compensate. It is well directed and co-ordinated, too.

Exactly four weeks after performing the Neumeister *Nun komm* cantata, Bach presented CANTATA NO. 152, his fine setting of Salomo Franck's *Tritt auf die Glaubensbahn* (Tread thou the road of Faith): since the text was published the following year, we must surely presume that it was written expressly for Bach's setting. The work opens with an instrumental ensemble headed "Concerto." The piece starts slowly and continues with a polyphonic Allegro ma Non Presto, yet is it not really an *ouverture* in style: indeed, its effect strikes the present writer as clearly Italianate (the inclusion of recorder, viola d'amore and gamba in quartet with oboe and continuo), a complete contrast to the opening chorus of Cantata No. 61 in rhythm, mood and instrumentation, and an *adagio* introduction of four floridly ornamental bars cannot be said to have the character of Bach's corresponding passages in clearly French pieces. What is clear is the relationship throughout this work between the text and Bach's music. The opening sinfonia does indeed have the quality of a joyful journey, and the fine oboe accompaniment to the first aria—for the bass, who represents both Christ and Biblical Authority throughout the work—continues this idea effectively. In the following recitative, the word "Israel"—which for Bach and his age had the meaning of "the local community"—brings the listener and composer into a seemingly closer relationship than is usual in a text so clearly derived from the scriptures: the demonstrative treatment accorded to the word "fall," and later to the words "stumble into Hell's dark hole," are, although pictorial rather than emotional, no less a part of Bach's expressive language than the confident manner of the recitative's conclusion, which refers to the Christ Child as the corner-stone through which we gain support and salvation through Divine Grace.

The soprano is introduced for the centrepiece of Franck's neatly devotional text, the aria of Faith "Stein, der über alle Schätze": we must remember that the singer would almost certainly be a treble, and that the relationship between the soloists is that of child to father, Christian to God as personified in the Christ Child. This aria displays Bach's habit of associating calm and devotion through the use of parallel lines which enrich the musical texture without cluttering the harmony, because they merely confirm the overtones that are already implied by the lower lines. The main feature of the following bass recitative is the striking harmonic illustration of the blind leading the blind—a clouding effect which is both confusing to the listener and also extremely beautiful as music:

(see example at top of facing page)

The final duet for the two soloists is the earliest of the preserved dialogue-duets between Christ the teacher and Man the believer, or the

die blin-de Lei-te-rin ver-führt die geist-lich Blin - den

Soul; we are reminded by its style of the contemporary operatic love-duets, which often took the form of a dialogue, thus enabling the composer to display his libretto to best advantage, and to extend the composition attractively by varying the material sung first by one participant in the other's reply. The dance-like lilt is a part of the conventional style of such duets.*

For Oculi 1715, Bach wrote his second preserved cantata for the day, CANTATA NO. 80a, *Alles was von Gott geboren ist zum Siegen auserkoren* (All that is born of God is destined for victory). The librettist was again Franck, and the text was issued in the same publication that year as *Tritt auf die Glaubensbahn*. Its structure is again quite direct and straightforward, and the piece has obvious symmetry—indeed, rather more than in its later (and much better-known) adaptation as the "Reformation Festival" Cantata No. 80, *Ein feste Burg*. Any adequate reconstruction of No. 80a must obviously be based on hypotheses, since the only surviving evidence of the early version is to be found in Franck's published text. The first aria is a vigorous and confident one as befits its text: the accompaniment for unison upper strings with an oboe *cantus firmus* (slightly decorating the chorale contours, in keeping with the work's cheerful mood) fits perfectly well into the already clearly regularised manner of Bach's commentary-movements. The actual obbligato line of the unison strings is very interesting: its violinistic energy seems to spring from Italian music of the Vivaldi/Torelli schools: indeed, Bach does seem to have become increasingly preoccupied with "modern" Italian music from about 1713 until the composition (early 1720s) of the English Suites, which show a strong leaning towards French

* An attractive recording by Amsterdam performers under Jürgens and Leonhardt was made in the early Sixties for Telefunken. The singing is a little too operatic and modern in the soprano, at times rather tentative in the bass, but the instrumental work is good: the opening instrumental concerto is—as always in Leonhardt's ensemble recordings—particularly pleasing.

mannerisms as well as Italianate features. There is also the interesting feature of its derivation from the chorale melody itself:

This, as we shall see, remains a feature of the Weimar scores—the subtle derivation of subsidiary materials from chorale contours. It is probably more sensible, however, to consider this as a method used by Bach, rather than as an expressive device which he wished either hearers, readers or even God to regard as particularly symbolic.

The recitatives have all the usual features common to other Weimar works: their length, their manner of vocal delivery, their style of notation and their structure—which starts in rapid declamatory style and only later melts into a slower *arioso* lyricism. All this reminds us of the surrounding works. One fact, however, is clear: the cantata would have been unperformable in Weimar in the key of its surviving Leipzig source (D). The reason is that the pitch used at Weimar was unusually high: a performance using parts in D would have required the bass soloist to sing up to modern concert f′ sharp or g′ during the opening aria. Probably the original work was written in C, with minor differences in instrumentation and disposition.*

The text of Bach's second preserved Easter cantata, CANTATA NO. 31, *Der Himmel lacht! die Erde jubilieret* (Heaven laughs! the earth rejoices), consists of three paired recitatives and arias, framed by an opening festive chorus and a concluding chorale taking the form of a welcoming song for the risen Saviour. This balanced structure is further enriched

---

* The Leipzig recording of Cantata No. 80 (*not* 80a, but its later reworking) is balanced and dignified, if slightly conservative in approach.

by Bach's proud Sonata, which is clearly intended to represent the contrast between heavenly and earthly rejoicing as described in the opening lines of the following chorus. The Heavens are represented by powerful unison and octave rhetorical figures in zigzag patterns similar, indeed, to laughter; the rejoicing on earth is celebrated by a division into full harmony, accompanied by trumpet flourishes—these represent the diversity of the nations and the worship of earthly riches as represented by the ruling classes (hence the trumpets). Trumpets are also appropriate to a cantata for this season because of Christ's role as God in earthly and heavenly triumph at Easter. The opening chorus is notable for its musical illustrations of the words "lacht" (laughs), "lebt" (lives) and "nicht verwesen" (uncorrupted) by simple *melismata;* the central *adagio* interlude is cleverly inserted into the otherwise rather impersonal and dogmatic fugal chorus.

The two bass solos treat the singer as interpreter and philosopher on the Christian message of Easter: the aria of praise foreshadows some of the solos of the Passion settings through the expressive rhythmic patterns of the bass-line. The tenor solos treat the theme of resurrection more evangelically; the joy of the bass aria is balanced by the urgent calls to repentance of the tenor's "Adam muss in uns verwesen," with its restlessly striving string accompaniment. Finally, the treble, speaking on behalf of the devout Christian, reflects on present and eventual union with Christ, and sings a song of yearning for personal resurrection at death; as a background to this effective aria of longing, unison upper strings play the melody associated with the chorale text "Wenn mein Stündlein vorhanden ist." The analogy is further stressed by the closing chorale harmonisation, which presents the same melody with the chorale's fifth stanza, "So fahr ich hin zu Jesu Christ." Much less romantic, but probably intentional, is the use of the note A in both solo voice and continuo accompaniment at the words "Das A und O" ("the Alpha and the Omega") in bar 8 of the bass recitative—a simple illustrative curiosity which will not have disappeared in the notation when the work was performed with the pitch possibly a minor third lower in Leipzig in 1724 and again later.*

---

* The Vienna recording under Harnoncourt has special interest in that it is performed at high Weimar Chorton pitch (Weimar C=Leipzig E flat). The string *timbres* are therefore of especial interest: Harnoncourt is right when he points out the suitability of the high *tessiture* to both oboists and singers, although the even shriller tone of the reproduction clarini could be said to more than compensate. The main idiosyncracy here lies in the strong contrasts of speed within the instrumental Sonata: although consistency is maintained within the movement, it is hard to see why the earth-bound multitudes should show less ready activity than the pompously unified Heavens. One is led to question the reasons for such wide fluctuations (brass difficulties?), and to conclude that they are suspect in authenticity if not demonstrably un-Bachian. Fortunately, a separate recording under Ansermet gives a contrasting reading of the Sonata alone.

Der Himmel lacht is richly scored, with its quintet of oboes and bassoon, its trumpet/drum brass quartet and a surviving bass-line clearly intended for a stringed instrument of double-bass pitch; the division of the treble soprano line in the opening chorus also gives the work a festive atmosphere, just as it does in the later *Magnificat*. The work contrasts strongly with the far more introverted expressive character of Cantata No. 4, *Christ lag in Todesbanden*, which is the only other surviving *Stück* for Easter Day: the only remaining Easter day *music* is to be found in the *Oster-Oratorium* (BWV 249). It is interesting to reflect on this contrast in works composed for the same season, for Bach habitually wrote pieces of a strongly contrasting character for similar occasions. Clearly this will have been dictated by expediency as well as artistic needs: Bach must have known that he was assembling a repertoire for future use, and he must have realised that different performance conditions, contrasting theological emphases in sermons, and even varying sociological situations, might require works of quite different character in future years.

CANTATA NO. 165, *O heilges Geist- und Wasserbad* (O fount of the Holy Spirit and waters), is designed for Trinity Sunday; the opening of Franck's text refers to the Gospel (John III, 1–15), where Christ advises Nicodemus: "Except a man be born of water and the Spirit he cannot enter into the kingdom of God." The work is of modest proportions, with accompaniment of strings with continuo bassoon, no sinfonia and no choral music apart from the final harmonic chorale setting, which has no preserved instrumental descant. The flowing lines of the opening salutation-aria for treble are clearly to be associated with the idea of flowing water: their arrangement in a fugal texture of running semi-quavers is similar to that used in a similar context in the "Leipzig Rivers" Cantata No. 206, *Schleicht, spielende Wellen*. The other two arias, for alto with continuo and tenor with unison violins over continuo, are separated from one another and the opening movement by bass recitatives. The second of these, "Ich habe ja, mein Seelenbräutigam," is the highlight of the whole cantata: indeed, the late Weimar works might be said to be generally more striking for their expressive recitatives than they are for arias as a whole. The decorative treatment accorded to the words "Hochheil'ges Gotteslamm" (most holy Lamb of God) is particularly fine and striking. The string support stresses the continuous uplifting character of the Spirit: this gives the music its special, elevated quality, which is reinforced through the various delayed resolutions to chains of quite bold discords—a very beautiful effect.

CANTATA NO. 185, *Barmherziges Herze der ewigen Liebe* (O merciful heart of everlasting love), is another Franck setting, this time on subjects closely related to the gospel of the day, the Fourth Sunday after Trinity (St. Luke VI, 36–42). The work has several strong Weimar characteristics and the alternating aria/recitative structure is made more symmetrical by Bach's ingenious addition of the appropriate seasonal chorale "Ich ruf zu dir, Herr Jesu Christ" to the opening duet movement: the same chorale, together with one of those caressing descants so characteristic of the Weimar years, concludes the cantata in harmony. The philosophical bass aria, No. 6, is constructed over a patterned bass-line containing repeated figurations in the manner of an *ostinato*—a device used particularly in the earliest group of cantatas. The opening duet of accord and thanksgiving resembles operatic duets of accord from the period, but its combination of taut rhythmic and contrapuntal organisation with warmth of expression are Bachian, rather than conventionally operatic, features; the echoing sighs and trills, in combination with the broadly flowing 6/8 rhythms and the mostly running bass-line, give the music strong character, and since these features (apart from the running bass) all belong also to the chorale projected in the background (by a solo oboe, not trumpet, at Weimar), the movement is especially agreeable. The alto recitative that follows is a complete contrast to this almost Brahmsian lyricism: notable are the *melismata* illustrating the words "melt"

and "measured" (meaning here "rewarded with")

Bach's alto must have been highly capable, for the recitative is quite long and its emphatic style demands a precise attack and not inconsiderable volume; the following aria, moreover, is slow and decorated quite intricately in both vocal and accompanying parts. Once again, we find that the alto *timbre* is considered as the voice of promise and intention. The style of this movement is lush and expansive: if it were better known, it might well be as popular as related movements like the Air from the third *Ouverture* ("on the G string") and the Good Shepherd aria from the "Hunting Cantata," which it briefly recalls at one point.

Although two lost cantatas presumably separated the composition of *Barmherziges Herze* and CANTATA NO. 161, *Komm, du süsse Todesstunde* (Come, thou sweet hour of death), their consecutive positions in the order of the preserved cantatas emphasise their similar features. These include the presentation in an opening solo movement of the chorale also heard at the work's conclusion, the juxtaposition of both traditional and more personal and modern styles between successive movements, expressive application of illustrative devices in recitative, the presence of a delicate descant above the final chorale harmonies, and the inclusion of important solo material for the (presumably boy) alto soloist. Cantata No. 161 is among Bach's most sensuous and directly appealing: Geiringer describes it as "even more transcendental" in character than No. 31, *Der Himmel lacht*. Perhaps too much of its high quality has been claimed to be the result of Bach's inspiration from Franck's text: in fact, texts expressive of the longing for Heaven through death were perfectly conventional, even somewhat old-fashioned, by the early Eighteenth century; possibly Bach wrote such apparently deeply felt and melodic music simply because the text contained such familiar material that he felt obliged to set it distinctively, rather than because of his own religious and psychological preferences. There is very little preserved evidence concerning Bach's exact personal feelings on such matters as belief, even less regarding his character.

The instrumentation is for two beaked flutes, obbligato organ, strings and continuo. The mixed four-part choir sings a fine example of the tuneful, direct, folk-music-styled chorus noted in earlier Weimar works, and the beautifully judged harmonies of the chorale round the work off effectively. The thematic material of the first, third and fifth movements (apart from the organ chorale line itself) has been shown by Alfred Dürr to be derived from the final chorale. The sighing semitone *appoggiatura* on the word "Verlangen" (longing/yearning) recalls poignant moments of No. 21, *Ich hatte viel Bekümmernis*, and No. 12, *Weinen, Klagen*: here, however, the accompanying instrument is the first violin rather than the oboe, an indication, surely, that the recorder parts were played by oboists in this particular work.* The musical style

---

* The violin part as written is none the less expressive, particularly as performed by Jaap Schroeder, who has taken the care to play on a modern instrument with appropriate style: highly emotional string accompaniments like this have been com-

of the opening movement has a commanding and moving sincerity, achieved through the flexible treatment of a rather Italianate trio- and quartet-style, into which the poignant chorale line is woven. Bach indicated his concern regarding the precise blending by noting (for him an uncharacteristic step) the chorale's registration on the organ: to be played on the Sesquialtera, possibly with conventional support stops. The Sesquialtera registration has a specially nasal and reedy quality associated both with mourning and with Christ's Passion.

The tendency already observed for Bach and Franck to highlight the subject-matter of a *Kirchenstück* in a recitative of flexible tempo and ornamental character is illustrated in the alto's "Der Schluss ist schon gemacht." As the singer describes the Christian's death as being taken into the arms of Jesus, both death and weariness are depicted by descending instrumental scales so that each of the images is enriched through the same device. At the reference to re-awakening, a fragment of the cantata's opening is briefly referred to, and at the conclusion, as the singer demands that the hour of parting may strike, the instruments sketch a vivid impression of the sounds one hears when one is conscious that a clock is about to strike: the various ticking and even whirring rhythms, particularly the repeated notes in the recorders, resemble strongly the kind of sounds that were made by wooden pendulum-clocks of the time.* The sense of expectancy that results from this illustration is barely fulfilled by the tidy, detached cadential chords that follow; it is possible that they are supposed to represent the actual striking of the hour, but a more likely explanation is that Bach deliberately restricted his artistic depictions to the physical and earthly: he would have been taught that to predict experiences beyond the grave was futile, to dwell on such subjects was to lack in Protestant purpose, and therefore close to sacrilege.

The most attractive feature of the chorus "Wenn es meines Gottes Wille" is to be found in the rippling joy of the recorder interludes; the patterns used to express longing in the opening aria of the work now express fulfilment, the soft flutes of mourning have become heavenly vehicles of pastoral peace. Set between two magnificent examples of Baroque musical elaboration, this short and very direct chorus—so direct that it is surprising that Bach did not set it as a bass aria—reminds us that Bach's musicianship was able to flourish at its customary inspired level in simple as well as complex situations. The straightforward melodic lines which might strike a newcomer to the work as

pletely transformed through the recent fashion for the recreation of "authentic" performing styles, with highly beneficial results.

* Today, the clock of the famous Bastille—almost the only surviving section of the palace Bach knew so well—still makes repeated mechanical noises before it strikes the hour. Bach may have been representing it here.

strangely contrasted with the rest of the music have a haunting beauty that stays in the mind even after the magnificent chorale that follows.

This chorale is among the most beautiful musical treatments throughout either choral or organ music. The meandering nature of the descant for unison recorders surely illustrates, or is derived from, the worms destroying the body in the grave, as described in the text. It is also possible for us to relate the falling intervals of a fifth at the start with the lowering of the body into the grave, and the elevated settling of the conclusion with the Soul's arrival at its heavenly destination, but the most important aspect is less pictorial than this: there is a marvellous sense of achievement, of suffering turned into joy, in this setting of this chorale melody.* On its own, the vocal harmonisation is sad and, until the customary modal twist in the concluding harmonies, rather final in effect, with its somewhat antique, bare perfect harmonies and its Phrygian/Aeolian treatment. The descant completely transforms it:

___

* The tune was associated with several texts in Bach's time, of which the most common was "Ach Herr, mich armen Sünder," a paraphrase of the penitential Psalm 6. Later, even possibly within Bach's lifetime, other texts ("O Haupt von Blut . . . ," "Herzlich tut mich verlangen") became better known.

*3: A violinist of Bach's period, by Pietro Longhi
(1702–85), chalk on brown paper*
(Janos Scholz Collection, New York)

4: Modern musicians playing an Eighteenth-century violin (using appropriate bow) and two-key oboe (Constantine, Birmingham)

Cantata No. 161 contains such a consistent level of inspired musical creation that it is little wonder that it has been consistently admired since its publication by Franz Wüllner in 1887. That Bach himself regarded the work highly is clear from its Leipzig re-use at least once, possibly many times, in and possibly from the late 1730s.*

---

* The established recording under Jaap Schröder is admirable for its polished suavity, its instrumental precision and its balanced, if not particularly immediate, recorded sound. That under Heinz Gottsche. however, has a far less cosmopolitan list of performers, and also less style, yet one is conscious here of the music's textual and religious contents, and of good, conscientious training by the choir.

CANTATA NO. 162, *Ach! ich sehe* (Behold, I see), is only partly preserved: the corno da caccia part is decidedly suspect, parts for one or two oboes may have been included in the original, and the final chorale may originally have included an instrumental descant. CANTATA NO. 163, *Nur jedem das Seine* (To each his due), has the same structural plan as *Ach! ich sehe*: Aria—Recitative and Aria—Recitative and Duet—Harmonised Chorale. The musical text is best known in the version published by Franz Wüllner for the Bach Gesellschaft, where the first violin part was quite unaccountably given to the oboe d'amore—an instrument that hardly existed at this date, and which Bach is thought never to have employed before his move to Leipzig in 1723. The accompaniment is for strings alone (with organ continuo, surely), and any danger that we might miss woodwind instruments is avoided by the fine writing that Bach produces for this medium. The opening movement is a tenor aria with a strong *concertante* dialogue character, achieved through the alternation of the solo violin, solo voice and accompanying ensemble. The bass aria "Lass mein Herz die Münze sein" is in Italian trio-sonata quartet style, where the two upper parts are played not by the customary two violins, nor even by the more French two gambas, but by two solo violoncelli—for the day an unusual combination. This aria produces a brilliant effect throughout, especially towards the conclusion, where the words "den schönen Glanz" and the following passage describing the work of the heavenly goldsmiths are clearly illustrated in musical terms. The duet-recitative and aria for soprano and alto are direct and operatic in their discussion of the contrast, which is now not between God and Caesar (as posed by the Pharisees in the Gospel), but between that which is heavenly and earthly Satanic values. The *arioso* recitative is a duet of perplexity: the participants are aware of their sinful inclinations and disturbed by them: tension is increased through the gradually increasing speeds dictated by the melodic rhythms and the changes of harmonic rhythm throughout the movement. The chorale-accompanied duet is an emphatic song of devotion, a love-duet where the singers address God rather than one another. The chorale that is intoned within their treble register by unison violins and violas is also one of devotion.

In CANTATA NO. 132, *Bereitet die Wege* (Prepare the highways), for the 4th Sunday in Advent, the opening *concertante* aria for soprano is similar in style to that of No. 163, *Nur jedem das Seine*. The highly dramatic recitatives for tenor (No. 2) and alto (4) recall No. 161, *Komm, du süsse Todesstunde*—another text that is forward-looking and full of yearning. In the bass aria "Wer bist du?" the intensive questioning of the soloist, here almost impersonating John the Baptist, has an industrious figured accompaniment for obbligato violoncello, reminding us of *Nur jedem das Seine*, where two virtuoso cello parts are similarly used, but to different expressive purposes. The *concertante* style of the opening aria is recalled in the alto's "Christi Glieder, ach bedenket," a trio with a characteristically instrumental ritornello structure. Here, the violin part, oscillating between the high and low registers, may be intended to illustrate various aspects of the Sacrament of Baptism (an outward and visible expression of a spiritual significance), or it may even be an attempt to portray Christ's own account of his Baptism in Jordan by John. There is no concluding chorale attached to this work in the score, but the libretto includes the first two lines of a chorale stanza:

> Ertöt uns durch deine Güte,
> Erweck uns durch deine Gnad, etc.

The reason for the omission of this movement in the original score is quite simple: Bach's surviving cantata took up the whole of three double pages of manuscript paper. The chorale was probably written out separately on a loose sheet, or copied straight into the lost vocal parts; it seems highly unlikely that Bach would have concluded a work that had started in A major with an aria in B minor.*

CANTATA NO. 155, *Mein Gott, wie lang, ach lange?* (My God, how long, alas, how long?), opens with a recitative derived from the Gospel words of Christ, "Woman, what have I to do with thee? My hour is not yet come." With his customary mastery of Lutheran conventions, Franck uses the first person singular for this post-Epiphany work: Epiphany, seen as God's revelation of Himself in Christ to the Gentiles, shows a particularly personal approach within this tradition. Bach highlights the involvement of the individual in his passionately expressive recitative—boldly drawn, even for a late Weimar work—made all the more poignant through its extended use of a tonic pedal-note below the opening, at times fiercely discordant, harmonies. In the later recitative for bass, "So sei, o Seele, sei zufrieden," conflicting moods (of suffering and relief) are expressed: this movement has the usual eloquent manner we associate with the period: the shuddering bass-line is a particularly vivid portrayal of currently experienced suffering. The duet and aria (second and fourth movements) are quite short, and relatively conventional in style. The bassoon obbligato and the patterned bass-line of the former give the duet a wistful detachment that reminds the present writer of the chorale-prelude section of the Finale of Act II of Mozart's

---

* In the Richter/Munich Bach Choir recording the continuo accompaniment to the bass aria "Wer bist du" is played on an unauthentically fierce registration, which destroys its dignity. The Barmen-Gemarke performance is here far more convincing. Munich's large-scaled, rather Handelian approach is also less appropriate to these rather intimate Weimar compositions than it is to certain of the more grandiose Leipzig works.

Die Zauberflöte; both are songs of witness. The soprano aria "Wirf, mein Herze" is a passionate aria of devotion—again a highly personal expression appropriate to the season—in which the strings produce vigorous rhetorical gestures illustrative of the text: the music is none the less dignified for this, partly because there are calmer sections which tell less of the abandonment of oneself to Christ than they do of his entirely trustworthy reception. The final four-part chorale setting is fairly orthodox, if such a word is ever appropriate to a form so varied as Bach's compressed miniatures. It is a good example of Bach's preference for enhancing the poetic climax of a verse at the penultimate cadence, and relaxing the harmonic tension effectively beneath the succeeding concluding line.*

Franck published three further texts associated with Bach in 1717. These do not include any recitatives in their printed source, yet Bach's preserved Leipzig versions are furnished with extensive recitatives. When any recitatives were first included in performances must be the subject of speculation; it is by no means certain that the entire printed texts were used in composition or performance by Bach at Weimar. It is, however, usually assumed that composition for the printed texts originated in Weimar. Possibly the traditionally penitential aspect of Advent resulted in an absence of recitatives at Weimar in 1716.

The three cantatas for Advent 1716 contain between them twelve arias, three fine choruses and closing chorale settings, of which, however, only that of CANTATA 70a, *Wachet! betet!* (Watch! Pray!), is apparently preserved in the Leipzig reworking. The opening chorus of *Wachet! betet!* and its arias Nos. 3 and 4 are all fine pieces of music in which there appear several features that emanate from Weimar. The chorus is a splendid movement in which the instruments, rather than the voices, first demand attention; they stress the watchfulness of the text. The choral writing is also highly dramatic, with its held notes, its imitative and fugal linear counterpoint, and its directness. Aria No. 3 is a striking *concertante* aria of faith for the treble soloist: the string accompaniment vividly conveys the sense of faithful expectation described in the text, and the rapid scales for a solo (surely) first violinist remind us of the similar *concertante* arias in the cantatas composed the previous winter. However, if this aria was sung by a treble at Weimar it would have had to have been subsequently transposed or rewritten for Leipzig, as the part of this later version, had it been used in Weimar,

---

* The recording under Helmuth Rilling with the Gächinger Kantorei, soloists and the Bach-Collegium, Stuttgart, has the rather operatic manner of performance that we connect with Telemann's Hamburg rather than Bach's Leipzig, let alone Weimar: an operatic style of singing, with a clearly feminine soprano in Ingeborg Reichelt, a florid harpsichord continuo realisation and a rhetorical projection throughout. However, the performance is very well managed within these conditions.

would have required a soloist with an exceptionally high treble voice.*
Aria No. 4, "Hebt euer Haupt empor und seid getrost, ihr Frommen!"
for tenor and strings with doubling oboe and continuo, has a particularly
broad, tuneful and expressive introductory ritornello:

It is striking that this melody, so similar to those of devotion in some
of the secular cantatas, is here clearly associated with those who are to
count themselves deservedly worthy. It is also striking that this resembles
in outline that of Schemelli's *Ich halte treulich still*, published with
Bach's collaboration in 1736, and other contemporary songs of steadfast
faith.

The Weimar setting of *Herz und Mund und Tat und Leben* (Heart
and voice and deed and life-style)—CANTATA NO. 147a—was directly
and effectively arranged so as to stress the evangelical message of
Advent. After a fine and communally expressive chorus, in which the
trumpet and ensemble dominate the outer sections and a more fluid
vocal lyricism is the basis of a contrasting central section, the four
arias may be summarised in single words: repentance—faith—preparation—fulfilment. Alto and oboe share the main expressive roles in the

---

* Even this range is not impossible: pitch was somewhat lower than it is today in
Leipzig—or at least, so we are led to believe by instrument-makers and the ranges of
many of Bach's vocal parts. A good treble can manage b″ with ease: the problem
here would be the consistently high writing of the whole movement, had it sounded
in G minor originally.

first, tenor and rippling obbligato cello in the second, soprano and eloquently evocative solo violin in the third. The final aria, for bass, with a stirring ritornello/*da capo* accompaniment for trumpet and strings. is similar to the opening *concertante* arias of Cantatas Nos. 162 and 163: here, however, the anticipation of service described in the text is heightened through the inclusion of the trumpet fanfares, associated with arias of resolve on the operatic stage. The inclusion of the trumpet in an Advent cantata is not so much festive as symbolic: it heralds the coming of the King of Kings.

Of the reconstructed early CANTATA NO. 186a, *Argre dich, o Seele. nicht* (Soul, deceive not yourself), the most striking movement is the fourth, an expressive aria for soprano. The text ("Die Armen will der Herr umarmen") speaks of God's prompt relief of the believer from burdening uncertainty; the accompanying unison line for violins starts with a vivid portrayal of the Christian struggling under his unwonted load

before rising in demonstration of his soaring spirits upon release.

Although the string *ripieno* line does not reach the dizzy heights scaled by the solo violin in the second movement of Cantata No. 158, *Der Friede sei mit dir*, it extends to notes rarely reached in Bach's second violin parts, and demands great dexterity and sensitivity. The actual similarity of the rising chromatic scales in these two pieces may well spring from Bach's association of Christ's peace with release from psychological burdens.*

---

* The decidedly hypothetical nature of BWV 70a, 186a and 147a has—not surprisingly—resulted in their not existing in their supposed Weimar forms on commercial recordings: however, some impression of the character of their presumed contents may be obtained by selecting appropriate movements from records of the Leipzig versions of *Wachet! betet!* (Gächinger Kantorei/Soloists/Stuttgart Bach-Collegium/ Rilling) and *Herz und Mund. . .* (Netherlands Vocal Ensemble/Soloists/augmented German Bach Soloists/Winschermann).

3: Cöthen Capellmeister

Cöthen was Bach's place of abode between early December 1717 and May 22, 1723. The period is noted for Bach's instrumental music, much of which will have been composed for performance at winter concerts in the Palace of Prince Leopold; the resident band cannot have been silent in the summer, either, and we have it on record that a very sensibly chosen and versatile ensemble accompanied the prince twice to Carlsbad, whither he went to take the waters.

Very little vocal music was required of Bach in Cöthen, and some of it—probably including a wealth of secular song—has apparently not survived. There were two occasions in the Cöthen calendar that were habitually celebrated with choral music and commissioned poetry: Leopold's birthday (December 10) and New Year's Day. The flattering homage-odes for the birthday were less devotionally worded than the New Year works, although both tended to refer to Leopold as a God-like figure: in the age of accepted Divine Right such attitudes were conventional and uncontroversial. Sometimes external forces were imported to Cöthen to assist in performances of such cantatas. Sometimes not one, but two such pieces were given on Leopold's birthday; on these occasions, one of the pieces was more religiously inclined than the other: it was probably performed by the same performers (the singers and instrumentalists of the Hofcapelle and imported specialists as available) but in the palace chapel and as part of an otherwise spoken service including a sermon. These more liturgically appropriate pieces were therefore prefaced by biblical texts.

CANTATA NO. 66a, *Der Himmel dacht auf Anhalts Ruhm und Glück* (Heaven provided splendidly for Anhalt's glory and fortune), is the earliest datable choral work here. Only the characters of three movements can be reconstructed musically. The work begins with a (lost) recitative of formal salutation, sung by an allegorical character representing Anhalt's Good Fortune; the following aria, "Traget, ihr Lüfte, den Jubel von hinnen," is given to the same voice in the later preserved parody. The speed and energy of the winds is illustrated in the gay *passepied* style of the opening, with its graceful oboe and violin gestures; the broadcasting of the good news is gently sketched in the syncopated patterns created by the tied rising figures. The central portion of the aria, which is lightly scored, would sound especially pleasant in the hands of a good Baroque first oboist like Rose. After a (lost) dialogue recitative, a duet follows between Fame and Anhalt's Good Fortune: in the later Leipzig parody the line attributed to the former is sung by a tenor, the latter by an alto. The duet is pretty and Italianate: it has a gently caressing *concertato* violin line, and the "happy ending" *hero-confidant* style which stems from Italian opera. After several lost numbers, the work ends in a rippling chorus in 3/8 time, which contains the D major opening bass flourish which Bach later reworked for a major Church Feast:

continuo  *etc.*

The New Year CANTATA NO. 134a, *Die Zeit, die Tag und Jahre macht* (Time, which creates the days and years), has partly survived in score, and it has therefore formed the basis upon which the other homage-cantatas of the period have been reconstructed.

A short recitative introduces the material of our contemplations and the two characters, Time (tenor) and Godly Foresight (alto). The first aria, given to Time, has the business-like style and the square phrasing that we associate with dances and marches: it is in 3/8 time, but is not really a *passepied*—more a "triple march," with alternating crotchet and quaver paces. The text exhorts us to rise and rejoice, and the similarity to certain pieces headed "la reveil" in contemporary French music makes one wonder if this was actually a specific type of dance and, if so, whether Bach knew. A second dialogue-recitative is followed by a duet with an industrious violin line in *concertato* style; the spaced primary triads at the start belong to this style, but also serve appropriately to illustrate the passage of time, the theme of the cantata's text. As in *Der Himmel dacht*, the duet being one of accord, it is presented in such a way that the two voices declaim the text with particular clarity in parallel consonant lines. The alto aria (number 6) is accompanied by continuo, and the time element is once again emphasised, this time in the repeated notes in the bass: number-symbolism fanatics will, however, search in vain for any special high-lighting of the number 19 (it was the first day of 1719), just as they cannot point with any certainty to a significant use of 24 in Cantata No. 66 (twenty-four was Leopold's age in 1718). It is well that we should observe the lack of such items occasionally, since there are those who try to make out that Bach could barely compose without them. The final chorus, with dialogue echoes for the soloists, is even more direct in appeal than the earlier *reveil*: it, too, is in 3/8 time, and it appears to demand an emphatic and fairly rapid style of performance. This movement makes a most interesting comparison both with its later modification in Cantata No. 134 and with the final chorus of Cantata No. 66, which is assumed to have been based on Bach's preceding homage-cantata for Leopold.

The less certainly datable CANTATA NO. 173a, *Durchlauchtster Leopold* (*Most* worthy Leopold), is remarkable in that it contains only two short recitatives—the introduction, sung directly by the soprano and a brief duet-recitative, No. 5, which soon develops the character of an *arioso*. The remaining movements do not lack either individuality or content—indeed, these include some of Bach's most striking choral pieces from this period.

Until recently it was assumed that the secular "Wedding Cantata," CANTATA NO. 202, *Weichet nur, betrübte Schatten* (Haste away, O gloomy mists) belonged to an unrecorded occasion in the Cöthen period. However, Dürr has pointed to notational evidence which indicates a possible origin by 1714 and Harald Streck has deduced that the text may be by Salomo Franck. If the work does come from the Cöthen years, as the style partly seems to indicate, it seems possible that the use of a Franck-influenced text is the result of a performance outside the town itself. The work is popular today, and its slightly self-conscious incorporation of folk-elements indicates—together with the text's avoidance of open flattery—a middle-class wedding which occurred in the spring. The most striking movements are the arias: especially the opening *pastorale* with oboe, the country-dance aria "Sich üben in Lieben," and the concluding Gavotte—headed thus by Bach, and, like the *tempo di minuetto* of *Durchlauchtster Leopold*, a piece in which the instrumental contribution to the dance is especially essential. The country dance is a particularly attractive movement, and when the oboe is joined by a bassoon with the continuo the strong characterisation is especially marked. The notion of a cantata consisting of alternating recitatives and arias is, of course, Italian: however, very little of the music in this work is particularly Italianate—the aria "Phoebus eilt mit schnellen Pferden" is the obvious exception, and this particular movement has a sonata-style (cf. BWV 1019, Finale) that is of traditional rather than recent association with Italian music. The secular purpose and the solo soprano line mean that this work was probably intended for the female voice—one that Bach had only rarely employed. It would be pleasant if we could associate it with Anna Magdalena Bach, or one of her two singing sisters. The opening of the cantata, in which the oboe and the singer enter successively on unexpected beats

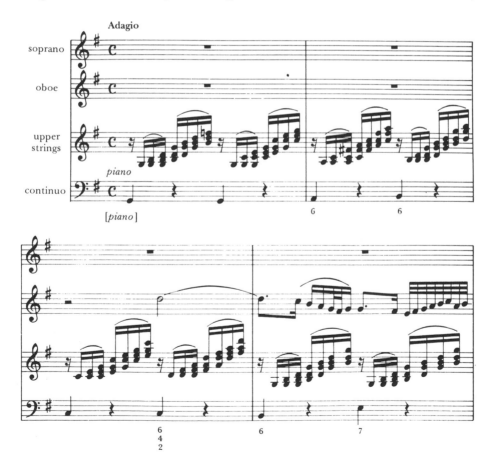

is particularly expressive, also peculiarly Schumannesque: it is a remark-able coincidence that *Dichterliebe* also opens with references to spring, illustrated in mildly dissonant arpeggios—and there are other points in common, also.*

We can only regret the loss of most of Bach's choral music for this period; this chapter has given only a glimpse of the skill with which the composer worked in praise of his most considerate employer.

---

* Three recordings to consider here: under Faerber with Ursula Buckel, under Schroeder with Agnes Giebel, and sung by Elly Ameling accompanied by members of Collegium Aureum. The first is at its best in the seventh aria, where the bassoon is helpful to the momentum of the movement even if it is played too smoothly; Buckel is strong in tone, but weaker in sense of contrast and even intonation: this account will not wear well. Ameling is safer, but the performance is rather lacking in gusto in comparison to the Schroeder/Giebel one, which has the stylistic assurance that we expect from Amsterdam.

4: Leipzig Direktor: The First Year

Bach's first year at Leipzig (*Jahrgang I*) was a period of immense productivity in the service of his Church, his new hometown and his colleagues in school, Church and the professional musical circles of the city. The impression of the first year is, moreover, one of diversity, rather than systematic variation on a standard framework—a contrast to the following year, in which the main interest might be found in the variety of treatments he applies to the chorale-cantata structure. Nevertheless, the various successive *Stücke* do relate to one another in some smaller groupings. Very probably these were arranged to correspond with sermon-series planned by the Leipzig clergy. We suspect —though we cannot be sure of this—that both Bach and his local librettists were in close contact with the clergy, and that preacher and cantor regularly collaborated in the preparation of the proper parts of the main Sunday service, the *Hauptgottesdienst*. It is particularly probable that Bach profited from good relationships with the clergy he met at Leipzig on his arrival, especially Pastor Christian Weiss, then the main priest attached to the Thomaskirche, and his assisting Archdeacon Johann Gottlieb Carpzov, a member of a distinguished and strictly orthodox family of clergy, whose famous uncle Martin Geier (1614–1680) had preached at the funeral of Heinrich Schütz.

Dürr, with characteristic perception, has traced three structural types within Bach's first Leipzig *Jahrgang*. The first, which is henceforth described here as Type 1A, is based on the outline:

```
┌──── biblical citation
│  ┌─ recitative
│  └─ aria
│  ┌─ recitative
│  └─ aria
└──── chorale
```

The second, henceforth 1B, has the outline:

```
┌──── biblical citation
│     recitative
│  ┌──chorale
│  │  aria
│  ┌─recitative
│  └─aria
└──── chorale
```

The third group, which is associated in particular with the texts supposed to be by Christian Weiss, our 1C, is as follows:

```
┌──── biblical citation (from the Gospel)
│  ┌─ aria
│  │  chorale
│  └─recitative
│  └─aria
└──── chorale
```

All three types are arranged symmetrically, as the diagrams make clear: Type 1A emphasises contrasting reactions to the text from two points-of-view (it matters little whether the recitatives and following arias are given to one or two singers: the effect is similar). Type 1B frames an aria in such a way as to stress its text's particular quality. Type 1C affords the same treatment to a chorale stanza, and is, therefore, a movement in the direction of the chorale-cantatas of *Jahrgang II* (the second annual series performed at Leipzig). Dürr categorises the cantatas thus, in our nomenclature:

    1A: Nos. 136, 105, 46, 179; 69a, 77, 25; 109, 89; and 104

    1B: 48; 40, 64; 153, 65; and 67

    1C: 144, 166, 86, 37, 44.

During his first year at Leipzig, Bach put to considerable new use music that he had composed at Weimar. This is hardly surprising when we observe the apparently uninterrupted continuity of his stylistic development in choral forms from Weimar to Leipzig: it is almost as though the Cöthen years had not taken place. Some commentators would not agree with this opinion: they might detect evidence of Bach's recent Cöthen instrumental experience in the early Leipzig pieces, or they might detect signs of influence from Italian or French sources which they would suppose to have been derived from the same period of Bach's life. Regrettably, we have far too little evidence regarding the artistic activities of the music-loving Prince Leopold—or, indeed, of the artistically and intellectually inclined Weimar princes—for it to be possible to trace such influences accurately. In the early Leipzig works Bach continued to set texts built on the model introduced by Neumeister and already well established throughout Protestant Germany:

1. Biblical quotation (e.g. Psalm text), or other discursive subject-matter forming the basis of the work, and also, ideally, the sermon which was to follow: *solo or chorus.*
2. *Recitative* (or occasionally *Aria*) in which either biblical or free poetic text expands the subject-matter of 1. Usually allotted to the bass or tenor voice by Bach—to present Christ and/or the priesthood.
3. etc. *Arias and linking Recitatives, usually of an even number,* closing with a Recitative before a concluding Chorale: some of the Recitatives were themselves set by Bach in compound structure (detached style followed by *arioso*, etc.), and the technique of combining chorale-based material with free verse as a commenting addition was also dear to him.
4. Concluding *Chorale* for choir and instruments, chosen for its appropriateness to the liturgical theme of the work: by no means necessarily a part of Neumeister's published text, but probably expected by him.

Such an arrangement had been common at Weimar, and was to remain customary in Leipzig: its musical outlines were dictated partly by its conventional poetic structure.

One aspect of Bach's settings is the way in which musical emphasis is often placed at the centre of the work. This has been said to reflect Bach's "sense of balance"—as though such a feeble notion of balance were ever essential to any masterpiece. More probably, it is derived from Bach's remarkable sense of individual response and responsibility. The centrally-placed arias almost always represent personal response to doctrine and challenge: they are less declamatory and dogmatic than the opening movements, less affirmative and structurally rigid, more personal and emotively responsive. One frequently encounters parallels in contemporary architecture, where the actual detail of apparently symmetrical buildings or arch-structures is found, on closer inspection, to be far from identical: indeed, it is an interesting feature of Baroque decoration that its centre is often more evocative, more individually expressive than are its framing materials. Two features noticeable in the early Leipzig works relate to Weimar developments in the composer's style. The final chorale is frequently embellished by an instrumental descant—a device which Bach ceased to use after 1723. Also the decidedly cheerful and dance-like styles of the last arias also relate to the Weimar choral works at least as closely as to the Cöthen chamber music.

The earliest compositions for Leipzig include, besides the whole of Bach's test-piece performed as part of his application (our Cantata No. 22), the first part also of Cantata No. 23, which formed the second part, in all probability, of this compound work: they also possibly include Cantata No. 59, *Wer mich liebet*, which Dürr considers may have been performed in the Leipzig University Church on Whitsunday in 1723 or 1724. This short setting of part of a text by Neumeister later formed the basis of the 1725 Whitsun *Stück* with the same title: CANTATA NO. 74, *Wer mich liebet, der wird mein Wort halten* (He who loves me will do my will). The early *Wer mich liebet* has a feature which associates it more strongly in our minds with 1723: this is its unusual instrumentation. We find Bach employing two trumpets and drums (rather than his later standard combination of three trumpets or two horns)—possibly a legacy of the Cöthen Capelle. There is the rather sketchy style of the brass writing, together with the particularly strong emphasis on trio textures, with treble and bass soloists balanced by important parts for first violins and continuo in both the duet and the aria; these could come from a Weimar cantata. Finally, in the choice of two solo voices, of which one is a capable treble, the other a bass fluent in the baritone register, we encounter two solo vocal parts which could have been sung by Friedemann Bach and any experienced student singer: Bach's own voice is supposed to have been of high bass register, but it is unlikely that he would have performed as a vocalist in any Leipzig church at this crucial stage in his career.

The two aria movements of Cantata No. 59 are graceful in style: the opening takes the form of a *concertante* dialogue between the instrumental and vocal paired groups (trumpets, outer strings and voices), the fourth movement is a flowing trio for violin, bass and continuo, in an instrumental style well suited to the violin, and somewhat reminiscent of the Sonatas for organ. Last, but in no way least, must be considered the very beautifully wrought soprano recitative, "O, was sind das vor Ehren," in which the power of the Holy Spirit to comfort is particularly aptly conveyed. This cantata is short and it has come in for unjustified criticism because Bach later chose to enlarge on its material. However, the longer work may only have been performed once whereas BWV 59 was probably performed three or more times.

For his Leipzig application, Bach was required to compose and direct a choral work as a sample of his abilities—a *Probestück*. It has recently been established that two pieces later performed separately, and published after Bach's death as separate cantatas, were both prepared for this occasion—our Cantatas Nos. 22 and 23, into which, however, the concluding chorale movement was not incorporated until later from the *Johannespassion*. The two cantatas probably formed two parts of the same *Stücke*, and the possibility arises that the very beautiful chorale setting well known to English-speaking musicians as "Mortify us by Thy Grace" was heard twice, but with an alternative text on its second appearance at the end of the work.* Since Bach was under perusal regarding both the *Probestück* and first performances in each of the Leipzig principal churches, it is interesting for us to compare them. All are magnificent pieces, and a comparison of Bach's different ways of approaching the problems of creating a satisfactory impression tell us a little, and imply much more, about Leipzig in his day.

If the fifth movement was repeated, CANTATA NO. 22/23, *Jesu nahm zu sich die Zwölfe* (Jesus called the Twelve to him), would have consisted of nine movements. CANTATA NO. 75, *Die Elenden sollen essen* (The wretched shall eat), is more extended—fourteen movements in all. Whereas the season of Estomihi occupies a Sunday during the series leading up to Passiontide and Easter, this later work, first heard in the Nicolaikirche, is concerned with a far more energetic and Evangelical theme—that of Dives and Lazarus. The last piece in the group, CANTATA NO. 76, *Die Himmel erzählen* (The heavens are telling the glory of God), only Bach's second work known to have been heard in the Thomaskirche, is likewise an extended piece in fourteen movements and two parts: from the relatively festive opening, the text turns quite early to contemplation of the duties inherent respectively in comradeship (derived from the Epistle) and response to God's calling (derived from the Gospel).

In its reconstructed form, Cantata No. 22/23 starts with reflection on self: the free arias and recitative of Part I all start with the word "Mein" (My): the emphasis is on personal responsibility and calling as Christ prepares his disciples for Easter in the first part of the Gospel. The freely composed biblical opening has an almost oratorio-like structure: the tenor soloist acts as Evangelist, the bass as Christ and the *ripieno* chorus as the Disciples. We lack recitative and the Disciples are described, rather than actually represented, by the chorus, but the style is still there, and it may have been this which was the reason behind a subsequently expressed opinion that on his appointment Bach must not write Church music that was "theatrical." The extremely expressive and beautiful chorale which closes this part—as well, possibly, as the other—of this rather sombre chamber-music work is clearly a musical illustration of the transformation referred to in its text, here

---

* This idea is the author's: the arguments are complex and unverifiable.

as in the comparable works a highly significant part of the overall scheme.

In contrast, the first part of No. 75, *Die Elenden sollen essen*, which is also very much concerned with self-examination and motives associated with suffering, is a far larger-scaled affair, with a rich assembly of contrasted images and a correspondingly less compact style: the interesting comparison here is with Part II of the *Probestück* whole and the similarly self-examining moments in Cantata No. 76. The Thomas-kirche cantata (No. 76) is by far the most extrovert and exaggerated in expression of the three. Whether this factor sprang from the libretto or not, it seems likely that this strong contrast was a result of the expected—and also probably the received—warmer response of both clergy and congregation at the Thomaskirche as opposed to the Nicolaikirche.

The warmth of expression of Cantata No. 76 contrasts with the magnificent power of No. 75, which is quite unaccountably neglected (in England particularly). Both works are full of subtlety, of internal contrasts and of inner riches, but it could probably be made out that there is more that points forwards stylistically in the earlier than the later piece. Bach's writing already conveys the influence of Reiche in the flowing trumpet lines, which flow lyrically in contrast to their previously punctuation-dominated role. There is also the per-vading influence, after the magnificent opening chorus, of the rising and falling scales of "Was Gott tut," which has been hinted at before it appears in such splendid clothing in the seventh movement, and dominates the musical discussion thenceforth. There is the structural notion of a freely descriptive opening chorus, in which there are no fewer than eight separate thematic motives. Although its constituent parts might each have come from a work composed for the Weimar Capelle, it has a new breadth which points forwards towards other Leipzig works, including the Passions. It seems almost unbelievable that no single surviving account of Bach's activities to have been written by a visitor or a member of the congregation, rather than a performer, mentions the scale and power of his church pieces. Here was the master of context producing what must surely have struck some as music of peculiar appropriateness, yet the most notable written praise that he received in his lifetime compared him to Johann Pachelbel and Buxtehude. The second most notable report was that associated with Cantata No. 75: this was simply a record that Bach's first music in Leipzig was heard in the Nicolaikirche "mit guten *applausu*."

The opening of *Die Elenden sollen essen* contains the same kinds of figures of restless suffering as the opening of Part II of the *Probestück*: the images are similar, the former being a portrayal of "the wretched" and the latter of the blind man who appeals to Christ in the Gospel

(Luke XVIII, 38). In the second part of the *Probestück*, the most unusual movement is the curious combination of recitative and chorale which forms the second movement. In order to indicate the position to the strings and oboes, Bach wrote *Recitativo a tempo* in the score: the uppermost strand of the accompaniment intones the melody associated with the Agnus Dei chorale "Christe, du Lamm Gottes." The idea of a firmly-projected *cantus firmus* line seems to have afforded Bach particular pleasure during the first two years of his Leipzig office. In Cantata No. 75, an original feature is the Sinfonia to Part II, a unique chorale setting without voices—or, at least, apparently without even the sopranos that might have been doubled by the surviving solo trumpet line. The arguments against this theory are: (i) the title Sinfonia, which does not imply vocal participation in Bach; (ii) the absence of any such indication in two surviving scores and the original parts; (iii) the fact that the movement is perfectly satisfactory as it stands. Bach may have chosen this particular form for the occasion because it was necessary to save the choir and soloists from participating. Two factors could have caused this: uncertainty regarding the formalities at the close of the sermon in the Nicolaikirche or, alternatively, some form of ceremony attached to Bach's installation as a citizen or a communicant parishioner of Leipzig which precluded his directing the *Hauptmusik* immediately after the sermon.*

In all of the early Leipzig cantatas discussed here, the most attractive aria is the lovely alto song of Christian devotion in the second part of No. 76, *Die Himmel erzählen*. The expansive serenity of the obbligato oboe d'amore and gamba, coupled with the associations of aspiring heroism in the youthful voice colouration, produces music that does indeed bring to mind the example of Christ:

---

* The *Probestück* Cantata has not been recorded in the form we suggest above, but its contents are included in the orthodox performances of BWV 22 and BWV 23 by the Tölzer and King's College Choirs. *Die Elenden sollen essen*, performed by soloists with the Frankfurter Kantorei, the Bach-Collegium Stuttgart and Martha Schuster under Helmuth Rilling, gives a good idea of the beauty and stature of the work, with particularly nice control of tempi and a reasonable, if a rather romantic and warm, balance of sound.

So well is the musical material wedded to the text that it seems improbable that this sensuous aria was ever joined with the Sinfonia from Part II in a separate work. The remaining arias of the early cantatas tend to be quite brief, and to express one primary affect in the text: contempt, anxiety, purpose, devotion, etc. All of them recall the slightly operatic language of similar movements composed at Weimar, and it seems probable that Bach revelled, during these first Leipzig activities, in the exploitation of his new resource—that of a choir of strong tradition and training—in familiar ways, at least as far as the solo movements were concerned.

The next set of works which we consider as a group is the series performed between July 18 and August 29 (Trinity + 8 to Trinity + 14): most of these are of the structure classified above as Type 1A. Between the early cantatas and the 1A group, Bach re-utilised Cantata No. 21, *Ich hatte viel Bekummernis*, No. 185, *Barmherziges Herze der ewigen Liebe*, and adapted the two late Weimar pieces, No. 147a, *Herz und Mund und Tat und Leben*, and No. 186a, *Ärgre dich, o Seele, nicht*, by adding new recitatives* which filled out their structures and added to their sense of communication to suit new purposes. During this period, Bach also composed new *Kirchenstücke* for Trinity + 4, and the Feast of John Baptist: for two Sundays for which we cannot otherwise account, Trinity + 5 and Trinity + 6, it is suspected that Bach re-performed those works which he had prepared for the preceding Thursday and Friday respectively, on the pretext that these two Sundays fall within the ecclesiastical octaves of their respective Feasts, John Baptist and The Visitation.

The two new cantatas are CANTATA NO. 24, *Ein ungefärbte Gemüte* (An unstained mind), and CANTATA NO. 167, *Ihr Menschen, rühmet Gottes Liebe* (Ye men, tell forth God's love). Each is built in one part consisting of a few symmetrically arranged movements grouped round a centre-piece. However, whereas the unknown poet of the second work uses a fairly orthodox order of aria (tenor), recitative (alto), duet (soprano/ alto), recitative (bass), chorale, the text for No. 24 is grouped around the biblical pronouncement "All things, then, whatsoever you would that men should do for you, so do to them." Around this central chorus, the cantata is arranged thus: aria (alto), recitative (tenor), chorus, recitative (bass), aria (tenor), chorale.† The central movements of the two pieces, Duet and Chorus respectively, have many points of interest, not the least being the quite different manners in which the music, having seemed to come into being to suit the initial ideas of the texts, nevertheless continues to illustrate them as it and they develop simultaneously. However, the chief delight of each of these fine works may be claimed to come not at the centre, but at the edge. In *Ein ungefärbte Gemüte* it is the emphatic (unison upper strings quasi-*ostinato*) opening aria calling for youthful vigilance that remains in the memory after the more lyrical and declamatory passages have faded from the mind; it is interesting that Bach should have combined the obvious alto voice with unison violins and violas, just as he was to do eight years

---

* It is not by any means certain that there had not been recitatives in the early versions, or in Bach's original and possibly uncompleted conception.

† With interludes and some curious brass fundamental effects: do these represent the passage of time, or the inevitability of prophesy and God's purpose, or some aspect of Christ's baptism?

later in Cantata No. 140, *Wachet auf!*, to express readiness. If the aria
"Ein ungefärbte Gemüte" had been published later in an organ transcrip-
tion, it might have become as famous as the "Zion" movement, for it
contains much of the same spirit. In Cantata No. 167 the material which
remains in the memory is all associated with the final chorale: the
penultimate movement—a bass recitative—which has been referring to
the miraculous restoration to speech of the aged Zacharias, ends with
the words ". . . Consider, Christians, the grace which God has given you,
And sing to him a song of devotion!" At these words, the contour of
the opening of the final chorale is most effectively introduced into the
vocal line *a tempo*. The full chorale follows, not in a simple harmonisation but in another beautiful orchestrally-enriched setting such as we
have noticed in Cantatas Nos. 22 and 75: here, the violin/oboe descant
is full of infectious joy, and we are reminded of those biblical texts
prized by Bach which commend the use of instruments as well as voices
in the expression of praise.*

From Trinity + 8 until Trinity + 14, Bach was concerned almost
exclusively with the 1A type of cantata. Musically, there is a
re-emphasis of dramatic characterisation in the opening choruses: this,
coupled with the continued expansion of recitatives, results in a musical
manner that is decidedly more dramatic, even though it is probably no
more operatic, in the sense in which a contemporary Leipziger would
understand that word. Partly, the new power accorded to the opening
choral movements may be attributed to their emotionally weighted texts:

> Cantata No. 46—
> "Behold, and see
> If there be any sorrow like unto my sorrow"
>> (Lamentations 1, 12)
> Cantata No. 25—
> "There is no soundness in my body because of thine anger,
> And no rest in my bones through my transgressions"
>> (Ps. 38, 3)

These opening texts are set in contrasting, rather than similar, ways.
CANTATA NO. 46, *Schauet doch und sehet* (Behold and see), has an
introductory chorus in prelude-and-fugue form; but here, the opening,
with its broad outlines behind the running recorder scales, creates a suitable atmosphere of sad witness that reminds us of the great preludes
to the Passion settings: the chromatically pointed, highly expressive,

---

* The Harnoncourt/Vienna performance of No. 24 brings out much of the character
of the work, although slightly tighter choral discipline might have suited the central
chorus better. There is, regrettably, no recording of Cantata No. 167 available at present
in Great Britain or the U.S.A.

fugue that follows contains that element of inevitability that we associate with the chromatic application by Bach of the formal motet style*; Bach himself recognised the mournful power of this section when he later incorporated it into the B minor Mass for the difficult "Qui tollis" text. CANTATA NO. 25, *Es ist nicht Gesundes* (There is no soundness in my body), which at first glance might be thought to have the least promising text of this group of seven pieces, probably starts with the most striking movement. The instrumental sighs and throbs speak Bach's language of mourning and grief, and when the oboes are joined in their lamentations by the voices, we are reminded backwards of the funereal intensities of No. 106, *Gottes Zeit*, forwards of the intense mourning of the Passions. There is an even closer reminder of the *Matthäuspassion* when a chorale ("Ach Herr, mich armen Sünder") is superimposed. The manner in which the chorale is introduced, despite its contrasting manner of presentation (in four instrumental parts, whereas in the *Matthäuspassion* a different chorale is heard as one *ripieno* soprano line with organ), is similar: it is the unsensational manner of the additional material that is so effective.

The concluding movements of the same seven cantatas (Nos. 136, 105, 46, 179, 69a, 77, 25) show Bach continuing to write the occasional descant over a chorale harmonisation; No. 136 includes a delicate violin embroidery rather like that in Cantata No. 76. He also continues (in No. 46, *Schauet doch*, and No. 105, *Herr, gehe nicht*) to explore the idea of brief commenting instrumental interludes in such movements: the setting of "Jesu, der du meine Seele" from the latter has a dramatically diminishing accompaniment of great beauty, which Karl Geiringer sees as almost a summary of the effect of the whole work. The effect of the final movement of Cantata No. 46 is completely different: here, the two flowing recorder parts (each of which is to be played by two players in unison) effectively sound continuous, as a semiquaver line: a similar effect occurs during the concluding chorale of Part II of the *Weihnachts-Oratorium*. The two final chorales under discussion are both straightforward settings in four parts, but their material could, again, hardly be more different: whilst No. 77, *Du sollt Gott . . . lieben*, concludes with a fine but fairly direct harmonisation, No. 179, *Siehe zu, dass deine Gottesfurcht nicht Heuchelei sei*, ends with what is, even for Bach, a remarkably poignant account of "Wer nur den lieben Gott lässt walten" (see music example on following page). The 1A structure automatically throws the two arias into prominence, and it is therefore hardly surprising that these are usually strongly

---

* Apart from many interesting examples which occur in Bach's choral compositions, the powerful Organ Prelude on "Durch Adams Fall" (from the *Orgel-Büchlein*), BWV 637, illustrates this mode of writing, and Bach's use of it, well.

contrasted musically: No. 46, for example, features first a veritable Dies Irae for militant bass, trumpet (almost certainly a slide-trumpet) and strings, followed by an ethereal "Dance of Blessed Spirits" for two recorders, alto and unison oboes da caccia in the bass. This latter effect will be encountered again, in such works as the *Magnificat*, the *Matthäuspassion* and the "Christchild" Cantata No. 154, *Mein liebsten Jesu ist verloren;* its association for Bach is one of heavenly activity.*

Sunday, July 18, was probably the date for which the well-known motet JESU MEINE FREUDE was composed. Bach's five-part setting of a text derived from Johann Franck's madrigalian text and Romans 8 (a neatly-worded passage contrasting earthly death and heavenly eternity through Christ) is as carefully moulded to the words as are the musical materials of the surrounding *Stücke* discussed above: however, to describe *Jesu meine Freude* as an "unaccompanied cantata"—as has often been done—is essentially inaccurate. First, it is highly unlikely that this, or any of Bach's motets, was performed without instrumental assistance; second, the choral writing does not resemble that of the cantatas in general—textures, styles and word-setting are guided by different traditions and concepts. The suggestion that certain sections of the motets are "instrumental" in character stems from these very differences, and should be considered only with caution: the idea is based on a Nineteenth-century notion of instrumental styles and sonorities, and also partially on a similarly anachronistic tradition of vocal performance of these very pieces. Although *Jesu meine Freude* has a general quality of consoling warmth, its music is rich in musical surprises: many of these are extremely beautiful and striking in themselves, and together they give the work a characteristic rugged yet expressive strength. It is to be regretted that the piece is known in English-speaking countries principally in the Troutbeck non-translation which starts "Jesu priceless treasure."

Leipzig's civic election was celebrated in late August in Leipzig on the Monday following St. Bartholomew's Day (August 24): Dürr reports that Thanksgiving Service could occur on the succeeding Friday. The *Ratswechselgottesdienst* took place in the Nicolaikirche, and

---

* Cantata No. 105 was recorded by Ansermet in 1966; the style is devout and respectful, but heavy and old-fashioned by today's standards. Harnoncourt's poised account of No. 25 is among his best recorded cantatas, really authoritative. In Cantata No. 46, his performance includes some strange features, most especially the very rapid tempo of the concluding chorale which should surely—on account of its content—be more close to that of the first section of the work. Helmut Kahlhöfer assembled for Cantate an outstanding group of musicians including Walter Holy —the narrow-bore trumpet virtuoso—Helmut Winschermann and Jakob Stämpfli. Stämpfli and Holy together in the militant bass aria capture the spirit better than their Amsterdam rivals, but the consistently tasteful playing of the Dutch/Belgian strings and the suave subtlety of their woodwinds is infinitely more pleasant on the ear.

it included the *Ratswahlpredigt* (Civic Festival Sermon) followed by instrumentally accompanied music. For the 1723 *Ratswechsel*, Bach seized the opportunity to employ a larger than customary group of performers. Indeed, to judge from the score of CANTATA NO. 119, *Preise Jerusalem, den Herrn* (Praise the Lord, O Jerusalem), one of the relatively few dated autographs, it seems probable that Bach augmented both his choir and his instrumental forces for this occasion: four trumpets with timpani, but also a continuo section listed as containing "organo, violoncelli, bassoni è violoni (*sic!*) col'organo." It is improbable that Bach had previously directed such a large ensemble.

The text has the exact structure of a 1A cantata up to the second chorus which, even though it is not a chorale setting, starts with figures which are distinctly reminiscent of "Nun danket alle Gott" (known in England as "Now thank we all our God"); up to this point, the text has contained a sensible proportion of biblical allusions—the number that we expect of a piece for a less specialised occasion. To this arrangement has (later?) been added a brief recitative for alto, introducing the final chorale —a setting of verse 4 of Luther's Te Deum paraphrase "Herr Gott, dich loben wir" (1529). This has so much internal energy that we must surely conclude that the (unpreserved) instrumental parts served some elaboratory accompanying role.

The grand and majestic opening chorus is in the style and structure of a French *ouverture*: the material is so complete in the instrumental parts that we are forced to consider the likelihood that this movement, like the equivalent opening of Cantata No. 110, started orchestrally as an instrumental whole without its text. It is in C major, a fact which leads us to recall that the instrumental ensemble *Ouverture in C* (BWV 1066) also stems from the years 1723/24. A comparison of the two first movements soon reveals interesting structural similarities and rhythmic resemblances. The second chorus of No. 119 also contains an interesting —if possibly coincidental—parallel with the *Ouverture*:

The similarity of both position and instrumentation is interesting, and in either context the sounding of this string fanfare is rather striking. As a piece of choral writing, this second *da capo* chorus is much more powerful than the central section of the opening movement; again, we are led to question the origins of that movement—it is by no means as suited to its biblical text as are settings of comparable texts from the preceding cantatas. The first aria, "Wohl dir, du Volk der Linden," has a special local significance through its utilisation of two oboes da caccia—an instrument recently invented in Leipzig by the instrument-maker J. H. Eichentopf. The second aria, "Die Obrigkeit ist Gottes Gabe," refers directly to the benefits (unchallenged in those days of Divine Right) of the city's "republican" form of civil administration, based on that of Rome and the Holy Roman Empire. In a strongly disparaging note on this aria, Arnold Schering claimed that the *staccato* markings in the two-recorder obbligato could not be intended as anything but humorous: in fact, these very markings stress the repeated note B flat, which is, indeed, remarkable and charming, but does not strike the present writer as being particularly humorous. The solution is probably to be found at bars 18–20, where the largest number of repeated B flats occurs: there are thirteen of these, and the Leipzig City Council, in which Magisterial Authority rested, had thirteen members.

Between Trinity+15 and the *Reformationsfest*, Bach presented a series of pieces which at first strike us as diversified in structure as well as style. In fact, they fall rather conveniently into two pairs (+15: Cantata No. 138; +16: No. 95; +21: No. 109;+22: No. 89) separated by an uncertain period (No. 148 is a probable candidate for Trinity+17; there is no such probability for +18 and the *Michaelisfest*) and two adaptations of Weimar originals with texts by Franck (Nos. 162 and 163). There is also the expressive, once again rather mournfully inclined, CANTATA NO. 48, *Ich elender Mensch, wer wird mich erlösen* (Unhappy that I am, who will deliver me?), which is the earliest preserved example of type 1B. The second and third movements of this work—the alto recitative and the following chorale—employ such unpredictable and soul-stirring chromaticisms that we must surely wonder what effect they had on contemporary hearers and the performers themselves. Robertson aptly compares the chorale's anguished harmonies to those of the famous setting of "Es ist genung" in Cantata No. 60. The other particularly striking movement of this work is the rhythmically and harmonically restless aria "Vergibt mir Jesus meine Sünden," a depiction of the constant and life-giving powers of the Saviour: in fact, we find elements in it from the slightly dogmatic motet style, from the dance, from French keyboard rhetoric, and else-where. This movement also compares in an interesting way with the Minuet of Mozart's Symphony No. 40, in that its phrases are built on three-bar groupings which result from an extension through syncopation of what would usually be two-bar units.

CANTATA NO. 138, *Warum betrübst du dich, mein Herz* (Why do you trouble yourself, my heart), and CANTATA NO. 95, *Christus, der ist mein Leben* (Christus, who is my life), both explore the incorporation of chorales in new ways. No. 138 presents settings of three verses of one chorale (including an exuberant setting of the third verse as finale). No. 95 incorporates four different chorales in representative stanzas related to death—the theme of the work (the Gospel for Trinity + 16 tells of the miraculous restoration to life of the widow's son at Nain). These two works are interesting both in that they form a pair of works presumably composed to explore similar ideas in both the Thomaskirche and the Nikolaikirche and also in that they show Bach experimenting with choral chorales in unconscious anticipation of his second *Jahrgang*.

CANTATA NO. 148, *Bringet dem Herrn Ehre seines Namens* (Bring to the Lord the honour of His name) has a particularly fine polyphonic opening chorus in D major for trumpet, strings and choir, followed by a graceful, moving tenor/violin aria whose text and figurations are comparable to the first soprano aria of the *Johannespassion*. If this work does indeed come from 1723, and not later, it marks Bach's first artistic association with the librettist Henrici (Picander): their collaboration in approximately forty preserved works, including the *Matthäuspassion*, indicates at least some degree of philosophical agreement between them. Henrici (1700–1764) was still a student attached to Leipzig University at this time; later he served as an official of the flourishing Leipzig Postal Service, before being made an important local government official in 1740.

CANTATAS NOS. 109 and 89 find Bach reducing the role of his chorus and intertwining his voices with elaborate instrumental counterpoint: this is especially so if we accept Arnold Schering's suggestion that the opening movement of No. 109, *Ich glaube, lieber Herr* (I believe, dear Lord), is more suited to solo, as opposed to choral, four-part treatment. The main subject of each work (faith in the first case; God's wrath and anguish at man's sin, his consistent love and forgiveness towards the repentant in the second) is strongly contrasted, but the musical techniques of these two cantatas, as also of No. 60, *O Ewigkeit*, which follows shortly, anticipate those of the third Leipzig *Jahrgang*.

One of Bach's least known significant works is the Störmthal/ later Trinity, CANTATA NO. 194, *Höchsterwünschtes Freudenfest* (Most desired festival). Our earliest textual materials from this sturdy and tuneful work stem from the performance given by a Leipzig performing ensemble on the occasion of the dedication of the newly-built little church in Störmthal, a village some sixteen kilometres from Leipzig. However, it is apparent that the origins of the piece are earlier: the two chorales, each of which is accorded the unusual luxury of two stanzas, were added for the Störmthal performance, and the scoring was somewhat altered; Bach also removed the movement whose incomplete existence is published in Dürr's commentary. *Höchsterwünschtes Freudenfest* starts with a movement structured like an *ouverture*, in which the voices take part only in the rapid central section and—a surprise entry, this—at the conclusion of the second Grave. The accompaniment is arranged so as to contrast the choir of three oboes and bassoon with the strings in the opening Grave : the unison string scales add a flourish to the sustained directness of the woodwinds, and the "double orchestra" is anchored in common consort by the shared bass-line, as in the preserved "early version" of the *Matthäuspassion*. When the reprise is reached, the roles of woodwind and strings are reversed, to pleasing symmetrical effect. The running instrumental scales will remind many listeners of the opening of the *Weihnachts-Oratorium*. No doubt these elements of contrast are responsible for Bach having headed the work *Concerto*.

Three of the movements for vocal soloists have a character closely associated with dances following an *ouverture*: No. 3 is something like a country dance, No. 5 like a Gavotte, No. 10 like a primly fussy Minuet. The fourth one, the aria "Des Höchsten Gegenwart allein," seems to have less of the character of a Gigue accorded to it by Neumann than that of a flattering homage-aria. It should be stressed, perhaps, that the actual music of most of this cantata is closer stylistically to the preserved Cöthen choral music than it is to any purely instrumental music and that the chorales were inserted for Störmthal rather than the later Leipzig version on Trinity Sunday. Certainly the cantata was heard—unchanged—as a celebratory piece for that festival. However, for Bach the main problem in its adaptation would not have been textual—the text is, indeed, quite well suited to the end-of-year associations of Trinity Sunday—but rather the transfer of the music to workable pitch at Leipzig : Störmthal pitch was unusually low.

The *Stück* for Trinity + 24, 1723, was headed by Bach : *Dialogus zwischen Furcht u. Hoffnung* (Dialogue between Fear and Hope). In fact, a third party is involved in the discussion, the comforting voice of the Saviour, quoted from John XIV, 13, and appropriately accorded to the bass voice. The two abstract characters are also carefully designated—to the two characteristically "heroic" voice-timbres from contemporary opera. CANTATA NO. 60, *O Ewigkeit* —for this *is* a cantata in the Italian sense—is conceived on an elevated plane. Its text and music are full of subject-matter for discussion: the symbols that are evoked, the quotations that are woven into the textures, are complex and richly presented. The two chorales were already rich in associations: "O Ewigkeit," almost a Dies Irae to the Lutheran Church, had associations of judgement combined with power (both of good and of evil), and was, as a congregational hymn, particularly square and forceful. "Es ist genung" has a special vigour and strength also; for Bach himself, it would have had important local associations as the chorale came from Thuringia. Dürr's note that the chorale melody starts by extending the interval associated with the first line from a perfect to an augmented fourth, thus creating a sense of exciting liberation, helps us to associate ourselves with the cantata's first hearers: the same kind of effect is used to convey despair at the start of the first recitative, and the "genung" *motif* occurs later in the same movement, both in disguised inversion and its basic form:

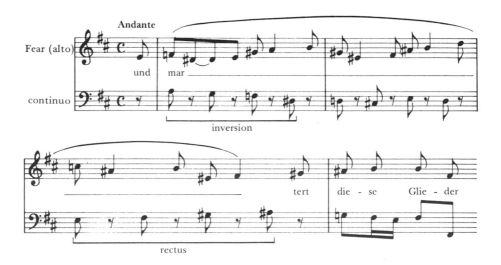

This particular work has been favoured by commentators with strongly contrasted philosophies and critical approaches; it is one of those works of art in which the "classical" and the "romantic" fuse, in which the detailed calculations of the creator are produced with apparent spontaneity. The biblical quotation by the bass, which has been anticipated at the conclusion of the first recitative, is beautifully incorporated, first, it seems, as a general epitaph, but soon, through its character and its extension verbally, as a message of hope and reassurance.*

---

* The Munich recording under Richter is of a kind that would surely have appealed strongly to Brahms—full of orchestral zest, *innigkeit* and disciplined tidiness: an interesting experience. There are, however, accentuations and bowings in the strings that would have seemed ridiculous to the point of hilarity to a violinist of Bach's day.

Between Trinity + 24 and Christmas 1723, Bach apparently composed one new *Kirchenstück* (Cantata No. 90) and utilised two earlier
compositions of which one (No. 70, *Wachet! betet!*) required the
addition of new recitatives and the other (No. 61, *Nun komm*) was
re-used without substantial re-structuring. CANTATA NO. 90, *Es reisset euch*
(A terrible end will seize you), is a compact work based on a text which
refers to various sources, but combines them effectively; here there
is no central chorale. The central aria, thus thrown into relief, is a
dramatic piece for trumpet and strings, a veritable Dies Irae which tells
of Christ purging the temple and which draws the traditional parallel
of God judging and punishing the world for its equivalent offences. The
clarino line (no particular instrument is indicated in the score) has
dazzling solos—last trump effects—which contrast the solidity of
arpeggiated chords with the fluidity of rapid scales. The earlier tenor
aria, with its fateful accumulating scales to illustrate God's wrath, is
throughout very tautly written for the strings, but the effect is less
fiery and dramatic, more elegant and dispassionate. The final chorale,
a rather smug stanza from the chorale "Nimm von uns, Herr," expresses
confidence that Leipzig in 1723, at least, has no reason to fear God's
wrath; this apparently self-satisfied philosophy is, however, completely
in keeping with some branches of orthodox Lutheran thinking in
Bach's day.*

*

The Advent season after the first Sunday and the Sundays in Lent
was an official period of repentance and self-preparation in the Lutheran
church; only on Palm Sunday was there likely to be any "elaborated
music" (in German: *Figuralmusik*) and in Leipzig even that occasion
was not usually celebrated. These periods provided for the preparation—possibly also for the composition—of the extended Christmas
pieces or music for Passiontide and Easter. To some extent Bach and
his associates would have had time to concentrate on practice and
self-examination regarding technical problems.

The main *Stück* for Christmas Day 1723 was Cantata No. 63,
Christen, ätzet diesen Tag (see Chapter One for discussion); this was the
first occasion on which its organisation was, with any certainty, that
which we know today. The other two pieces linked with this Christmas
are the festive SANCTUS IN D (BWV 238) and the MAGNIFICAT with
interpolations (BWV 243a). The *Sanctus* is compact, but energetic in

---

* The Schroeder recording has the clean instrumental delivery and energetic musical
vitality we expect from the Amsterdam musicians; the Hamburg singers are at their
best and there is some good solo work.

expression. The words "Sanctus Dominus Deus Sabaoth" are set in a formal style with obbligato violin above the voices*: its required speed is by no means clear, as is the case with the equivalent passage of its more famous successor of the following year. There is another parallel in the more obviously polyphonic "Pleni" which follows; the main theme of this presumably faster section will immediately strike many keyboard players as similar to the tail of the F major fugue subject from Book II of "The 48" (BWV 880, 2).

Although the vernacular was of essential importance to Reformation philosophies, Latin had continued to play an important part in public worship during and after Luther's lifetime. The well-loved Ordinary was not forgotten, and, no doubt, its international and almost dialect-proof character was appreciated by all but the most radical reformers. The weekly *Hauptgottesdienst* at Leipzig included the Kyrie, Gloria, Gospel (intoned) and Creed (Plainsong) all in Latin, in keeping with Lutheran policy that "In our churches Mass is celebrated every Sunday . . . when the sacrament is offered to those who desire it . . . We keep traditional forms, such as the order . . . we keep Latin for the sake of those who study and understand it." At the non-festal *Vespergottesdienst* (afternoon service), however, there was no Latin on ordinary Sundays. The *Magnificat* was customarily sung in German to the short chant known as the *Tonus peregrinus (noni toni)* with straightforward, repeated (possibly antiphonal) chordal accompaniment: usually, this was in a harmonisation by the great Renaissance Leipzig composer Johann Hermann Schein, although Bach himself seems to have written similar chant-like settings himself. On the main religious Feasts, however, the Vespers *Magnificat* was heard in verse-settings: semi-dramatic, elaborated musical settings with orchestral accompaniment. These *followed* the Vespers sermon, whereas a festive *Stück* preceded it, or both preceded and followed it. It is not certain whether even the three main festivals always demanded a festive *Magnificat*, that this was customarily by Bach himself, or whether an orchestral accompaniment was always present (especially if a cantata with two parts was also involved). Nevertheless, it is rather surprising that only one such setting has come down to us from Bach—although its two versions almost justify consideration as separate compositions.

In 1723 the earlier E flat major version was performed. This work is clearly related to Leipzig and Christmas: both connections relate to Kuhnau's Christmas cantata *Vom Himmel hoch* of 1721, which had

---

* The recording by the London Bach Society under Steinitz does not project the first section successfully, owing to apparent ill-digestion of the styles involved: the treatment of the violin line, especially, is unsympathetic as well as technically ill-at-ease. The second section fares better, although the choir is too big and the engineering does not help it to sound as though its members care.

employed spaced choirs including a "chorus angelorum" (probably a small semi-chorus), and from the text of which Bach apparently drew for his own interpolations. These all have strong traditional and textual associations with Christmas: "Vom Himmel hoch" and "Freut euch" with the annunciation to the shepherds, "Gloria in excelsis" with the angel chorus and "Virga Jesse floruit" with the cradled Christ-child as the fulfilment of the hope of ages. "Vom Himmel hoch" also has general Christmas associations, but the other pieces and their links with the story of the shepherds are appropriately Jewish in accent. This has two important aspects: first, Mary is a Jew, and her song of praise links Jewish teaching and Old Testament teaching to Christian teaching and the New Testament through its emphasis on the significance of Christ's birth; second, the state of Israel seems clearly to have been considered as a symbol of local society—the city, the parish, the state—in Lutheran teaching of Bach's time: Lutheran theologians even contested the subject of how restricted the "chosen people" of Christianity were.

Bach's *Magnificat* is one of his most striking pieces of music in many ways; yet its especial interest lies in its widespread incorporation of traditional devices. The illustrative approach to the text is particularly interesting from this point-of-view. In "Magnificat ... Dominum" the long held notes in the first trumpet strike us first, the gradual accumulations within the harmonies only later as illustrating the word "magnificat." The first two notes of the leading trumpet, which rise from mediant to dominant, the emphatic use of four upbeat quavers and the held descending scales are probably all deliberate references to the *tonus peregrinus*:

Tonus Peregrinus (E♭ pitch)

The string and trumpet fanfares have a special Italianate brilliance well worth individual study; the two oboes (no flutes in the E flat version) play quicker music to depict an active response. However, it is the bass-line of this chorus that gives it its heart and its energy: nearly all of Bach's basses are of melodic, as well as harmonic, interest, but this one is particularly expressive. In "Et exsultavit ... salutari meo" the exultation is parallel to the magnification: it starts with the same three notes (NB. the latter two). The little bass-line flourish seems to be a special musical gesture to signify special pleasure, the charming melisma on "exsul-*ta*-vit" etc. to convey emotion. The singer is the second soprano—there is one soloist from each of the five voices of the chorus. Possibly a slightly mellower treble is required here in comparison to the one called for in the "Quia respexit."

The first interpolation, "Vom Himmel hoch," is a *cantus firmus* treatment of the chorale with the soprano parts united over an accompaniment that is entirely choral, and which anticipates each line. The movement balances the "Suscepit" which is placed third from the end. There is no certainty about the number of voices expected in either of these movements, nor, indeed, through most of the work, although some of the movements would barely sound balanced if soloists were not employed. The rhythmic vitality and the illustrative descending lines of this "Vom Himmel hoch" are particularly well suited to the season. In "Quia respexit . . ." the obbligato line given to oboe surely stresses humility; the lyrical minor lines and harmonies are really full of joy, although it is none too easy for us to notice that after two-and-a-half centuries of contrary emphasis by expert composers. The start of the oboe's notation in dotted rhythms almost certainly indicates that the semiquavers are to be played unequally in some way, but we cannot be sure how; furthermore, it would be incorrect to assume that these rhythms provide a performer's blueprint for the later D major version, which also has important differences in its actual notes. This version suffers from its unfamiliarity; it should be brought to life by capable performers.

"Omnes generationes": to set just two words as a whole movement would be curious but for the fact that it illustrates its text through particularly energetic counterpoint. The short *fugato* is rich in emphatic *stretto* and vigorously uncompromising lines: the fierce unresolved dominant minor ninth chord at bar 24 is especially heightened by the following snatch of "choral cadenza" after the fermata. The accumulation at the end expresses the overwhelming power of God as implied in the text. Whether the long *melismata* on "potens" and "magna" in "Quia fecit mihi magna" are designed to illustrate either or both, they certainly do. Less obvious is the traditional scaffolding behind the pattern-bass of the continuo; taking it from the bass' entry, we find the following melodic line:

The new expressive figure introduced by the voice at "et sanctum nomen eius" might also be derived from the *peregrinus*, as it resembles the contours of its responsorial line. In the second interpolation, "Freut euch," the little dancing figure which gives the continuo bass-line its lightness is, rather like that of the "Et exsultavit," a portrayal of rejoicing that is physical and earthly : above, the message of the angels is emphasised in the selection of high-pitched voices (the bass, or basses, are silent) and the interweaving of the soprano lines—indeed, of all of the vocal parts. If this is a motet style, it is of a particularly spirited kind. Its material compares in various ways with the eighth and ninth movements : the opening three notes in the imitative soprano parts are those noted above in the first two movements, but now in the dominant key (B flat).

"Et misericordia . . timentibus eum" : the string accompaniment in 12/8 time is pastoral in style—a characteristic one for the illustration of appreciative gratitude, even though there are no flutes in the score here (the music would fit only awkwardly on the beaked flutes employed later in the "Esurientes"). The shimmering chromatic trill on the tenor's final "timentibus" did not survive in the revision, but a textual oddity —"eum" for "eius"—did. In "Fecit potentiam . . . dispersit superbos mente cordis sui" the power of God, vividly painted in the vocal writing, is related closely to his upheld splendour. The restraint with which Bach reserves the trumpets and drums for specially significant moments is ingenious. The splendid climax at the telling words "in the imagination of their hearts" contains nothing that could not—in detail and out of this context—have been composed by many of Bach's contemporaries : it is the whole in context that is so personal to him.

The third interpolation, "Gloria in excelsis deo," sums up the essence of the *Magnificat*'s relevance to Christmas. The violin descant line, taking the texture into six real parts, relates to the similar effect in the *Sanctus in D*. The homophonic style is emphatic and festive, the rhythmic kinship between descant and bass is an Italianate feature which was probably instinctively included as it was an established expressive vehicle. However, this movement gives the impression of containing elements of which we do not know : could it not be that it incorporates music by another composer (Kuhnau?)? In "Deposuit potentes . . . et exaltavit humiles" the two verbs are illustrated musically : "deposuit" by scurrying downward scales of fierce rhetoric, "exaltavit" by flourishing *melismata* that rise in answer. The unsoftened leap of a minor ninth at "deposu-*it*," which was eliminated in the later revision, is a parallel to the harmonic emphasis on the same interval in "Omnes generationes" (the fourth movement out of twelve; this is the eighth). In the next movement, "Esurientes implevit bonis," the upper accompanying lines are here in the plural, probably to represent the hungry. Because the text describes God's merciful bounty towards the righteous, the motives are refined and joyous, and the sweet flutes are an inspired choice, together with the continuo bass-line sensitively punctuated with rests. The alto blends with this ensemble to particularly graceful effect, and the resulting style is beautifully serene and balanced, rather like Bach's own experiments with the Polish style in instrumental music. The dismissal of the rich without reward is far more gently portrayed than the descent of the mighty, but again the unsympathetic reception is conveyed through downward scales. The words "sent empty away" are illustrated by a sudden silence of the recorders at the end.

The last interpolation, the Latin hymn "Virga Jesse floruit," is traditionally associated with the rocking of the cradled Christ-child, and the gentle rocking nature of the quasi-*ostinato* bass-line represents this element. The text also refers to God's chosen people. The preceding and succeeding movements also stress the same concept.*

In "Suscepit Israel . . . misericordiae suae" the interweaving lines of the three vocal parts create the impression of a musical Jacob's ladder —an apposite one here. The slightly *affettuoso* repeated notes of the violins-and-violas bass-line convey a feeling of involvement. Above, the trumpet (da tirarsi) intones the *peregrinus* in steadily projected dignity. The harmonies are at times very bold, but the contrapuntal web is so skilfully woven that we only notice the effect, which is extremely sensuous. The "recordatus" motive (introduced by the alto/altos at bar 18) is related to the second line of the *peregrinus*; it is also of the pattern sometimes described as a "cross-*motif*" but, more important, it has so strong a character of sympathetic support—almost a gesture of consolation. The slightly inconclusive conclusion (half "modal," half tonally imperfect) surely implies that God still sustains His people.

The dignified and even slightly archaic fugue in "Sicut locutus est . . . in saecula" conveys an appropriate atmosphere of formality for the description of God's covenant with Abraham. It is also very cleverly placed from the point-of-view of the *Magnificat*'s musical structure: it separates the three foregoing movements (which are rather gentle and contemplative, even though they certainly involve us) from the "Gloria patri." It also returns us firmly to E flat major (the key of the opening *two* movements) and marks the conclusion of Mary's words in Luke 1. A specially interesting detail is the apparently deliberate quotation of the falling scale from the last line of "Vom Himmel hoch" in the first soprano from bar 41. In "Gloria patri . . . et in saecula saeculo. Amen" the rhetorical opening to the doxology is effectively coloured by the

---

* "The proud" would probably be associated with the infidel Turks, "the rich" with the secular powers of Rome to Lutherans of Bach's time, whereas those who had humbly hungered for Christ during Advent would, in local experience, be seen to be Lutherans. The very special affection with which Bach treats this portion of the text is only explained by assuming that he saw "Israel" as representing collective groups of which he was a member.

accumulation of harmonic suspense until bar 19, by which time all Three Persons have been glorified. There follows a cleverly compressed reprise of materials from the first movement ("as it was in the beginning")—another traditional device but here put to particularly good use. The organisation of the triplets in the introduction is, however, the most remarkable feature here: an impression is given of an olympian ceremonial preparation for the apparently familiar "commonplace" of the doxology. This must have been deliberate. The *Magnificat* is, indeed, a song of glorification for all ages, the battle-hymn of the Word. The test of composers who strive to set it has always been the challenge of making The Word live. Nobody has made better Flesh of this Word than Bach.*

*

The remaining *Stücke* from Bach's first Christmas season are Cantatas Nos. 40, 64, 190, 153 and 65: they stretch forward to Epiphany, the celebration of the Gentiles' homage to the infant Christ. The feast of St. Stephen, the first Christian martyr, coincided with the customary celebration of the second day of Christmas. The latter aspect accounts for the use of a pair of horns in CANTATA NO. 40. *Dazu ist erschienen der Sohn Gottes* (The Son of God appeared so as to *destroy the work of the devil*); however, these are cleverly restricted to those movements having some element of festivity——their *concertante* dialogue with the two oboes in the opening chorus is well organised. The remainder of this work is dominated by the rearing head of the serpent: the bass aria, actually addressed to the serpent, has a sinister and demoniac character which compares with the two arias of Cantata No. 90; the tenor one, in contrast, is gentle and intimate in its festive charm. Of the three chorales, the final one is by no means familiar to English hearers melodically. The first one, a verse from Füger's *Wir Christenleut* is most expressively harmonised to emphasise the nature of its text: usually, this is a festive and enthusiastic melody, treated in a popular carolling style.

CANTATA NO. 64, *Sehet, welch eine Lieber*, is the first of a series of pieces with the textual structure 1B. In the opening scriptural text—"See then what love the Father shows us, that we are called Sons of God"—the word "Sehet" (see) is spaced for emphasis at the start. Later, at bars 98–99, occurs a dramatic general pause to introduce the final phrase of the text—an equivalent procedure to that written at the conclusion of the *Magnificat*'s "Fecit potentiam." The rest of the cantata concentrates

---

* See under Recommended Recordings for discussion of performances of the *Magnificat* on disc.

on the insubstantiality of earthly treasures as opposed to heavenly riches. The rapid scales in the continuo part of the alto recitative "Geh, Welt" and later in the violin accompaniment to the soprano aria very probably illustrate the temporary aspect of the former: comparison with Cantata No. 26 is relevant here.

The New Year *Stück*, CANTATA NO. 190, *Singet dem Herrn* (Sing to the Lord), which must have been a splendidly celebratory work, only partly survives. The opening movement, which blended elements from the Psalm-chorale of the title, the Te Deum melody and a Hallelujah with *concertante* and fugal materials, must have sounded especially grand. The orchestra included the full four-part trumpet-and-drum choir.

For the Sunday after the feast of the Circumcision, the Gospel at Leipzig appears to have been Matt. II, 13–15, the account of the Flight into Egypt. The subject of CANTATA NO. 153, *Schau, lieber Gott* (Behold, dear God), is the Christian beset by adversity: the first two chorale texts come from the mid-Seventeenth century, when German literature was dominated by the Thirty Years' War, the second aria (for tenor and string orchestra) conveys the majesty and turbulence of a storm in sophisticated chamber-music imagery. The bass' recitative returns text and music to trust in Kod (in the person of Christ) after the disturbing storm-aria for tenor. The alto's penultimate song is one of optimism and good cheer: the accompaniment now has a confident swagger and an extrovert finesse.

CANTATA NO. 65, *Sie werden aus Saba alle kommen* (They will come *in droves* from Sheba), is a highly approachable festive piece for Epiphany. The reference to Sheba seems to have inspired Bach to attempt special coloured and visually representative instrumentation: two beaked flutes (in F), two oboes de caccia with their exotic bells and two horns (in C—an octave below Haydn's beloved ones in C alto), with strings. The instruments are used very effectively: the horns to convey majestic mystery and antiquity, the flutes possibly to represent the high pitches much exploited in Eastern music, and the gurgling tenor oboes to represent the shawm-like double-reed instruments of Asia and the Near East. This special instrumental colouring is evident in the opening chorus and the tenor's extremely attractive summarising aria "Nimm mich dir . . . hin," which has the style of a purposeful dance and a splendid array of *concertato* effects. In the opening chorus, an imitative, yet essentially homophonic choral opening is followed by a tuneful fugue—a form often used by Bach to illustrate abundance, as we have seen. *Sie werden aus Saba* must have sounded especially rich tonally after its strings-with-continuo predecessor of four days earlier. It was also fitting that Bach ended this last composition for his first Leipzig Christmas with a fine tenor solo: the singer had been supplied with particularly demanding solos throughout the season. CANTATA NO.

154, *Mein liebster Jesus ist verloren* (My dear Jesus is lost), may incorporate some Weimar materials; it is, nevertheless, a splendid example of the type 1B, and its text has the appearance of being well planned in the context of its surrounding pieces. Later we encounter literary materials which refer less directly to the Epistle for the day (Romans XII, 1–6), a passage concerned with the Christian doctrine of the relationship between belief and behaviour. In the ensuing recitative the tenor introduces the more personal aspect of separation from Christ: the words "Verlangen" (yearning) and "empfindlich rühren" (touch to the quick) are appropriately set to affective harmonies and melodic lines requiring conventional *appoggiature*. The core of the cantata lies in the next three movements: the alto aria contains an illustration of separation from Christ in the deliberate omission of the organ continuo, and the writing of intertwining textures for two oboes and *ripieno* upper strings around the voice. A part for cembalo survives for this aria, but it is not known whether this was employed in the 1724 performance or a later one. Bach's preference for the bass voice (customary for God or God in Christ) in preference to the more apparently realistic treble soprano is notable, and gives rise to interesting contemplation of his view of the *Kirchenstück* as alternately "dramatic" or "liturgical" in emphasis. The return of the tenor voice brings back musical motives associated with his opening aria (the falling diminished fifth in the bass, for example) and his earlier recitative (the words "ich war von Schmerzen krank" are treated similarly to the earlier "Verlangen"). This recitative's text is an extended theological contemplation based on the love of Christ as derived on the opening line from the Song of Songs, on the yearning for Christ fashionable since the Seventeenth century in German literature and theology, with its madrigalian imagery, and an ingenious interpretation of Christ's words as representing the Bible, of the Temple as representing the Sanctuary. The tenor and alto join for the duet "Wohl mir, Jesus ist gefunden": the jubilant style, with its instrumental flourishes and the consonant parallel vocal lines, reminds us of those satisfied duets from contemporary operas. The final chorale takes verse six of Keymann's text "Meinem Jesu": it has an affirmative character, achieved especially through the constant quaver movement in the bass within each line.

For Epiphany + 2 Bach re-utilised a Weimar piece, Cantata No. 155, *Mein Gott, wie lang, ach lange*. The libretto, by Salomo Franck, is directly related to significant points in the Epistle and Gospel, the subject-matter follows that of the preceding Sunday particularly aptly. For Epiphany + 3, was composed CANTATA NO. 73, *Herr, wie du willt, so schicks mit mir* (Lord, do just as you wish with me), which is concerned with self-dedication throughout. The two most striking movements are the first—which is a complicated chorale for homophonic chorus, with

derived as well as independent accompaniment and particularly striking
use of recitative interpolations—and the recitative-with-aria for bass.
This pair of movements, expressive of the poet's joy even in death at
God's wish, is remarkable in that it is unusually outspoken emotionally
for a bass aria with a text which is really (despite its personal recitative
introduction) taken from the Bible. The various detached notes (*pizzicato*
does not necessarily denote plucking of the strings in Bach's music) at
the words "so schlagt, ihr Leichenglocken" (Strike then, o funeral bells)
depict agitation and rising tension, possibly the ticking of a clock, even
perhaps the striking of the bells themselves.* The whole aria is fluid
in texture and of an intensely emotional motivic structure. One wonders
whether Bach realised that his telling opening vocal phrase was identical
to that of Stölzel's *Bist du bei mir* (which Anna Magdalena later entered
into her second album).† Certainly this is a profoundly stirring
movement.

In CANTATA NO. 81, *Jesus schläft, was soll ich hoffen?* (Jesus sleeps,
where *lies my* hope?), we encounter another work with a strikingly
involved emotional style. The subject-matter is based on the Gospel
(Matt. VIII, 23–27), which tells of Christ's sleeping, the development of
a storm, and His summary stilling of it when awakened. The same
subject-matter of the soul's communion with Christ therefore appears
again—probably a set of related sermons on this theme was responsible—
but it is treated with intense, intimate drama in the music. The opening
aria has an accompaniment of sighing *motifs* similar to those employed
at the start of Cantata No. 25: Christ's sleeping gives the soul cause for
deep anxiety. The tenor's recitative and aria adds terror and alarm to
the alto's apprehensive pessimism: the string accompaniment to "Die
schäumenden Wellen von Belials Bächen" is a more excited chamber
portrayal of a storm than that in Cantata No. 153. In those short interludes, which Bach marks *adagio*, the poet even seems to question basic
tenets of Christianity: Bach apparently recognised this and hurled all
his energy into a suitably Belial-like portrayal. The following biblical
arioso is superbly restrained, dignified and comforting in immediate
juxtaposition. Even here, though, the style is warmer and more emotional
than is customary, and this becomes even more apparent when the
biblical *arioso* transfers without interruption or change of person into
an elaborated madrigalian aria. A short summarising recitative—in which
we return to listen to the alto—and the homophonic chorale end the
work neatly; the latter is Stanza II of "Jesu, meine Freude," the melody

---

* Compare the alto solo at "Schlage doch" in Cantata No. 161.

† This aria, long considered to be Bach's own, and an extremely good example of
Eighteenth-century German song in its own right, is a secular love-song: "When you
are by me I flourish happily."

of which had been heard in a contrasting setting only six weeks earlier (in Cantata No. 64).

For the Feast of the Purification of the Blessed Virgin Mary, the Gospel included the account of Christ's presentation in the Temple and of Simeon's song, the Nunc Dimittis; the Epistle foretold of the Lord's sudden arrival in the Temple (clearly relevant). CANTATA NO. 83, *Erfreute Zeit im neuen Bunde* (O joyful day of our new salvation), is chiefly preoccupied with Simeon's ready acceptance of the Christ-child and of his own death: so festive is the occasion of our meeting with God, the poet argues, that we are happy during the period of waiting that precedes our death. Again we encounter the "God with us" theme of the series of *Stücke* under examination, and again, Christ's presence may be considered as felt intuitively, as experienced at the Eucharist or as reassuring contemplation on death. The main movement in No. 83 is the "Intonazione e Recitativo" on the Nunc Dimittis for bass. It is a fluidly-planned chorale commentary for one singer, with canonic accompaniment for unison upper strings and continuo, making use of one of the nine Gregorian Psalm-tones habitually associated with the text in the Leipzig services: it is one of Bach's most difficult movements to organise rhythmically in performance. The use of the bass voice is predictable by now. This movement comes second: on each side of it is an aria with prominent solo violin which contemplates with joy the prospect of union with Christ—the theory that the violin lines once belonged to a (lost) violin concerto must be reported, but the style of the first is hardly right, the structure of each is a fairly strict *da capo* form, and the words are illustrated decoratively. Bach integrated so many different styles, types and structures into his music that we should not be surprised by concerto figurations and flourishes, even less by *concertante* virtuosity, in the context of a church cantata.

Bach's "Concerto" for Septuagesima 1724, CANTATA NO. 144, *Nimm, was dein ist, und gehe hin*, opens with an imposing contrapuntal chorus in Bach's vigorous motet style. The text—"Take what is thine, and depart"—is from the Gospel for the day, which tells of the parable of the unequally treated labourers in the vineyard. The two arias both employ expressive devices from secular styles to convey atmosphere; the string-accompanied alto one in dance-style is simple and direct, the lovely soprano one with oboe d'amore in sonata style is so extremely joyful that we are not surprised to find that it is in B minor. The expressive feature of this work, however, is the way in which the falling major scale from the sixth to the tonic is exploited in the opening movement—itself a finely-wrought, close-knit structure. CANTATA NO. 181, *Leichtgesinnte Flattergeister rauben sich des Wortes Kraft* (The irresponsible and frivolous deprive themselves of the Word's power), is built around the parable of the Sower. The aria (for bass) is rhetorical in style, rather than dramatic or restrained, to suit the text, and there is a somewhat light-headed swagger about its instrumental music. There were no woodwinds at the first performance. The central movements contemplate the serious dangers of irresponsibility, philosophically in a flexible alto recitative, with grim caution in the tenor's aria with continuo, and more straightforwardly in the soprano recitative. The final movement is not a chorale but an independent contrapuntal choral movement in praise of the Word: it is in *da capo* structure with a central (solo?) duet section; for this movement, Bach calls for a trumpet in D to join the strings. The entire cantata is remarkable for the absence of any chorale or apparent space for one. The congregation of the Nikolaikirche had probably not witnessed the performance of such an unusual *Stück* for a very long time.

The remaining two *Kirchenstücke* before Lent 1724 were for Estomihi and the Feast of the Annunciation. For the former Bach again used the material today catalogued as BWV 22 which had been composed for his Leipzig "examination" the year before. A circulated text, preserved in printed form in Leningrad and only recently discovered, indicates that it was at this stage that it reached its present form. The Leningrad booklet also contains the text of a cantata for the Feast of the Annunciation, but no music by Bach has survived for that occasion. We move on, therefore, to the *Johannespassion*.

*

Bach's musical apparatus was so much involved with tradition that we tend not to notice his originality. The *Passio secundum Johannem* of 1724 is an example in point.

The Eighteenth century's new kind of Passion Music was similar to its new and operatically-derived *Kirchenstück*: it introduced, besides the traditional biblical text and chorales, madrigalian poetry set for soloists and chorus in the manner of Italian oratorio. The main centre for Passion Music composition was Hamburg, where, around 1720, as many as four or five settings might be heard in one year. Leipzig's first representative composer of the century, Johann Kuhnau, had composed church music of a rather traditional, un-operatic kind in general, but had eventually written a *Passio ex Evangelista Marco* in 1721: music of an elevated Schütz-like detachment which, despite some "modern" features, would have seemed old-fashioned to Bach. This had been the only Eighteenth-century Passion performed in Leipzig before Bach's installation. Nor could he seek examples or specialist advice from his relations: his settings were the first from the Bach family.

Today the JOHANNESPASSION (BWV 245) suffers from too much ill-considered comparison with the *Matthäuspassion* and too little consideration alongside the cantatas and its original context. The text, which is apparently more of a compilation than an original work of art in itself, is anonymous; it seems to have been written in collaboration with Bach, or carefully adapted by him, but there is really no evidence that Bach himself aspired to any literary pretensions. Briefly, the biblical account (from John XVIII and XIX, with additions from Matthew on Peter's remorse and the earthquake at Christ's death—except for the third performance, for which these additions were excluded) contains minor verbal inconsistencies which make it precisely match no preserved printed Bible text: however, the librettist does seem to have referred to the John-Passion text printed in Vopelius's "Neu Leipziger Gesangbuch" of 1682.

Much has been written concerning the architecture of the work, which is certainly awe-inspiring and economical. However, the claim that it fits easily into a symmetrical design (as a whole or in its central core) does not really stand up to investigation: Friedrich Smend's ingenious theories of around 1950 may now be said to have been discredited. There is no real reason why the Passion story should be organised into such a pattern: indeed, this of all subjects is incomplete, and there is no reason why it should be more appropriately illustrated by the symmetrical Cross than by the complex but irregular Crown of Thorns.

The *Johannespassion* is built out of dramatically presented recitatives, chorales, *arioso*- and aria-movements, a few combinations of these types, and choruses. The recitatives are of a kind which Bach had hardly ever used: the Evangelist, represented by a tenor, is joined by Christ (not surprisingly a bass) and the choir, which, as well as representing the crowd, in the *turba* choruses, also supplies soloists for the smaller individual roles. The material of the biblical narrative is all delivered in a recitative style; even the choral passages are rhythmically of this character, and they show in their treatment of tonality and in their instrumental writing other characteristics of accompanied recitative; together with their memorable harmonic boldness, these features must have made them seem highly challenging, if not perplexing, to their Eighteenth-century hearers.

The two recitatives to be discussed here as examples open the narrative portions of the two parts: "Jesus ging mit seinen Jüngern" (Jesus went with his disciples) and "Da führeten sie Jesum" (Then they led Jesus). They therefore have some purposes in common: to present the subject-matter of the next scene to the congregation, and to engage the interest of both listeners and performers. The two compound movements also involve some description, some dialogue and two crowd-contributions which are similar, and on related topics. Recitative has conventions of performance (notation, timing, speed, ornamentation, disposition of the accompaniment, etc.); it also presents us with interesting problems regarding its precise interpretation. It may be pure coincidence that resulted in Bach opening the action of his first Passion with a reference to the "Bach Kidron" (brook Kedron); on the other hand, we do know that Bach is supposed to have referred to his later pupil and young friend Johann Ludwig Krebs as "the only crab [= Krebs] in the brook," and also that one of the composer's earliest Leipzig compositions had started with the words "Murmelt nur, ihr heitern Bäche" (Murmur on, contented streams). The fact that this opening phrase of the Evangelist's text is set to a signature of fourteen notes will probably not have passed unnoticed, either, but a remarkable possibility in the accompaniment probably has—an anticipation of the Passion's first chorale implied by the figuring of the continuo harmonies:

However improbable all these speculations may seem, it is surely no coincidence that the first word of the action is "Jesus," the first word of the second sentence is "Judas." They are the principal characters of the first scene of the drama; they are also, inasfar as Judas represents sinful man, the main subjects of the entire work. "Jesus" is set to an arpeggiated falling *minor* triad (by tradition a symbol of the Trinity and hence God); "Judas" to a falling *diminished* triad (spanning the diminished fifth, known as *diabolus in musica*). This is no more a symbolic portrayal than a well-managed expressive treatment of St. John's rhetoric. St. John's comment that it was Judas "der ihn verriet" (who betrayed Him) is repeated at bar 24; Bach here expands some of the nature of the "tierce" harmonies, and produces a strikingly more plaintive (rather than more savage) effect. Passing rapidly over the high *tessitura* accorded—in typical Baroque manner—to the high priests, we reach the splendidly aloof modulation at Christ's first utterance: aloof from what we expected, but, again, with the warm association of harmonies employing a conspicuous major third.

At a first glance the other recitative under consideration might seem to start completely differently. It is true that Jesus is named first, and in the first phrase, and also that the Jewish community (representing mankind) is the subject of the second sentence, but the harmonic and melodic patterns initially strike us as quite different. In fact there is a strong rhythmic similarity (partly the result of the text, but not wholly so); there is a resemblance in the way in which the succeeding phrases balance, yet become more detached and rapid to portray action, in the way in which words of significance are treated specially. In "Da führeten sie Jesum," the word "Richthaus" (courthouse) twice concludes with a sumptuous *appoggiatura* (implied), the word "Ostern" (Passover and Easter are identical in German) is set with unusual delaying harmonies, "nicht unrein" (not defiled) is illustrated in the melody and harmony also. Pilate's dignified entry is finely set: perhaps it is no coincidence that the word "Menschen" (man) is set to a (probably decorated) minor triad: to define Christ as human does not signify the whole truth.

Each recitative now introduces the chorus. In Part One the pair of choruses signifies the repeated answer of the crowd seeking to arrest Jesus; the second, whilst not strictly a repeat of the first, is very similar. The activity and positive effort of the search for Christ is conveyed by the flute with violin line and the accompanying oboes and lower strings, whose material gains in activity as each little choral section progresses. The harmonic basis of the second chorus and its recitative is a descending tetrachord (G, F, E flat, D/C, B flat, A flat, G), preceded by chords establishing the keys respectively of G minor and C minor. The broken divisions above disguise this essentially chaconne-like figure, a veritable *cliché* of the period, but the real interest lies in the vocal writing, which is closely arranged harmonically and so that the main accent of the quadruple metre is shifted from the start of the bar to the centre: each bar of the vocal writing starts with a rest, stressing the urgency and the energy of the crowd's quest (also, in a completely different sense, the congregation's quest). The extremely expressive part-writing of the final choral phrase (bar 34) helps to remind us that this is high art as well as high drama. The choruses in Part Two are more extended and far less orthodox harmonically than their rough equivalents in Part One. Some of the chromatic twists in the part-writing of both no doubt may be traced back to operas and motets of the preceding century but some, most assuredly, may not. Not only chromaticisms are employed: the rhythms are of dramatic rhetorical power and conviction, the melodic lines employ sequence—so often associated with moments of the most exquisite gentleness and tenderness in Bach—to convey determination and irascibility. Again, the actual material is not identical, but the two successive effects are so similar that together they seem colossal. Some of the harmonic effects created through the contrapuntal force of simultaneous chromatic movement (see around bars 20–21, etc.) are as dramatically unpredictable as those of the harmonised chorale "Es ist genung" (in Cantata No. 60) of exactly five months earlier. The striking treatment of "nicht" in the first chorus (at bars 35–36) is built over the falling tetrachord discussed in relation to the earlier pair of choruses above.

The space between the choruses in Part Two is much shorter than that between those in Part One: the second chorus has an added feature which points back to Part One in the new independent part for first violins and flutes, which has clearly reminiscent patterns. The next stage in both parts starts with dominant harmony moving from root position to first inversion. Christ's first answer, to the crowd (in Part One), has a powerful restraint in scope and manner; the harmonies then lead the music on, to the end with the same cadence that was interrupted at Christ's first words. The parallel passage in Part Two very soon reaches the reference to Christ's prophecy concerning the manner of his death: this is accompanied by a jagged bass-line in the pattern which modern scholars refer to as a Cross-symbol, for clear reasons:

The last especially significant section of this recitative is to be found in the *arioso* elaborations of Christ's reference to the military behaviour of earthly kings, during which even some of the majesty of His true identity is lost in an illustrative flourish of *arioso*. The passage might be said to anticipate both the matter and the manner of the significant middle section of the later alto aria "Es ist vollbracht" (It is finished). It also shows how, in Baroque music, even a dialogue-recitative with choral interjections (and quotation from Christ for performance in church) was thought a perfectly proper place for what is essentially a cadenza. It also seems unlikely that Bach accidentally followed two similarly-placed recitatives with contrasting settings of different stanzas of the same chorale. This brings us to the next aspect of the *Johannespassion*: consideration of the chorale settings.

In written studies of Bach's Passion Music it is usual for commentators to dwell upon two particular aspects: the texts of the stanzas which Bach sets (with reference to those which he does not) and comparisons between contrasting settings of identical melodies within either Passion. Both subjects are fascinating in themselves: in the *Johannespassion* the different versions of "Jesu Leiden" and the significant keychange of "Christus, der uns selig macht" may be added to those referred to above as fascinating because, once again, detailed comparisons show Bach's reactions to comparable stimuli but in different contexts. The two movements to be compared now have been selected *because* of their contexts: they frame the sermon as Nos. 14 and 15 of the whole work. Although the texts and melodies are *not* identical, in metre and verse-structure they *are*:

It would be futile to pretend that the contexts are identical; clearly the Good Friday sermon concentrated on certain aspects of the inadequacies of Man, probably taking the immediately preceding subject-matter (Peter's betrayal) as a starting-point. This would account for the slightly more positive nature of the first chorale, and the more philosophical and contemplative one of the second.

Besides the position within the service and vis-a-vis the Gospel, there is the position within the musical-dramatic structure. "Jesu Leiden" closes a scene of the action that has disturbing subject-matter set in such a way as to lead our attention towards the chorale: the text is tellingly illustrated in respects both general (disturbing ends of lines; contrasting approach to Christ in comparison with Peter; downward leaps; spacing designed to hold the listener's attention) and particular ("weinet"; "will"; end of line 4 leaves Peter on a chord renowned for its pathos; "Böses"; a natural cancels a G sharp on "nicht" in line 6). "Christus, der uns selig macht" stands at a point of regeneration—of our attention, our involvement, the musical momentum, etc. The character of the setting is mellow and less arresting harmonically, which might lead us to compare it with the great opening chorus of Part One, but it also somehow transmits a feeling of *continuation*, and there is an emotional restraint here that is also new. Such a setting gives immediacy to the recitative that follows, where the opening chorus had separated itself from the account: the chorale has been subtly transformed into a prelude that is, in its own way, no less striking than the poised instrumental prelude to the Cantata No. 4, *Christ lag in Todes Banden*.

A chorale was, by its nature, full of associations for a Lutheran musician of Bach's time and background. Some of the ingredients of Bach's settings mentioned above were not original, but had been derived consciously or subconsciously from the vast literature of contemporary and earlier settings. Once again, however, we find the depth of Bach's perception and the thoroughness of his execution exemplary: Reinhard Keiser's setting of "Christus, der uns selig macht," set to precede the sermon in his *Marcuspassion*, is certainly not too remote from Bach's either in outline or in detail, but the total effect is spoiled in comparison by a lack of overall proportion and vision.

(raised a major 2nd)

A special feature of the harmonisation of Bach's "Christus, der uns selig macht" is its re-quotation, slightly modified, later as "O hilf, Christe Gottes Sohn" (with the eighth stanza as text); there, the interesting aspect is the key—the rare tonality of B flat minor, almost unheard-of in choral music of those times. The usual explanation of this feature is that at this point Christ's soul is in purgatory—a strange situation, and the most "remote" that Christ has been from Man. In the language of keys and temperaments (exact tuning) known to Bach and his listeners, this key would, indeed, have been invested with an "other-worldly" quality.

It is impossible to generalise on the arias of the *Johannespassion* since each is uniquely designed for its place. "Von den Stricken meiner Sünden" is an alto song of devotion: the bonds of the New Covenant are represented by sturdy, rather traditional counterpoint—the "Jewish Law" style of "Sicut locutus est," but invested with an added purpose by the emphatic repeated notes in the bass. "Ich folge dir gleichfalls" is a treble aria of faith stressing the importance of the imitation of Christ. It is comparable to "Wer ein wahrer Christ will heissen" from Cantata No. 47 and other examples; the style probably owes much to arias of intention in contemporary operas. Its opening *motif* seems to have impressed itself upon Bach's mind so strongly that he was to re-use it in some of the more biting crowd-choruses later in the Passion. "Ach, mein Sinn, wo willt du endlich hin" is one of the composer's many tenor arias of agitated perplexity: it is certainly one of the finest examples, but it calls for exceptional technical and stylistic ability from its performer. Again, the style-source will have been operatic. "Betrachte, meine Seel, mit ängstlichem Vergnügen" is a song of loyal mourning for bass which is coloured by affective conventional instrumentations (they were changed for different performances). Similar movements occur in Cantata No. 106, *Gottes Zeit*, and the *Trauer-Ode* (BWV 198). Although the *lamento* had come from opera and its predecessors in secular music, it had also been an established type of music in the Lutheran church since the time of Schütz. "Erwäge, wie sein blutgefärbter Rücken" is another effective tenor aria on an anguished subject: the viole d'amore of the accompaniment are given music that is concentrated in both internal organisation and outward expressive effect; there is nothing quite like this in the gamba-writing of *Gottes Zeit*. "Eilt, ihr angefochten Seelen" combines the bass soloist with choral (or semi-choral) forces: the dialogue-text, closely derived from Brockes, indeed calls for such treatment. Handel's *Brockes Passion* had been similarly treated, even though its musical effect had been more detached, but also more graceful and elegant—ingredients better suited to Hamburg. The Bach dialogue is among his most emotionally extrovert pieces for the days of early polyphony: it had been present in Lutheran church music long before the time of the Italian sacred symphonists of the early Seventeenth century. "Es ist vollbracht!" is an aria of changing character with clearly defined contrasting sections—a very effective operatic device. The alto soloist is cast as hero, or even as anti-hero, for he represents mankind. The aria starts with music and text from the preceding recitative—"It is finished!" from the "Christus"—which is cunningly echoed at the start in a new harmonic garb:

The whole of the opening is in richly decorated trio style: both the gamba and the alto concentrate on the tessitura known in France as the *taille*. The main contrasting section is a portion of battle-aria in D major ("Der Held aus Juda siegt mit Macht"): as often in opera, the accompanying fanfares are given to the strings rather than actual trumpets or trumpet + strings (the trumpet itself would be completely ineligible for Passion Music). The shortened return to the opening (a summary *da capo*) brings our attention back sharply to the subject-matter of Christ's farewell and death, between which actions the aria is set. The expressive application of the ornaments is beautifully refined. The key-sequences, from the preceding recitative (starting in F sharp minor) away and back again to the death of Christ, provide yet further evidence of the careful attention Bach lavished on every aspect of the whole work. The two recitatives are flanked by contrasted settings of the same chorale, the same "Jesu Leiden, Pein und Tod" which has been quoted and discussed as the chorale preceding the Sermon above. The second of these, setting the last stanza of Stockmann's text of 1633, is a free commentary for the bass soloist upon a simple harmonisation of the chorale for four-voice choir (or possibly semi-chorus). In the setting, the genial yet emphatic *quasi-ostinato* of the bass's commentary is related both to *opera buffa* and to certain chorale-variation types cultivated by organists around 1700.

"Zerfliesse, mein Herze, in Fluten der Zähren," with its throbbing repeated notes, its restless character and its many anguished *melismata* is a refined example of the delicate application of the Italian *affettuoso* style—a kind of aria used in opera of Bach's day for heightened emotion of any kind. The precise notation (*staccato* dots, full slurrings, etc.) comes from the supposed fourth working, and would seem incredibly prophetic from any composer writing in 1724, yet the style itself is written into the music without these conventionalised additions: Bach's music is, indeed, amazingly advanced, as well as being assured, and the only useful comparison that can be made here is with the trio-sonata of the *Musikalisches Opfer*, by Bach himself, composed twenty-three years later. The possibility that the aria was originally conceived for beaked flutes is entirely attractive and would do nothing to diminish its originality: there is no certainty regarding details of orchestration from the first performance. There are many instances of recurring musical figures in the *Johannespassion*: the relationship between a figure introduced in this aria (bar 4, etc.) and the opening of the whole work is obvious, yet generally passes unnoticed. Its psychological effect is not diminished by our ignorance of whether or not Bach inserted it consciously.

Each of the soloists not involved directly in the drama therefore has two or three solos in a modern performance. There is no certainty that the same four individuals were employed in the Nikolaikirche in 1724, however: possibly the arias were shared out between members of the choirs. The full chorus itself has two important commenting movements—the two which frame the essential drama of the whole work, "Herr, unser Herrscher" and "Ruht wohl."

"Herr, unser Herrscher" (Lord, our Master) combines many features related to its context: the instrumental opening establishes a devotional mood (the key of G minor; the slow and dignified harmonic changes), a distressed reaction to the occasion (dissonant woodwind imitations; restless string gestures), a funereal solemnity (the tolling repeated bass-notes in overlapping patterns) and a cumulative sense of epic grandeur (the low remoteness of the throbbing bass and its nine-bar harmonic pedal on the note G). The text reinforces these impressions, and the choral voices, at first singing in a serious style of grand solemnity, seem to fill a hitherto unnoticed space between the continuo bass-line and the melodic instruments. The apparent repeat of the instrumental opening between bars 19 and 31 is actually varied and enriched apart from the addition of the choir: the string parts are raised to balance the chorus, for example. The fluent response to the essentially rather square rhythms of these preludings is introduced at bar 33 in the bass voices: this is far more vital rhythmically (syncopations; *détaché* upper-string accompaniments; a rhetorical treatment of the text that exploits wider intervals in all voices) but also subsidiary to the restless string figure that flows through the whole movement and only ceases briefly at the rhetorical general pause (bar 58)—which is, on its second arrival, the end of the movement. The section before of the *da capo* is not independent in material, although there is some effective development of ideas only previously heard complete in the introduction (see bars 85–93), and the increases in contrapuntal density in the choral writing are carefully placed at those moments where the text refers to the immensity of Christ's achievement as Saviour despite the most appalling suffering: the superlatives are stressed in the music to which they are declaimed. This opening chorus is full of life and movement. It involves us as listeners even when—as often—it is played in lifeless fashion; when it is heard with the appropriate rhythmic motion towards the strong accents, the warmth of correct, period string articulation, and the sweetness of Eighteenth-century woodwinds, it is a beautiful and a moving introduction. This is how Bach envisaged it. It is, however, certainly a prelude: it could not be effective anywhere else in the work; it beckons us into the drama, leans towards it structurally and stylistically.

"Ruht wohl" (Rest secure) is also tailor-made for its place. In no sense is this a final movement, but then the account of Passiontide is itself essentially inconclusive: to a Lutheran, who believes in Justification by Faith, even more than to the general Christian, who sees the

Resurrection as evidence of the Hope for Mankind, this is an important aspect of the contemplation of Good Friday. "Ruht wohl" is a lullaby in triple time, yet an epic style of lullaby as a comparison with the "Schlafe, mein Liebster" of Cantata No. 213 soon shows. The textures are soft and woven—a strong contrast with the opening chorus—and the lilting lines and rhythms (almost in 6/4 time) are slightly reminiscent of a Brahms Intermezzo or Serenade. The essentially ternary *da capo* structure involves the treatment of the first twelve bars as a ritornello corner-stone. Of the many beautiful transformations which this music undergoes, there is a particularly tender version accompanying the words "Das Grab, so euch bestimmet ist" (The grave, which was prepared for you).

The *Johannespassion* as a whole has a tender and deeply human quality. The music which portrays the disgrace of Judas, of Pilate and of Peter is imbued with a spirit of pity rather than anger: only the crowd choruses—sung by "our" representatives in the Nicolaikirche gallery— have a quality of bitterness, and this bitterness is reported to us in a manner that does not seek to explain or to express disgust; rather, we are led into involvement, so that the reaction becomes our own responsibility. That is one of the special qualities of John's account; Bach has captured it with precise and sympathetic exactness.

*

The Easter celebrations of 1724 saw Bach returning to earlier material. On Easter Day he certainly performed Cantata No. 31, *Der Himmel lacht* (composed in Weimar for the same purpose), in the two Hauptkirchen, and very probably he also performed No. 4, *Christ lag in Todes Banden*, this time with the addition of a choir of three trombones and soprano cornetto for tonal colouring (a traditional one, capable of grave subtlety) to the more dignified vocal counterpoints.

For Quasimodogeniti 1724 Bach's composition was CANTATA NO. 67, *Halt in Gedächtnis Jesum Christ* (Hold in affection Jesus Christ).* Its subject is doubt as opposed to faith, inspired by the Gospel's account of the doubts of St. Thomas and the risen Christ's moral. There is an excellent *arioso* with chorus, "Friede sei mit euch" (Peace be with you), in which the four repetitions of the words of Christ (sung by a bass, but with special embellishments to emphasise His risen nature and woodwind accompaniment conveying pastoral calm) are set back from more agitated string passages with semi-choral or ensemble interjections after Christ's first utterance. The absence of bass voices, also of

---

* A work that is especially familiar in England through its early publication by Novello and its recording by the Jacques Orchestra with Kathleen Ferrier in the Fifties.

bass instrumental foundation, is deliberate: as in Cantata No. 154 this symbolises separation (here through doubt) from God.*

CANTATA NO. 104, *Du Hirte Israel, höre* (Hear, thou shepherd of Israel), is, like all of Bach's three works for Misericordias Domini, pastoral in essence. The instrumentation of the opening ritornello is striking, and has appeared to some writers to represent shepherd-music; however, it is clearly derived more directly from the text, with the *staccato* passages (which are by no means restricted to the woodwind) drawing attention to the word "höre" (hear ye), whilst the flowing triplet-patterns alone represent the "shepherd of Israel." This is confirmed when the chorus enters, but would be obvious beforehand to a contemporary musician. The combination of musical *motifs* implying "give me your attention" and "he is industriously going about his labour of caring" convey the contrasting elements of restlessness and reassurance in both Epistle and Gospel.†

For the following Sunday, Jubilate, Bach again made use of his setting of Salomo Franck's *Weinen, Klagen, Sorgen, Zagen*, known to us as Cantata No. 12 and discussed earlier in Chapter Two. Next follow four *Stücke* constructed around the structure 1C, Nos. 166, 86, 37 and 44. In these, the elaborate chorales are all interesting: that in CANTATA NO. 166, *Wo gehest du hin?* (Where are you going?), is in a trio-structure, with unison upper strings and soprano in dialogue above the continuo; that to CANTATA NO. 86, *Wahrlich, wahrlich, ich sage euch* (Truly, truly, I say unto you), is for soprano again, but this time the chorale is heard against a trio-sonata combination (with the upper parts mainly in consonant thirds and sixths) for two oboes d'amore and continuo; in CANTATA NO. 37, *Wer da gläubet und getauft wird* (Those who believe and are baptised), soprano and alto have the chorale melody above a freely-running continuo bass-line—a challenging task for the organist, this; finally, the fourth movement of CANTATA NO. 44, *Sie werden euch in den Bann tun* (They will cast you out from their temples), is for tenor who decorates the chorale "Ach Gott, wie manches Herzeleid" over a bass-line of a chromatic and expressive *ostinato* character. There are many other striking moments and movements—the fine aria in No. 86 with its arpeggio-chords for a virtuoso violin soloist, the preceding

---

* Richter's performance gets to the musical heart of the cantata well, with the rather Handelian manner of the opening chorus well co-ordinated, good ensemble in the sustained recitatives (Bilgram at his best) and good solo work from Reynolds, Schreier and Fischer-Dieskau. The important brass part marked *corno da tirarsi* (slide-horn) is played on a modern trumpet by Pierre Thibaud—not a bad compromise, since there is no certainty regarding Bach's precise requirement, but the line is too prominent in both volume and treatment.

† Richter's Munich recording has too romantic a tone-colour and too symphonic a conception to bring out the subtle beauties within this gently expressive piece: would that the Concerto Amsterdam had recorded it with Amsterdam Baroque woodwinds!

dignified and formally treated saying of Christ for bass and instruments ("Wahrlich, ich sage euch"), the entry of the chorus after the opening duet of perplexity in No. 44 and the especially impressive opening chorus on the striking text "Wer da gläubet und getauft wird," the *motifs* of which are so woven as to sound as challenging as their text, yet which contain elements that represent the words in detail. The chorales, however, have a lightness of texture that would have seemed quite "modern" at the time: they anticipate the patterns of G. F. Kauffmann's *Harmonische Seelen-Lust* (published 1733–37) by ten years.

The last three *Kirchenstücke* of the first Leipzig cycle had all been performed before and have therefore been discussed earlier. The Whitsuntide piece *Erschallet, ihr Lieder* had been composed and performed in Weimar (our No. 172); the shorter *Wer mich liebet* (No. 59) had been performed, in all probability, in the Paulinerkirche the preceding year; and the Trinity Sunday piece was a textually unaltered version of the Störmthal Dedication and Organ-Dedication Cantata *Höchsterwünschtes Freudenfest* (No. 194). The end of Bach's opening year in Leipzig was thus concluded in masterly fashion.

5: Leipzig: The Second Year

Bach's second academic year at Leipzig was, in its requirements, similar to the first. However, this did not mean that it resembled it in all respects. Clearly, the interpretative nature of the extended sermons in the *Hauptgottesdienst* resulted in neither a similar series of subjects nor a similar discursion in adjacent years. There may have been other differences in Bach's position. Possibly he found it difficult to obtain the collaboration of a poet for regular libretti. More probably, the end of the academic year resulted in his collaboration with a new poet who specifically flourished in the adaptation of available material but shunned original philosophical verse. Perhaps the textual success—for such it must have been—of the *Johannespassion* made him negotiate for the services of its author, who was certainly knowledgeable of a wide range of chorales. We cannot be sure of any of these details: the important point is that the style of Bach's libretti did change, and that he came to depend, for the first portion of the year at least, very heavily upon the type of composition to which we refer as the *chorale-cantata* (*Choralkantate*). By this we understand a piece in which the outer two movements set the same chorale; the intervening movements include at least one, usually more, of which the text is recognisably derived from intervening stanzas of the chorale text. Many chorales are, of course, themselves seasonal in association; others refer directly to scripture. The resulting works therefore relate to the seasonal Epistle and Gospel, but through the orthodox Lutheran interpretation of the chorale.

Bach's series of chorale-cantatas stretches, effectively uninterrupted, from Trinity + 1, 1724, to Palm Sunday 1725. The preserved pieces number forty-one, a figure which would be wildly greeted by the number-searchers of our times had not two works evidently been lost. The *Sanctus* (BWV 232^{III}) is excluded from the list, but was, along with certain additional compositions, also performed. The chorale-cantatas are those which we know as Nos. 20, 2, 7, 135 (apparently performed in Bach's absence), 10, 93, 107, 178, 94, 101, 113, 33, 78, 99, 8, 130, 114, 96, 5, 180, 38, 80(?), 115, 139, 26, 116, 62, 91, 121, 133, 122, 41, 123, 124, 3, 111, 92, 125, 126, 127 and 1. No preserved works are attributed to Trinity + 6 or + 12, and there is no record regarding the identity of the "Ratswechsel Cantata" for 1724. The chorales seem to have been selected with due attention to Benedikt Carpzov's criteria of 1690: to be appropriate, they had to be good, beautiful (poetically), old, *evangelisches* (=of appropriate orthodoxy) and Lutheran (a reference to the origin rather than those qualities already covered).

The setting of a chorale, rather than a biblical, text did not in itself prevent Bach from employing the same stylistic variety that he had displayed hitherto. Although the number of chorale-commentary recitatives increases, the recitatives and arias which are chorale paraphrases are no less inhibited in music or text than earlier ones setting biblical paraphrases. The opening choruses are at once subtle and immediate in impact. Dürr's implication that the opening four pieces of the second cycle were intended to serve as demonstrations of musical *genres* appears to be a little fanciful, although his tenet that Bach was definitely starting a series is born out by the musical organisation:

Cantata	Opening Movement
20	French *ouverture* (chorale in soprano)
2	Motet-like *cantus firmus* movement (ch. in alto)
7	"Violin concerto" (ch. in tenor)
135	Chorale fantasia (ch. in bass)

The first movement of CANTATA NO. 20, *O Ewigkeit* (Eternity), has an interesting character that could hardly be described as belonging to one nation: it is too lightly and airily managed to be properly described as French, and it is hardly typical of German or Italian types. Although Bach's variety in the application of the *ouverture* structure is considerable, and his employment of it in important opening movements (this one opens the *Jahrgang* as well as an important *Stück*) much discussed,

this one could hardly be described as a demonstration-piece. The motet-like treatment of the opening of CANTATA NO. 2, *Ach Gott, vom Himmel sieh darein* (O God, look down from Heaven), is, indeed, somewhat antiquated and strongly characteristic; yet it is for Bach an altogether orthodox treatment of venerable material. The exact extent of its actual originality is (along with various companion pieces in Bach's output) uncertain, but if it is designed as an example of its type this would hardly have struck contemporary hearers as anything particularly unusual; it would certainly have seemed well-managed and expressive, however.* The beginning of CANTATA NO. 7, *Christ unser Herr zum Jordan kam* (Christ our Lord came to the Jordan), is a far more complex movement than the description "violin concerto" conveys: it is a *concertato* movement but tersely designed in dovetailing sections, including instrumental *tutti* themes of a ritornello character, chorale polyphonies with accompanimental passage-work (a modern style of treatment for the time) and antiphonal dialogues between the oboes and strings. The movement certainly compares in interesting ways with Bach's own preserved (and presumably earlier) violin concerti, but, for all its traditionally Italianate structure (in the *concertato* element) this is a highly cosmopolitan movement. Its opening has a vigorous robustness like Lully's *Alceste* Overture but it is certainly not French.†
The fourth opening chorus of the series, from CANTATA NO. 135, the "chorale fantasia" on *Ach Herr, mich armen Sünder* (O Lord, for my grievous sins *condemn me not*), is a setting of the tune which we know as the "Passion Chorale"; this would, however, be its most familiar text to Bach and his contemporaries. The term "chorale fantasia" is itself only slightly less loose than "chorale," since examples can be long or shortish and since the accompanying materials may be derived or underived from the chorale-line. Bach's example here certainly makes effective use of the melody itself, which permeates all the instrumental parts. The resulting style is really less of an orchestral and grand one than a chamber and lyrical one: the triple metre and the emphasis on horizontal movement (reinforced effectively by the way in which the oboes and voices overlap within the textures) have an agreeable

---

* Both Harnoncourt and Rilling treat the opening as too monumental: surely a less pretentious and more gracefully pointed treatment would have worked better. Harnoncourt's soloists are at their best (Equiluz especially), and the clearer contours make more attractive music than Rilling's modern, well-controlled group. The lyrical lilt of Rilling's approach makes for much attractive detail, especially in the bass aria, "Gott ist gerecht."

† Nos. 2 and 7 afford an opportunity to compare the interpretative approaches of Harnoncourt and Leonhardt: the choral sounds are both rather soft-centred and often insensitive to the styles within the music, but the chamber-music quality of Leonhardt's Dutch team is very neat when all is going well, the slightly more unanimous orchestral style of Harnoncourt's Vienna Concentus rounder and more confident.

Seventeenth-century sense of proportioned progress. Once again, however, the music could hardly be said to "represent" any type for all its conspicuous sensitivity to context.

The incorporation of chorale-based materials into arias and recitatives would be obvious to Bach's congregations. For example, the traditional text might be referred to or incorporated into recitative or *arioso*, as it is in the fourth movement of CANTATA NO. 127, *Herr Jesu Christ, wahr' Mensch und Gott* (Lord Jesus Christ, truly Man and God). The text, a dramatic portrayal of the "last trumpet" ("Wenn einstens die Posaunen schallen"), refers directly to the fifth and sixth stanzas of the chorale text to represent the comfort then afforded to the believer through his faith in Christ:

> *Fifth and Sixth Chorale Stanzas*
> Ein frühlich Urstand mir verleih
> Am Jüngsten G'richt mein fürsprech sei
> Und meine Sünd nicht mir gedenk
> Aus Gnaden mir das Lieben schenk
> Wie du hast zugesaget
> In deinen Wort das trau ich dir.
>
> Fürwahr, fürwahr, euch sage ich:
> Wer mein Wort hält und glaubt an mich;
> Er wird nicht kommen ins Gericht
> Und den Tod ewig schmecken nicht . . .
>
> *Recitative*
> Wenn einstens die Posaunen schallen,
> Und wenn der Bau der Welt
> Nebst denen Himmelsfesten,
> Zerschmettert wird zerschalten,
> So denke mein Gott, im besten;
> Wenn sich dein Knecht einst vors Gerichte stellt,
> Da die Gedanken sich verklagen,
> So wollest du allein,
> O Jesu, mein Fürsprecher sein:
> Und meiner Seele tröstlich sagen:
> *Fürwahr, fürwahr, euch sage ich:*
> Wenn Himmel und Erde im Feuer vergehen,
> So soll doch ein gläubiger ewig bestehen.
> *Er wird nicht kommen ins Gericht*
> *Und den Tod ewig schmecken nicht . . .*

Further, in any kind of movement, the chorale's melodic contour may be quoted musically: in the recitative quoted above the opening fragment of this contour appropriately sets the quotation of "Fürwahr, fürwahr, . . ."; later, however, the same passage of the tune is combined with the third line of the sixth stanza ("Er wird nicht kommen . . .") —with which it is not heard in the chorale. Even more interesting are the ways in which the various melodic patterns and cadences of the chorale may be developed motivically by either instruments or voices.

CHORALE

oboes I & II

oboes I & II

continuo

recorders I & II

Für-wahr, für - wahr, eudi sa - ge ____ ich

The derivation of all these examples from Cantata No. 127 is no accident, although it is, apart from its multiple quotation of chorales, as "typical" as any single work can be by a man like Bach in a time like his. The reason for their inclusion is to draw special attention to the work, one of the last of a highly significant and creatively consistent series, one which contains some of the most challenging of Bach's music to perform in anything approaching authentic instrumentation, and one that is consequently little-known today.

The interpretation of the chorales was almost as complex as that of the Bible in Lutheran theology. Our only evidence of Bach's responses to either comes from his settings. The old chorale "Nun komm" of CANTATA NO. 62 (Come, O Saviour of the gentiles), for example, has associations of Advent and Christmas, but also of the related themes of (a) salvation, (b) light in darkness, (c) expectancy, (d) God's practical care for his people (=Israel/Leipzig, etc.), and, through its association with Luther, (e) personal faith and meditation. No. 62 has five movements: of these, the first (a, b, c, d, e) and sixth (a, d, e) are taken directly from the chorale text. The contrapuntal nature of the first stresses the subtly organised nature of God's works, the second unsensational harmonisation our expressive response. The work is designed for the appropriate first Sunday in Advent, which marks the start of the traditionally very special preparation for Christmas in the Lutheran Church.

The eponymous chorale "Schmücke dich, o liebe Seele" of CANTATA NO. 180, a more lyrical and personally expressive Seventeenth-century product, is today quite well known through Bach's fine organ setting (BWV 654) and through the rather characterless adaptation by Winkworth and Vaughan Williams in *The English Hymnal*. Its link with Trinity + 20 concerns the reference in the Gospel (Matt. XXII, 1–14) to the fate of the man who came ill-clothed for the meal in the parable of the king's great wedding-feast, but its relevance also to the Epistle (Ephesians V, 15–21), which is concerned with true spirituality, cannot have passed unnoticed in conjunction with the poem and Crüger's beautiful setting.* Here, all of the associations blend most effectively, but the whole is capable of various musical/emotional interpretations. Bach's cantata is full of joyful elaboration both textually and musically, and is therefore illustrative of the Epistle ("communicate in psalms, hymns and songs; sing and make music in your hearts to the Lord") seen through the chorale. The opening chorus in F (the usual key of this chorale—also that at which the E flat organ-setting would have sounded in Leipzig's two main churches) is a gently woven movement in the reassuringly positive style of Cantata No. 65's "Sie werden aus Saba." The falling and returning scale through a major third which opens Crüger's melody is subtly interwoven from the start into the heavenly chorus of the woodwinds; it is also possible to trace its outline, stretched almost into "O Ewigkeit," in the unison upper strings ritornello figure beneath. In this chorus the voices are apart from that thematic link, independent of the instruments. The chorale is heard as a soprano *cantus firmus* and the accompanying voices are loosely imitative and anticipatory. The whole effect is one of gentle joy.

In the tenor aria with flauto traverso which follows, the second strophe of the chorale is paraphrased: this starts "Ermuntre dich: dein

---

* One realisation of the original by the author is to be heard in conjunction with the famous organ-setting on Argo: the performers are The Alban Singers and Peter Hurford.

Heiland klopft" (Arouse yourself: your Saviour knocks), and the emphatic octave summons in the bass-line, together with the quick-silver fanfares, are clearly derived from this picture. The soprano recitative leads attractively towards a direct quotation of the chorale's fourth stanza, heard as an *arioso*: this movement is embroidered with rich ornamentation of the chorale by the treble soloist and by the arpeggiated accompaniment of the piccolo cello. Here, as before, the gentle embellishment exploiting consonant intervals conveys the warm assurance of Divine Blessing. The alto recitative, "Mein Herz fühlt" (My heart is overwhelmed), has a slightly agitated quality: Bach's pictorial illustration of this is heard in the first flute's rhythmically free version of the chorale's first two lines:

At the triumph of joy ("Freude") over fear ("Furcht") which concludes the movement, all is resolved, and the last line is heard in a far more consistently decorated form:

The fine, dancing soprano aria, "Lebens Sonne," might well have come from a Cöthen homage-cantata, so graceful is its use of tied melody notes against a steady triple metre. However, the strongly assertive ritornello theme of this *da capo* aria is yet again based firmly on the contours of the chorale itself, as inspection quickly reveals. Even the (apparently contrasting) rhetorical vigour of the penultimate recitative is independent of neither text (it paraphrases the eighth stanza) nor the opening *motif* of the melody: the important word "gedenke" is repeated to it:

In the "straightforward" chordal setting of the ninth stanza which concludes the work, we find an entirely apposite spirit of trusting reassurance: the deployment of the minor seventh at the word "Gast" in the final line is especially beautiful.

The above examples can only imply the rich beauties and the complex expressive methods of the chorale-cantata series. There are no weak works, and to select outstanding ones is very hard. CANTATA NO. 101, *Nimm von uns* (Take from us), has a magnificently proportioned opening chorus of motet-like solemnity combined with highly dramatic rhythmic momentum: perhaps it anticipates something of the spirit of the funeral motet, *O Jesus Christ, meins Lebens Licht* (No. 118), perhaps it recalls some of Bach's forbears, for its effect is certainly striking. CANTATA NO. 10, *Meine Seel'erhebt* (My soul doth magnify), which is based on the German Magnificat with the *tonus peregrinus*, compares very interestingly with the festive Latin Magnificat of the preceding year. CANTATA NO. 93, *Wer nur* (He who lets God alone control), is a strong warmly human work on a fine chorale that Bach set admirably for keyboard instruments and elsewhere in the choral music. The Reformation re-working of Cantata No. 80a, *Alles, was von Gott*, as CANTATA NO. 80, *Ein feste Burg* (A firm stronghold), is much admired, although partly in the version employing Friedemann

Bach's blunt trumpet-writing in the opening movement: this chorus has some of the vigorous archaicism of *Nimm von uns*, too.

*

The Passion Music for Good Friday 1725 consisted of a modified version of the *Johannespassion* from the preceding year: new—or very probably newly-deployed—materials were introduced, including an opening chorus built on the chorale "O Mensch, bewein dein Sünde gross," and there were several later modifications* (the main changes

are printed in the Bärenreiter scores). Although Bach apparently removed most of the new material later, we do have strong evidence regarding the nature of the whole for the first time in 1725, and it is clear that Bach was gradually improving the detail of the music as he reconsidered it. The main reason behind the changes was probably the desire not to be repetitive rather than any dissatisfaction with the work as it had first stood. The great chorus on "O Mensch" was later incorporated (ca. 1736) into Part One of the *Matthäuspassion*, of which it formed the conclusion: we know it well in this second context today.

The *Oster-Oratorium* (Easter Oratorio) and its conception-twin, the Birthday *Tafel-Music* (*sic*) for Duke Christian of Weissenfels, are both so well suited to their purposes that, as elsewhere, specialists have recently concurred that they were composed—at least from the psychological point of view—simultaneously; the additional restraint of complex requirements seems to have especially stimulated Bach, and it appears that he found it attractive to make these requirements more complicated on occasion. The OSTER-ORATORIUM is essentially a longish *Kirchenstück*—CANTATA NO. 249, *Kommt, eilet und laufet* (Come hasten)— with biblical soloists but without biblical commentary: the tenor represents Peter, the bass John, and it is through their dialogue and alternation with Mary the mother of James and Mary Magdalene that we—also disciples—are drawn into the subject-matter of the work. Because this is a philosophical and self-examining approach, the rather unusual opening (essentially a duet with chorus added to a lively 3/8 concerto finale) is particularly effective, whether we see the beautiful preceding Adagio as symbolic of the anguish of Passiontide or of the beauty of God's infinite resourcefulness. The text is probably, like that published with regard to the birthday pastorale, by Picander: it seems probable that both were prepared simultaneously with the aim of twinned composition from the start. The musical expression of the arias reinforces this impression. Here, indeed, Bach has effected a most

---

* There is at present no recorded performance of this version: perhaps some enterprising group of performers will rectify this.

striking "compromise"—striking because no compromise is involved. The main soprano soloist in Weissenfels was Pauline Kellner, a brilliant soprano of national stature; the leading violinst was Kammermusikus Johann Adam Andrae, a member of a family of distinguished string players. The remaining Weissenfels musicians were all highly skilled: the tenor Ebert, the bass Ehrhardt (who had worked under Bach in Weimar), the Altenburg-Nicolai-Wilcken trumpet-choir, etc. The material of the arias—both vocal and instrumental—had to be so planned that it could be performed with adequate technique and expression by the Leipzig treble, unchanged alto, and younger maturing tenor and bass, to accompaniments from an ensemble which, if more regularly drilled in ensemble, lacked the distinguished names of the Ducal Court's employees. The arias are among Bach's most warm and motivically striking collections within any one work: they compare in tunefulness and in openness of expression with those of the "Hunting Cantata" (the earlier Weissenfels homage-composition) and would, at the same time, have produced a most effective foil to the chorales and arias of the second version of the *Johannespassion*; the latter, with its emphasis of the pity of Passiontide, is neatly countered by the oratorio's involved approach to the comfort of Easter. The *Oster-Oratorium* is surprisingly little-known: it makes an obvious answer to the often-heard expression of regret that "the *Magnificat* is the only Bach work of its length and for its approximate forces which is readily acceptable to us today."*

The *Kirchenstücke* between Easter 1725 and Trinity divide into two groups, of which the first shows textual resemblances to the previous year's compositions and the second consists of settings of the Leipzig poetess Mariane von Ziegler (1695–1760). Ziegler's texts tend to be rather clumsy in expression and overloaded with imagery. It is often assumed that Bach's many simplifications and adaptations indicate that the composer himself revised them; it is, however, no less probable that Bach sought expert advice from one of his clerical or literary associates.

The group opens with the striking and today quite familiar CANTATA NO. 6, *Bleib bei uns* (Stay with us). This work, together with No. 4, *Christ lag in Todes Banden* (now incorporating the cornetto and trombone choir), completed the formal Easter and Passion series of performances. The collection has a characteristic warmth and emotional gentleness: the less rhetorical opening of the Passion, the rather peacefully managed spiritual deliberations of the oratorio, the whole of *Bleib bei uns* and the introduction of the brass "halo" to *Christ lag* all point

---

* The oratorio has been very well recorded by Münchinger with Ameling, Watts, Krenn, Krause, the Vienna Academiechor and the Stuttgart CO. This is arguably Münchinger's best Bach on record; the entire performance is full of life and sparkle, and, if we are still awaiting a good "authentic" rendering, at least the soloists here bear some resemblance to the secular ones expected by Bach at Weissenfels.

in the same direction. The opening of *Bleib bei uns* is especially interesting for its thematic and textual resemblances to "Ruht wohl" in the
Johannespassion: our pleas to Christ, whether in Paradise or in risen
majesty on earth, have a parallel quality. The remainder of the
cantata is built on the pattern dictated by the text, which we have
mentioned as Type 1C above. CANTATA NO. 42, *Am Abend aber desselbigen
Sabbats* (On the same evening), for Quasimodogeniti, has a striking
instrumental Sinfonia, which has been linked with the opening aria
and hailed as preserved evidence for an otherwise lost instrumental composition. After the Sinfonia, the text again adheres to the structure of
Type 1C, but Bach's setting for duet of the central chorale text does
not appear to include any significant references to the melody usually
associated with it. The penultimate bass aria is reassuring in manner;
the music effectively conveys its mood in lightly expressive arpeggiated
trio-work. The third of the set is the cantata for Misericordias Domini,
CANTATA NO. 85, *Ich bin ein guter Hirt* (I am a Good Shepherd). The
material is, as in 1724, centred around the view of Christ as Good
Shepherd—the Gospel of the day relates the parable. Once again the text
follows the 1C pattern, but this time the opening biblical quotation
(which in Cantata No. 6 was given to the chorus and in No. 42 to a
recitative) is heard as a bass aria: the effective opening *motif* has a
remote kinship with the well-known dialogue "Mein Freund ist mein"
from Cantata No. 140, *Wachet auf*—itself composed later. The bass
aria should probably not be taken too slowly. The most striking
movement of *Ich bin ein guter Hirt* is, however, the beautiful
and wondering tenor aria, "Seht, was die Liebe thut" (See what love
achieves): it is so aptly expressive of the spirit of the preceding few
weeks' music that it may be said to summarise them. Certainly this is
an extremely economical portrayal of profound experience.

The Ziegler series contains some movements of especial interest—by
no means all in conjunction with her best literary work! CANTATA NO.
103, *Ihr werdet weinen und heulen*, for Jubilate, has a dramatic opening
chorus* to the evocative but expressively challenging text "You will *all*
weep and lament, but the world will rejoice: you will be downcast,
but your sorrows will be turned to joy." Various commentators, noting
the unmistakably mournful opening of the voices (compare *Weinen,
Klagen*) have tried to find "joy" in the woodwind patterns for beaked
flute in consort with two oboes d'amore. However, Bach's illustration of scripture is not as over-simplified as this: the joy here is both
beneath the surface (in the harmonies, the textures and the rhythms)

---

* Graulich's Stuttgart/Heidelberg performance fails to capture the expressive life of
this chorus, the instrumentalists sound mechanical, and although the choir strives
valiantly—it sounds a fine ensemble—the styles of the surface are lost and the essence
beneath barely permeates.

and in that striking recitative interruption starting "You, however . . ."; most of the rest of the material is built from figures associated with tranquility. CANTATA NO. 108, *Es ist euch gut* (It is for your good), contains three well-characterised arias for the lower voices, each of which is supported by a sensitively-coloured obbligato. The third (alto) aria, "Was mein Herz" provides a good example of the rhythmic fragmentation which skilled composers of the day exercised to heighten the emotion within a text: in this case, the technique considerably enriches an undistinguished verse. The highlight of CANTATA NO. 87, *Bisher habt ihr nichts gebeten in meinem Namen* (Up to the present you have asked nothing in my name), has two colourful arias, but its main highlight is the second quotation of Christ (John XVI, 33) which is most beautifully set for bass and continuo. Movements like this and the "Wist ye not . . . ?" setting from Cantata No. 154 (see Chapter Four) are unique to Bach.

The Ascensiontide *Stück* CANTATA NO. 128, *Auf Christi Himmelfahrt allein* (From the Ascension of Christ alone), contains two movements of special interest: these are the opening *concertato* chorale chorus, which would have fitted quite happily earlier into the cycle, and the dramatically interrupted battle-aria for trumpet and bass—the central portion suddenly plunges into rhetorical recitative, before the music of the ritornello returns. The choice of paired horns for the outer movements could have been prompted by either the necessity to save the full effect of the trumpet choir for Whitsunday, or because of their association, through hunting, with the notion of the quest: we marvel and seek to explain Christ's disappearance.

The Whitsun cantatas (Nos. 74, 68 and 175) show Bach still struggling to write music in combination with Mariane von Ziegler's texts: now, however, he sets himself even more complex problems by combining these with music originally composed for quite different purposes. CANTATA NO. 74, *Wer mich liebet* (He who loves me), is actually an extension of Cantata No. 59 of the same name: after the opening festive *concertato* with trumpet choir (expanded from the original duet of No. 59), the most interesting new material is that of the alto aria, "Nichts kann mich erretten," with its violent declamatory passagework—here Bach approaches the stormy styles of Emanuel and Friedemann in the 1740s. In CANTATA NO. 68, *Also hat Gott* (God so loved the world), the most striking music sets two texts from the Gospel for the day (John III, 16–21). These are the outer movements of a five-movement piece; within, two arias flank a reference to the Epistle (Acts X, 42–48). The two arias are freely adapted from the Weissenfels *Tafel-Musik* which we know as the "Hunting Cantata" (No. 208), together with that composition's associated instrumental movement (BWV 1040). The contemplation of Christ's description of the behaviour of the Good Shepherd, CANTATA NO. 175, *Er rufet seinen Schäfen mit Namen* (He calls to his sheep by name), also contains an incorporated movement—the tenor's "Es dunket mich," which is a transposed version of the seventh movement of the Cöthen homage-cantata *Durchlauchster Leopold*. This last Whitsuntide piece is a curious work, in which the musical and theological make-up are ill-matched by the poorly-managed arrangement of words: even if the last aria, as well as the central one, is incorporated from an external work—and we cannot be sure that this is so—there are surely better ways in which the text of both of them could have been combined with the music than that apparently chosen by Bach. On the other hand, the striking triple portrait in the arias of Christ the Good Shepherd as respectively Comforter, Forgiver and Master is so masterfully conveyed in the music that we feel no lack of communicative rhetoric. The opening aria, which is pastoral in its unique instrumentation, and of infinite expressive subtlety in all respects, manages to convey an atmosphere of dismay and confusion that is also a precise musical portrayal of worried sheep. The year ends rather less strikingly, with CANTATA NO. 176, *Es ist ein trotzig und verzagt Ding* (It is a stubborn and truculent thing, *this heart of Man*): here, apart from complex theological arguments that must be related to the sermon, the most striking movement is the opening choral fugue, with its dour message from Jeremiah (XVII, 9). The images are complex: the canker of evil is illustrated by the rising entries and the increasing momentum, the ominous portent and the antiquity of the warning are conveyed in the contrapuntal form and its severe delivery. The remainder of the work leaves an impression of restriction and awkwardness. Possibly here, again, Bach was making further use of otherwise lost earlier materials.

5: *View of Leipzig from the road by which Bach arrived in 1723*
(Historical Museum, Leipzig)

Doch Königin! Du stirbest nicht,
Man weiß was man an Dir besessen,
Die Nachwelt wird Dich nicht vergessen,
Biß dieser Weltbau einst zerbricht.
Ihr Dichter, schreibt! wir wollens lesen:
Sie ist der Tugend Eigenthum,
Der Unterthanen Lust und Ruhm,
Der Königinnen Preis gewesen.

M. Joh. Chr. Gottsched.

6: *Final chorus of the* Trauer-Ode *(BWV 198) as in
the printed text-folder (note the larger print for
the unison sections)*
(Bach Archive, Leipzig)

7: *Bach in 1747, by E. G. Haussmann (this is the only certain likeness of the composer, of which there are two copies)*
(Historical Museum, Leipzig)

8: *Fanciful impression of Bach at a young age, aimed
to capture the spirit and possible bone-structure of
the composer around 1718, by Barbara Money, 1974*
(by permission of the artist)

9: *Autograph of the* Credo *section of the Mass in*
B minor, c. 1747
(State Library, Berlin)

10: *The Weimar palace before the great fire of 1774, based on old engravings and published in A. Doebber's history of the Wilhelmsberg (1911)*

11: *Interior of the Weimar palace chapel* (Town Art Collection, Weimar)

*12: Exterior of the Thomaskirche (Bach lived in the
school beyond)*
(Art Collection, Leipzig)

13: Interior of the Thomaskirche
(Collection of Art and Archives, Berlin)

*14:Leipzig's City
Church, or
Nicolaikirche, from
the West
(Church Archives)*

*15: The organ gallery,
from where the* Stücke
were performed
(by courtesy of
Breitkopf & Härtel,
acting for the
copyright owners)

6: *Leipzig: From 1726 to the Last Decade*

Predecessors of Bach such as Vivaldi, Couperin and Buxtehude had already perfected musical development as it was applied in Baroque art. In completely individual ways, each had exploited both larger and smaller elements within extensive artistic units: sometimes these materials had been clearly defined and "thematic" in essence, sometimes they had been less clearly projected, more motivically developed.

A glance at such diverse works as the Fifth Brandenburg Concerto, the first setting in the *Orgelbüchlein* or the G major *Partita Praeambulum* for harpsichord might lead us to conclude that Bach's thematic essentials are presented within the first few bars. However, even in these works, all is not derived of necessity from the opening, and even where that might appear to be so, the manner of achievement is such that it could rarely be said to be predictable. Bach's compositional strategy, too, was consistent with his previous methods, yet never entirely predictable. In many respects, the problems that had occurred before the summer of 1725 would recur, and the challenges be met in a similar way. Thus, no proper consideration of the *Matthäuspassion* is complete without discussion also of the *Johannespassion*; no thorough consideration of the

Weihnachts-Oratorium should omit reference to the *Oster-Oratorium*; no series, or even cycle, of cantatas should be treated in such a way as to imply that one common factor is more important than many disparate ones, or as if, once again, there are no precedents. On the other hand, Bach's creative energy was such that it would be surprising if he did not at times appear to break new ground, to have been presented with some new situation or opportunity, or even to have responded to a familiar situation in a way that would have surprised even his closest friends and family.

Modern commentators have discussed Bach's organisation of *Kirchenstücke* into *Jahrgänge* after 1725. There certainly seems to have been a Picander cycle, and the fragments that remain indicate a unifying factor in the form of ambitious and elaborate opening choral movements. However, as previously, pieces designed for the two Leipzig Hauptkirchen often gather themselves more conveniently into smaller groups within each whole year. This is not a new feature at all, as we have seen above, and it is obvious how such groupings must have come about through the essential relationships between the liturgy, the carefully organised series of sermons in Leipzig's churches, the traditional associations of both, and the necessity for regular sophisticated musical expression.

The so-called Third Annual Cycle appears to have started with a lost *Kirchenstück* on the First Sunday in Advent, 1725. It did not, therefore, follow the Second Cycle immediately; older texts which seem to have been unset for the Sundays after Trinity of 1723 or 1724 formed the framework of the intervening half-year. Of these CANTATA NO. 137, *Lobe den Herren, den mächtigen König der Ehren* (Praise to the Lord, the mighty King of Glory) stands out as remarkable in that the (to Englishmen) familiar chorale melody, as well as its text, is clearly recognisable within each movement; the only other preserved piece of which this could be said is the altogether different Cantata No. 4, *Christ lag in Todes Banden*. The Reformation Festival of 1725 was celebrated in grand style by CANTATA NO. 79, *Gott der Herr ist Sonn und Schild* (The Lord God is *our* Sun and Shield*). The structure of this work is straightforward, and its message is direct. The wished-for togetherness of God and Man as illustrated in the duet for treble and bass is highly effective, whichever of the two we consider as earthly or godly. The most remarkable feature musically is the manner in which the apparently independent orchestral opening of the choral first movement later combines to greater expressive effect with the seasonally appropriate chorale

---

* Adequate translation is impracticable: "Schild" also means a coat-of-arms in German; "Sonn" conveyed many complex associations in the Eighteenth century: most of the Lutheran altars of the period were crowned with the godly emblem of the Sun, including that of the Thomaskirche.

"Nun danket." The repeated drumbeats are used on their first appearance in each movement in such a way as to draw attention to their actual number (twenty-eight). Possibly these represented the twenty-eight articles of the Augsburg Confession, the most essential public statement of the Reformation; the first diplomatic movements which led up to the Augsburg Confession of 1530 had occurred around 1525, the bicentenary of which year the Leipzig clergy might have had reason to celebrate.

One striking feature of the Third Annual Cycle is the presence of compositions that are not by Bach, together with their apparent influences upon his own writing. During the year, both the Good Friday Passion Music (Reinhard Keiser's *Marcuspassion*) and at least fifteen *Kirchenstücke* (by Bach's Meiningen relation Johann Ludwig Bach) were prepared for performance by Bach's usual resources, and heard in the Leipzig Hauptkirchen. It is hardly reasonable to suggest that Bach's selection of this material for inclusion among his own works was the result of laziness or any sense of disillusionment with his Leipzig employers. Possibly he was busy as a composer in some other respect (the Sonatas for Organ, the Partitas and the so-called "English Suites" for harpsichord may all have been assembled during this portion of his life); perhaps he decided that an over-emphasis on his own works might be interpreted as some form of pride; possibly he was trying to improve the singing of his choirs during the spring of 1726, or maybe he was encountering some difficulties with his instrumentalists (the works by Keiser and Johann Ludwig are comparatively modest in their demands on the accompanists). That fewer instrumentalists *are* required is a feature of the third *Jahrgang* as a whole, as well as the incorporated items, but this may simply have been because the set would therefore be adaptable to a wider range of circumstances than the two preceding cycles, both in Leipzig and in the surrounding smaller towns. In any event, it seems clear that, during the period under discussion, Bach no longer benefited from a regular literary collaborator and was compelled to find texts (possibly in collaboration with the clergy) for himself

Later in 1726 the texts appear to be influenced strongly by those set by Johann Ludwig, as William Scheide has shown. Scheide divides Johann Ludwig's cantatas into a "long" form (Old Testament text —recitative—aria—New Testament text—strophic poem—chorale) and a "short" one (Old Testament text—recitative—aria—New Testament text—less expansive poem—recitative—chorale). Of Bach's own preserved works (and we should remember that from 1726 an increasing proportion is missing or unrecorded almost every year) only Cantata No. 43 involves the strophic poem; the shorter form is used in Nos. 39, 88, 187, 45, 102 and 17. CANTATA NO. 43, *Gott fähret auf mit Jauchzen* (God ascends with rejoicing) is itself an extended (two-part) treatment of the "long" structure, in which the six stanzas of the poem "Mein Jesus hat nunmehr" are alternately arias and recitatives for soprano, bass and alto; each aria is preceded by a recitative for the same soloist, including the first stanza, which is an aria following the New Testament text; the final stanza is also a soprano recitative—a rounding structural device. The three arias and their recitatives demonstrate very clearly that a metric text need never inhibit the melodic character of a movement: although each vocal entry consists of a quaver following one-and-a-half beats' rest, and five of the six movements are cast in 4/4 time, their styles are strongly differentiated. As if to emphasise the traditional nature of the text, Bach concludes with an almost unmodified chorale setting from Vopelius's *Leipziger Gesangbuch* (1682): the stylised use of strings and oboes with at most one trumpet, also gives the chorale an effectively Seventeenth-century impression.* The virtuoso bass and trumpet aria (seventh movement) is a challenge for the singer as well as the instrumentalist: Nikolaus Harnoncourt has aptly drawn attention to the deliberate cultivation of the "imperfect" seventh harmonic (B flat) to illustrate the text at "Qual und Pein." The tender and beautiful consonances of the oboe-duet obbligato to the alto aria is another instance of traditional illustrative materials used to optimum effect. It is possible, incidentally, that the eleven movements were designed to represent the eleven apostles mentioned in the gospel as witnessing the risen Christ before His Ascension.

The larger group of texts of the "short" structure clearly exploits the difference between the more generalised Old Testament texts and the more personally interpretable New Testament ones: the opening chorus has in each case something of the older and more expansive motet style—especially within the choral writing; nevertheless, each also has a distinct character stemming from the orchestral contribution, which, especially in CANTATA NO. 39, *Brich dem Hungrigen dein Brot* (*Distribute* your bread to the hungry), has a far more strongly characterised and dramatic quality. The *concertante* contrast between these elements is rich, and it might profitably be more emphasised in performance than is usually the case. The personal, New Testament side of these works is partly illustrated in the musical styles adopted, partly in a clear reduction from orchestral- to chamber-scaled proportions in the respective movements. The actual New Testament texts are central to the Lutheran teaching of each work, and are treated with the delicacy and restraint that we have come to expect. At the centre of the same

---

* Harnoncourt's performers show this admirably on record, with the violin obbligato to the third aria especially well played. The singing of the bass Ruud van der Meer is, however, far less tidy than that of the rest of the basses in the series. Harnoncourt's notes explain the above remarks concerning the single trumpet.

Stück there is St. Paul's exhortation (Hebrews XIII, 16), attractively set as an aria of beautiful proportion and restraint for bass with continuo. CANTATA NO. 88, *Siehe, ich will viel Fischer aussenden* (Behold, I shall send out many fishermen), has the quality of an oratorio excerpt, with the tenor representing the Evangelist and the bass representing Christ: the flourishes at Christ's reference to Peter of his future role as a "fisher of men" are notable; also the gentle caress with which the upper strings join the Evangelist to introduce Christ's words of comfort. In CANTATA NO. 187, *Es wartet alles auf dich* (All these wait upon Thee), Christ's instruction to the disciples not to be anxious concerning earthly necessities is treated in a flowing, Italianate, slightly archaic manner (possibly because this is direct teaching); the resemblance of the opening to that of the chorale "Von Gott will ich nicht lassen" can hardly be accidental. In CANTATA NO. 45, *Es ist dir gesagt, Mensch, was gut ist* (He has told you, O Man, what is good), the second part starts with Christ's prophecy of the futility of self-justification through acts at the Day of Judgement; the *arioso* has an accompaniment of impatient character, forcefully underlining Luther's attitude to the abuse of indulgences which had been based on just such a philosophy. (This piece contrasts strongly with the specially gentle nature of the opening movement of the same *Stück*.) The fourth movement of CANTATA NO. 102, *Herr, deine Augen sehen nach dem Glauben* (Lord, thine eyes are set in faith), is a questioning *arioso* of despair at the hardness of Man's heart; this movement calls for a highly accented style of *affettuoso* playing of the full strings: material of such an artifically dramatic type would apparently never have been selected by Bach to set the words of Christ. In CANTATA NO. 17, *Wer Dank opfert, der preiset mich* (He who offers thanks glorifies me), the Evangelist Luke's account of the grateful healed Samaritan leper is treated directly as a tenor recitative: this is nine bars in length, and in the following tenor aria the soloist is surely intended to represent the tenth figure in the drama—the leper who does voice his thanks.*

During 1726 and 1727 Bach devoted special attention to church music for one solo voice and instrumental ensemble, and to the obbligato

---

* The Leonhardt ensemble's performance of Cantata No. 39 includes some of the best soprano treble singing on record from the unnamed Hannover soloist; the rest of the piece is effectively managed, sometimes very beautifully, although a stronger contrast might profitably have been drawn between the two clear sections of the opening chorus. In Cantata No. 45 a similar ensemble fares rather less consistently, with some uncharacteristic lack of precision in the continuo, yet excellent violin co-ordination in the bass *arioso* mentioned above. The account of Cantata No. 17 features good singing (especially from the youthful tenors of the Chorus Viennensis) and expressive use of the Concentus Musicus's strongly characteristic articulations in the first movement; possibly the final chorale could have been delivered with more rhythmic character—it is a fascinating example of Bach's skill in varying traditional harmonies and rhythms to revitalising effect.

use of the organ in his *Stücke*. The solo cantatas—for these pieces really do approach the real Italian meaning of *cantata*—are popular and relatively familiar today because of their convenience to financially economic performance, and also because they provide a satisfactory concert item comparable to a short song-cycle for one soloist. In contrast the pieces employing obbligato organ are relatively unfamiliar, because of various performance difficulties. In two works, CANTATA NO. 170, *Vergnügte Ruh, beliebte Seelenlust* (Delightful rest, *and* longed-for balm of souls), and CANTATA NO. 35, *Geist und Seele wird verwirret* (Soul and spirit are perplexed), a solo alto and obbligato organ music are combined specially effectively. *Vergnügte Ruh* has some of the tender polyphonic intricacy of the concentrated *Orgelbüchlein* chorale preludes: the alto voice is especially expressive when heard in interwoven textures, and in the third movement ("Wie jammern mich") the organ is added in rare (for Bach) three-stave notation. However, the fifth movement ("Mir ekelt mehr zu leben") uses the organ in a far more *concertante* manner, which adds effectively to the vigorous effect of the whole. *Geist und Seele* is so planned as to require close positioning and careful ensemble between the singer and the obbligato organist. The right-hand part for organ is used as a duetting soloist in three movements, and plays a solo role also in the two *sinfoniae*. The atmosphere of the work has a distinctly small-scaled character, and the dynamic indications in the score also give an impression that a quiet organ-registration was envisaged by Bach. The first aria is an extremely effective slow movement.

Of the other works for solo voice, CANTATA NO. 82, *Ich habe genug* (I am satisfied/I have suffered enough*), for bass, is especially fine. The beautiful self-administered lullaby, "Schlummert ein, ihr matten Augen," was so esteemed by Bach's wife Magdalena that she copied it twice into her album, transposing it to keys more suited to the pitch of her own soprano voice. The use of gentle, repeated notes conveys time, repetition, stress, the rhythm of life and of sleep: this might be said to be an Italian-derived feature, although *Gottes Zeit* includes it also. Certainly, our understanding of such passages is greatly clarified when the instruments are played sympathetically with baroque bows and fittings. The "Kreuzstab" cantata, CANTATA NO. 56, *Ich will den Kreuzstab gerne tragen* (I will gladly bear the cross), again casts the bass voice in a role of discipleship. Later, a recitative returns to music from an earlier aria to stress the common subject-matter. These two *Stücke* are often considered as companions, and it is hardly surprising that recent

---

*This title is virtually impossible to render in English: the best illustrations of the exact meaning are to be found in Bach's music here.

research has established that they were apparently composed in close proximity.

Whilst on the subject of the small-scale cantatas, mention should be made also of contemporary dialogue-cantatas; the preserved three works of this *genre* are all for soprano and bass. We have already encountered the type in CANTATA NO. 60, *O Ewigkeit*. From 1726 come CANTATA NO. 32, *Liebster Jesu, mein Verlangen* (Dearest Jesus, *source of my yearning*), and CANTATA NO. 49, *Ich gehe und suche* (I wander, searching with longing), and from 1727 CANTATA NO. 47, *Wer sich selbst erhöhet* (He who raises himself). Some of these solo cantatas end with a harmonised chorale.

Further organ obbligato movements of special interest occur in Cantata No. 47 (mainly a dialogue work), 169 (a solo for alto) and 49 (another dialogue). In No. 47 the second movement, the aria "Wer ein wahrer Christ will heissen," portrays meekness and gentleness in materials that recall the fluidity and the freedom of part-writing in the harpsichord suites. In No. 169 the most interesting application comes in the third movement, an alto aria in which the obbligato line weaves a decorative web of appropriate warmth and fervour: here the *Duetto*, BWV 802 (*Clavierübung III*), is anticipated. In Cantata No. 49, *Ich gehe und suche*, the first aria of that name is similarly a duetto treatment for organ, this time accompanying the bass voice; the vocal soloist here represents the Faithful Believer, so that the similarity in expression to the last-mentioned movement is hardly surprising. Possibly this association of the particular style with profound belief and Christian truth contradicts the notion that the four *Clavierübung Duetti* have no spiritual significance in that collection. There is little that is more like them in Bach's other music than these organ obbligati, or, indeed, in the whole musical literature of the period. The close identification with the text would also appear to imply that the music was conceived to set these words, rather than as a part of some lost concerto. Again there can be no certainty: Bach's ability in adapting his earlier compositions is so masterly that even this kind of "evidence" cannot be assumed to be final.

Eight motets by Bach have survived, BWV 225–231 and BWV 118, which was erroneously treated as a cantata by the Nineteenth-century editors. Of these only four can be related with any real certainty to specific occasions, and there is every doubt about some of them. The purposes and dates are diverse, and so are the characters of the individual motets. We must assume, also, that some considerable proportion of Bach's output in this *genre* is lost. However, what we have makes good sense in the light of our more representative knowledge of the *Kirchenstücke*. First, Bach knew well the rich tradition of German motet-composition of the mid- and late-Seventeenth century: *Jesu, meine Freude* (BWV 227) is often admired for the exquisite restraint of its outer movements, yet the harmonies are so close to Crüger's original (Berlin, 1653?) that it seems likely that Bach did not consider these portions of the work as his own original work at all. Second, the traditional style is restrained, yet Bach uses it in association with the most intense emotions—great joy, profound sorrow, extreme doubt, absolute faith. There is a strength in these works that derives from the sensitivity with which these apparent contradictions are moulded into the most delicate and sensuous expression by Bach: this reminds us of the similar mastery displayed in the Passions, where cruelty, suffering, sacrifice, anxiety and terror are combined with beauty and poetry in such a way as to heighten our experience. Third, the motets provide recurring evidence of the high quality of expressive singing, the well-trained discipline and the actual technical competence of the First Choir in Leipzig during Bach's service there.

The work which can be most closely related to its context is the funeral motet for Ernesti (*Der Geist hilft*, BWV 226), a well-respected member of Leipzig's academic community who had been Bach's closest neighbour for six-and-a-half years, and may well have been affectionately regarded by Bach's family. The motet's text makes an impressive intellectual statement of orthodox faith contemplating both the living and the dead: the concluding chorale stanza is the only excerpt from Luther's writings in any of the preserved motets, a re-affirmation of Ernesti's stand for orthodoxy and traditional values but also profoundly relevant in its exhortation to God not to relieve us from affliction but rather to strengthen us to meet it. Bach's setting of the chorale is *concertante* and "active" in style. It has the rhythmic life that would appeal to the non-specialist, the intricacy of motivic expansion that would appeal to the intellectual, the involvement inherent in a text in the first person plural and the highlighting of certain words and figures that would have appealed to the teacher and the orator.

Jesu, meine Freude (BWV 227)—especially in the Novello translation "Jesu priceless treasure"—is easily the best-known motet; and this particular work has remained especially popular in the Nine-Nineteenth and Twentieth centuries, partly because of its conciseness (each movement is almost a tone-poem for voices) and its direct manner of address. Indeed, the texts of all of the motets lack the elements that some have found an obstruction to their appreciation of the cantatas; they have continued to be performed in the Thomaskirche since Bach's lifetime as no other category of his music has. To the student of musical styles, the derivation of the various elements within these works is a fascinating subject; clearly, influences from Venetian music and Schütz or his contemporaries are remote, but are the works of later Seventeenth-century German masters really any closer to Bach? We are left wondering—as often—about the limits of Bach's knowledge of the various traditions within which we might be tempted to include his own examples of the *genre*.

*

The years around and following 1730 include the composition of the *Matthäuspassion* and its subsequent adaptations, the assembly of the *Missa* (a short Lutheran Mass—"Kyrie" with "Gloria") which was later expanded to form the celebratory B minor Mass, the composition of a number of homage-odes directed at Dresden (the *Trauer-Ode*—Cantata No. 198—and nameday or birthday pieces for the Dresden kings or princes), the assembly of the *Weihnachts-Oratorium* and the composition of the *Himmelfahrts-Oratorium*. The regular church-music continued to be performed, and although preserved new compositions are now far less numerous, there are interesting additional developments: for example, the chorale-cantata type seems to have dominated the academic years 1730–32, the bi-centenary in 1730 of the signing of the Augsburg Confession was attended with ceremonial music on a scale associated with the major church feasts, and the death of the King (August "der Stark," on February 1, 1733) and the crowning of his heir (August II of Saxony, III of Poland, on January 17, 1734) both occasioned responses from Leipzig's churches.

The precise evolution of the MATTHAUSPASSION (BWV 244) is tantalisingly obscure. Parts of the musical materials seem to have been in existence by late 1726, and the music of certain numbers appears —from literary evidence—to have been shared with the lost Bach funeral music for Leopold I of Cöthen, which was performed on March 24, 1729, after only four months' notice. It may well be that those numbers common to both works were jointly conceived for two purposes—a similar process to that employed earlier for the *Oster-Oratorium* (BWV 249) and the *Schäferkantate* (BWV 249a). There are other movements in the *Matthäuspassion* that appear to be parodies of earlier compositions, and which are lost in the alternative versions. By 1729 a version of the work with one continuo group shared by the two choirs and ensembles was apparently complete, although 1730 is a possible alternative which would put that version's performance into the Nicolaikirche —an attractive notion, since most of Bach's monumental masterpieces were first heard there, and its acoustics are today warmer and more attractive for *concertante* choral music. This early version is today referred to as BWV 244b. BWV 244 itself strictly belongs to the version of the work with two continuo sections, a longer concluding chorus to Part I (taken and transposed from the second version of the

Johannespassion) and other more detailed alterations. The church records in Leipzig contain a list of Passion performances with the significant entry :

> 1736. St. Thomae mit beyden Orgeln
> (=1736. At St. Thomas's with both organs)

This is considered to have been the first performance of the enlarged version: the evidence is also supported by the preserved performing materials. Quite which two organs were used is unclear: antiphonal performance between the West and East ends of the Thomaskirche nave might have been practicable, but the older East-end organ was apparently not much valued, since, despite attention in 1727/28, it was finally dismantled in 1740/41; besides, it is unlikely that its gallery could have accommodated one of the two choirs involved. A more probable explanation is that some form of chamber-organ was already in regular use in the church—perhaps as a temporary measure—and that this was used; an instrument could also have been brought in specially.

One surprising feature of the *Matthäuspassion*—especially if we compare it with the *Johannespassion*—is the relatively slight extent of the differences between the "1729" and 1736 versions. Indeed, the setting of St. Matthew's account has a very strong character throughout its various transformations, a character that is quite distinct from that of the re-workings of the St. John setting. It is both longer and (despite great emphasis on personal response in *arioso* and aria) more monumental. It is also in some respects a more traditional setting of the Passion story. The characterising of Christ's words through sustained string and organ accompaniments, the greater emphasis on personal commentary from diversified sources (more arias, in particular). the dramatic as well as musical dialogue effects between the two ensembles of instruments and voices, even the monumental scales of the opening and closing choruses—all contribute to this effect. Most writers have seen this special character as some kind of extension of ideas tried earlier in the *Johannespassion*. Whilst there can be little doubt that the scale is more extended, and that, for example, the lullaby Finale is closely related to the penultimate movement of the *Johannespassion*, it is surely a mistake to view the later setting as an attempt to improve on the earlier one. The character of the *Matthäuspassion* is that of the gospel that is being set: it contrasts strongly with the *Johannespassion* in the very same ways—length, mood, treatment of subject-matter, philosophical approach, relation of the Passion of Christ to its traditional contexts. Furthermore, its individuality is achieved through musical means expressive of its text. The music of the

Johannespassion provides us with a massive study of Christian compassion; that of the *Matthäuspassion* focuses our attention on contrasting aspects of Christian witness.

Various attempts have been made to analyse the architecture of the *Matthäuspassion* symbolically, but most of these could be said to reveal more about the commentators than about Bach himself. The dramatic and interpretative aspects of this commanding work are best stressed in a discussion that divides it not into categories, but into scenes (here using the NBA numbering).

Introduction (Nos. 1–4b). The opening chorus stresses the aspect of witness, and reminds us (through the vernacular paraphrase of the Agnus Dei) of the essential relationship between the sacrifice of the Passion and our belief. The first recitative shows Christ prophesying His crucifixion at the Passover. The reaction of the congregation having been invoked and represented in the chorale, we are brought back to the harsh reality of Passiontide with the plotting of the chief priests and scribes to take and kill Jesus "mit Listen" (with subtlety).

The Anointing at Bethany (Nos. 4c–6). The ways of God are not always as simple as even well-meaning disciples might expect: the alto's commenting recitative and aria of repentant humility is effectively placed to remind us of our involvement at a stage where we might be in danger of witnessing events in too external and impersonal a way. The central heart of this scene is, of course, the disciples' reaction and Christ's masterly yet slightly mysterious answer—a characteristically mystical detail for St. Matthew.

The Last Supper (Nos. 7–14 and 15–17). A symmetrical scene:

7: Judas plots the betrayal
8: Soprano aria: Man, who seems as innocent as a child (treble solo, NB) has nevertheless betrayed Jesus
9a–e: Christ is asked where he proposes to spend the Passover; the preparations; Christ begins to speak of the disciples' forthcoming betrayal, and they ask, "Is it I?"
10: Chorale: "Ich bin's . . ."
11: Christ continues to speak of the betrayal and is directly questioned by Judas; the institution of the Eucharist
12 and 13: Soprano recitative and aria of dedication
14: Christ prophesies his desertion by the disciples, but also the Resurrection

is followed by a symmetrical sub-scene:

15: Chorale of devotion
16: Peter's affirmation—an ironic touch between the two chorales (after all, Peter represents us)
17: Chorale of dedication

The placing of the movements, as well as the individual character of each, is tellingly executed and on the whole concisely proportioned. The chorales occupy special positions in either part of the scene, and the materials—both text and music—have been selected with the same skill that we have already noticed in the *Johannespassion*.

Gethsemane (Nos. 18–28). Again, the movements pair off symmetrically: the heart of the scene is Christ's acceptance of his role as Saviour (during No. 24). On either side are the bass recitative and aria concerning the Christian's readiness to suffer for Christ and a chorale of faith. Christ's agonised prayer to the Father (No. 21) balances the second discovery of the sleeping disciples and the betrayal most strikingly; the dialogue for tenor and chorus (No. 19) which has introduced the whole subject of Gethsemane is placed opposite the far more agitated dialogue between soprano-with-alto and chorus at the betrayal. The recitatives at the extremes of the Gethsemane scene similarly contrast the reflective ("Tarry ye here and watch") with the active—even the violent (the episode of the servant's ear. Christ's reaction, and the subsequent desertion of the disciples). Here, after a concluding movement (in our "usual" version, the choral chorale-prelude on "O Mensch, bewein," but in the version 244b a commenting chorale), Part One ended, and the Good Friday Vespers sermon was preached. Part Two opens with two shorter scenes.

Christ before False Witnesses (Nos. 30–35). The central chorale is philosophical and priestly; the alto aria with choral assistance (No. 30) is agitated and active, which makes an effective contrast with the tenor's recitative and aria (Nos. 34–35) which reflect on Christ's exemplary forbearance.

Christ and Peter Contrasted under Direct Interrogation, with Added Reflections (Nos. 36–40). The biblical accounts numbered 36a–d and 38a–c stress the essential contrasts; the chorale (No. 37, "Wer hat dich so geschlagen?") stresses the completely blameless and guiltless nature of Christ. Peter's behaviour, whilst it is accorded far less restrained dignity, is given special feeling and emotion—he, like us, is human. Such clear contrast between the divine and the all-too-earthly naturally leads into a prayer for forgiveness ("Erbarme dich") and a hymn of devotion.

Christ before Pilate (Nos. 41–50). Another symmetrical scheme, centred on the emphatic united cry of "Barabbas":

41a–c: Christ is delivered to Pilate. The remorse and suicide of Judas
42: Bass aria of emphatic regret. The priestly voice is none the less eloquent simply because its manner of delivery is almost academically tidy and understated: indeed, there is calculation behind this very element in the music
43: The purchase of the Potter's Field; Christ is questioned, at first sympathetically, by Pilate

(Nos. 41–43 themselves form a symmetrical sub-scene in which the history of Judas is neatly framed within more essential things concerning Christ, whose character forms the subject of the aria at its centre)

44: Chorale of devotion and trust
45: The whole of mankind (for the two choirs have at times clearly represented Judaism and Christian believers respectively) pronounces a preference for Barabbas over Christ, and calls for His crucifixion
46: Chorale of wondering worship that the Master, although innocent, is sacrificed for the faults of his vassals
47: Pilate questions the crowd regarding their motive
48–49: Soprano recitative and aria: Christ's perfection renders the sacrifice perfect, consequently the power of evil affects only the imperfect sinner
50a–e: Under pressure, Pilate abandons his impartial idealism for the sake of expediency: he ironically washes his hands since he cannot escape responsibility; on the other hand, the crowd, whose responsibility is actually indirect, pretends that it has the power to assume it

Nos. 44–46 form a central trilogy, Nos. 47–50 a later one. The crowd's unison lies at the centre, devotion to Christ at the heart of the first subdivision, the hope of Easter at the heart of the third. The actual tension and drama within the account is handled in masterly fashion within the recitative solos and choruses (the so-called *turbae*).

Contemplation of the Scourging (Nos. 51–57). The heart of this scene is to be found in the two verses of the chorale. The mockery of Christ as an earthly king lies in the great Passion recitatives on either side, and the two arias with recitative preludes contrast strongly: the alto's (No. 52) starts with an emotional reaction to the drama of the situation and continues more reflectively; the bass's solos (Nos. 56–57), however, start in a more contemplative way and end actively, whether we see the singer as representing Simon of Cyrene, ourselves, or both.

Golgotha (Nos. 58–66). The symmetry is again striking; the proportions and balances of expression are precisely controlled, even by the standards evident earlier within the work:

58a–e: Arrival at Golgotha; Christ mocked by the crowd, also the malefactors; the partition of His garments and the attachment of Pilate's "notice of accusation"
59–60: Alto recitative and dialogue aria with chorus in which the misery of Golgotha is contrasted with God's generous protection of mankind through Christ
61a–e: Darkness at the sixth hour. "Eli! Eli! . . ."; the sponge of vinegar. The death of Christ
62: Chorale of personal appeal and commitment to Christ
63a–c: The earthquake. Joseph of Aramathea seeks and obtains Pilate's permission to take the body of Christ
64–65: Bass recitative and aria commenting on the eventide act of redemption atoning for Adam's (traditional) betrayal of mankind at an equivalent time. Aria of devotion to Christ in death

66a–b: Joseph takes the body for burial; the Pharisees caution Pilate concerning Christ's promise to rise from the dead within three days

The whole work's *Conclusion* is none the less effective for its direct brevity:

67: Recitative *arioso* and chorus (almost in some kind of folk-style)—a reminder of both our personal and communal witness, and of the strong links between the family and Christianity

68: Tutti lullaby-chorus: this most effective idea, which relates closely to the similar penultimate movement of the *Johannespassion*, probably came originally from the Kuhnau *Markuspassion* of 1721. The dialogue element that is added here is specially effective, partly because it stresses that awareness of others that is essential to the work and its subject-matter.

Tabulation and division may help us to follow Bach's masterpiece with greater ease and some sense of proportion, but it can seem out-of-place—an interpretative incompatibility—applied to music that flows so expressively. In various respects the *Matthäuspassion* seems conscious of musical tradition, as stated above; yet its originality is also striking, even though it is disguised with such art (even, perhaps, deliberate humility) that it is easily missed. Dramatic outbursts like the cry of "Barabbas" (a powerful and unexpected diminished chord), the lyrical devotion of the famous "Erbarme dich" (No. 39, "Have thou mercy") or the grave pathos of "Ach Golgotha" (No. 59) may strike us as anticipatory of Wagner's intense expression or Beethoven's directness of appeal, but we see such elements with hindsight. Even if that delicately calculated final rising *appoggiatura* in the last bar of the whole work draws attention to itself as something which is disturbing or original, few of us will pause to wonder what question it poses (whether Christ really is, or was, sleeping? what are we to make of it all? simply a conventional expression of pathos?). However, all of these examples have the quality of surprise within the work: they have been included partly to draw our attention. If we look instead at the far less obvious aria "Können Tränen meiner Wangen nicht erlangen" (No. 52, "If the tears on my cheeks can achieve nothing"), we find no less musical originality or character: indeed, the music is here most especially refined and characteristic of its composer. There are three main *motifs*, each of which undergoes significant transformations. The first *motif* is essentially an embroidered descending arpeggio:

The second is essentially a rhythmic effect designed to depict weeping or sobbing:

The third, of which both the rhythm and the wide leap are essential ingredients, is again an illustration of sobbing emotion:

Unison violin themes that eventually expand into elegant polyphonies may not be unique to Bach (Vivaldi made good use of this idea), and are certainly not in his case restricted to this work or this aria; however, the lilting delicacy of the whole opening ritornello has a special transparency. To the uncritical eye the aria might therefore seem agreeable and charming—as, indeed, in a sense it is. However, interesting harmonic astringencies are contained within the movement,

the curiously tortuous word-setting must be intended to convey deep anguish,

and the strongly directional discord within the bar shown below

fails to resolve correctly, according to Bach's habitual practice, with a specially expressive result:

The *da capo* marking at the conclusion and the instrumental ritornello remind us that this aria is yet another example of the *da-capo*-cum-ritornello type favoured by the composer since Weimar. Also characteristic is the manner in which the fluid vocal line becomes more expressive whilst still developing the opening *motifs* in the central (unrepeated) section. The conclusion of that section is especially lovely: the two upper parts start in gently-coloured homophony, then diverge into a remarkable burst of interdependent melody—a magnificent musical representation of heartfelt, heaven-sent communion.

*

Close in character to the arias of the *Matthäuspassion* is the dignified TRAUER-ODE (BWV 198—Ode of Mourning). The dead Electress Eberhardine, wife of August "der Stark," had been regarded with particular sympathy throughout Protestant Germany, and the work was commissioned by a young nobleman studying in Leipzig from Bach and Johann Christoph Gottsched, a young poet and critic of great promise who was later to become of considerable international significance. Gottsched's none-too-inspired text was unusual for Bach in that it was not written in alternating recitatives and arias with choruses, but rather as a dense, strophic poem in nine eight-line stanzas (see Plate 6). Bach divided it in two at the end of the fifth stanza, then set the opening and closing half-stanzas of Part One as choruses, the first dignified and stately, with lyrical homophonic chorus-work sometimes compared to the openings of the two Passions, the second as an ensemble *colla parte* fugue with a central section for instruments alone separating two contrasting expositions of similar material. The final movement of the work, a setting of the last of Gottsched's nine stanzas, has a warmly assertive popular style (this is a *contredanse* rather than a *gigue* or a *giga*, surely). Its highlight, and indeed one of the whole work, is reached at the words (in bold type in the printed Gottsched text) "Sie ist der Tugend Eigenthum, der unterthanen Lust und Ruhm" (She was of unparalleled virtue, a cause of joy and pride to her subjects), most beautifully set for suddenly unison voices with a warm accompaniment: a fine portrayal of sincere communal feeling (see Plate 6).

The Leipzig chronicler Sicul recorded that the Ode was composed "nach Italianischer Art . . . , mit *Clave di Cembalo*, welche Herr Bach selbste spielete, Orgel, *Violes di Gamba*, Lauten, Violinen, *Fleutes douces* und *Fleutes traverses* &c. . ."* : the Italianate element can barely refer

---

* After the Italian manner . . . with *Clave di Cembalo*, which Mr. Bach himself played, organ, *Violes di Gamba*, lutes, violins [=violins, violas, celli], *Fleutes douces* [=recorders] and *Fleutes traverses* &c. . ."

to the styles of the movements, even though the throbbing bass-lines of the first two movements, the precise nature of the dotted figures of the first chorus, the almost *cliché*-ridden bass-line of the aria and the use of two recorders and flutes throughout do show a degree of Italian influence. The work is dominated neither by Italianate aria (after Vivaldi or Scarlatti) nor by sonata (Corellian or Handelian), even though the movements depend heavily on solo singing and string accompaniments. Rather, it is in the profusion of continuo and colouristic effects—the instrumentation directly referred to above, in fact—that the work displays Italian characteristics. Apart from an unusually heavy employment of minor keys (all movements but one conclude in the minor), the work appears to hark back to Bach's early maturity. The "bell" recitative might remind us loosely of the "clock" aria of Cantata No .161 or similarly orchestrated passages of the *Actus tragicus* (Cantata No. 106). Here, the intention is to convey the catastrophe of the Queen's passing, and the whole orchestral resources of the work are most strikingly used to portray bells: especially remarkable are the two oboes (probably d'amore), which produce a solemn tolling, and the recorders. The beautiful tenor aria, "Der Ewigkeit saphirnes Haus," has a text that was surely inspired by the catafalque bearing the dead Queen's emblems which was present at the memorial service. The picture of Heaven among the stars of the heavens, and where the Queen is envisaged amid a halo of suns, surely inspired from Bach that magnificently evocative melody for flute. The bass-line is part-*lamentoso* (the falling tetrachords), part-reassuring (the rising scale-fragments, the gently rocking trochaic rhythms, and the seemingly timeless sequences beneath seventh-chords); the sudden hastening quaver-figures before many of the cadences add to the impression of intricacy as well as beauty. Above this harmonic bass the two gambas weave their ornamentation of it, sometimes digressing independently but mostly embroidering the fundamental bass: it seems probable that the latter was played by the organ, celli and lutes together—a beautiful, and indeed a characteristically Italian, effect.

The *Trauer-Ode* may well have been close in composition to the first versions of the *Matthäuspassion*, and some similarity has already been indicated. The materials partly found their way into the lost *Markuspassion*, which has been laboriously reconstructed from this and other sources as a frustratingly incomplete torso. Other secular homage-cantatas have been preserved from the last two dozen years of Bach's service in Leipzig. Generally, this corpus of material is little known, apart from the agreeable but hardly representative "Bauernkantate" (Peasant Cantata), CANTATA NO. 212, *Mer hahn en neue Oberkeet* (Happen we got us a new squire), written for the wedding-feast of an apparently spirited and wealthy village squire. "The Kaffeekantate" (Coffee Cantata), CANTATA NO. 211, *Schweigt stille* (Be quiet and stop chattering), which is often included in this group, is really a rather different kind of composition, since it is not written to flatter so much as to entertain— the closest that Bach came to the composition of commercially-orientated opera. The two works are frequently discussed together despite their diversity of purpose, mainly because the combination of a story with an important national institution (the coffee-house) and with *couleur locale* appealed strongly to late Nineteenth-century taste, and as a result their charm was readily appreciated. Together they also serve to remind us of the difference between the earnest and parochially diplomatic town life of the time (portrayed in the "Kaffeekantate") and the unashamed lack of sophistication then attributed to the peasantry.* In an important sense the "Kaffeekantate" is a parody, but what are its precise targets? It may well be that some actual work was the object of Bach's humour—an aspect that is absorbing with regard to the similar parody, CANTATA NO. 201, *Der Streit zwischen Phoebus und Pan* (The contest between Phoebus and Pan), which seems to be intended to mock rigid aesthetic evaluation in the arts. A closer study of Leipzig's academic and cultural climate around 1725–35 might well lead to interesting conclusions here. In the case of the "Bauernkantate," it has emerged that the work contains modified and developed quotations from a substantial number of folk melodies. There are parallels in this respect between the delicately comical and *risqué* cantata-suite and the last of the famous "Goldberg" variations for harpsichord, which is headed *Quodlibet*.

The actual homage-cantatas also frequently took the form of *drammae per musica*, with named characters from the mythological gods or abstract virtues. Their music is partly familiar through transcriptions and paraphrases in sacred pieces—a process we have already seen in the Weissenfels "Schäferkantate" (No. 249a) and the *Oster-Oratorium*. We may count ourselves especially fortunate that both scores and parts are preserved for three homage-cantatas, CANTATA NO. 214, *Tonet ihr Pauken! Erschallet, Trompeten!* (Resound, ye drums! Ring out ye trumpets!), CANTATA NO. 213, *Lasst uns sorgen, lasst uns wachen* (the "Hercules at the Crossroads" cantata), and CANTATA NO. 215, *Preise dein Glücke, gesegnetes Sachsen* (Reflect on thy good fortune, O blessed Saxony). The delicate soprano aria of No. 214, "Blast die wohlgegriffnen Flöten" (Sound forth the deftly handled flutes!), contains some of the composer's most intricately tender music for transverse flute duet. The final rondo-chorus of the "Hercules" cantata is a spirited homophonic dialogue between the chorus and the bass soloist in *gavotte* style; its materials are reworked from a Cöthen homage-cantata, where they

---

* The Concentus Musicus Vienna performances of both cantatas are extremely tidy and entertaining, if just a little deficient in rhythmic gusto.

formed the sixth movement of the only partly preserved Cantata No. 184a. Only two movements of No. 215 are preserved in other forms, however, and in both cases there are substantial differences between the workings of similar material: the opening double chorus is an expansive and vigorous fugato on the *motif* later developed in a more succinct way as the "Osanna" of the B minor Mass; the beautiful soprano aria with flutes, "Durch die von Eifer entflammeten Waffen," is reworked as a bass aria in Part Five of the *Weihnachts-Oratorium*, but here it has a specially tender heroic quality that was probably intended to be French in style (a tribute to the favour accorded to the French flautist Buffardin at the Dresden court?). The earlier bass aria is much more positive and military in style, and the splendid tenor aria, "Freilich trotzt Augustus' Name," is a virtuoso showpiece for its soloist. This last is in ternary form (ABA), clearly underlined in the selfconscious cadences at the end of each section—the "A" section actually makes use of the device (rare in Bach) of an essential augmented sixth chord. The piece's opening flourish stresses the three essential notes of the triad in a way that recalls the opening of the first chorus: all of these threes were probably included to flatter the king, August III, for whom the work was produced by torchlight as an evening serenade.

The remaining homage-cantatas include many whose music has not been preserved, some the music of which can be partially reconstructed, and a few miscellaneous works including the "Wind" and "Water" cantatas—CANTATA NO. 205, *Zerreisset, zersprenget* (Shatter, burst forth) and CANTATA NO. 206, *Schleicht, spielende Wellen* (Flow calmly, ye rippling currents)—delicate allegorical works reflecting the growing use of natural phenomena as subject-matter for literature during the lifetime of Bach. These occasional compositions belonged to a traditional repertoire nourished in the near-feudal society of the time. The performances on these occasions often resulted in rich rewards, new employment or enviable publicity for performers (either vocal or instrumental), which meant that to be selected to compose or perform in one was a special privilege.

*

From the secular cantatas we pass naturally to the WEIHNACHTS-ORATORIUM (BWV 248) of 1734/35, partly because of the actual parodying of movements and *motifs*, but partly because there is also an attitude of proclaimed affirmation about the two kinds of composition. Although the oratorio is a discontinous work, designed to be heard on six different days, it is not quite a set of regular *Stücke*, even though it fulfilled the same role in the services as six of them usually did. In considering the differences, it is useful that in J. G. Walther's musical "Lexicon" we have a local definition of "oratorio":

A sacred OPERA or a representation IN MUSIC of a sacred history, performed in the chapels and chambers of PERSONS of substance, with speech, SOLI, DUO and TRIO, RITORNELLOS, fine choruses &c. The musical COMPOSITION must throughout be so richly inventive that the impression created is appropriate and integrated. . .

If for "speech" we substitute "recitative,"* we have an interesting description which—apart from the reference to chapels and chambers— fits the Easter and Ascensiontide oratorios by Bach as well as the Christmas one. It certainly helps us to see that secular cantatas and oratorios of special artistic elaboration were quite compatible for Bach and his contemporaries.

One feature of the *Weihnachts-Oratorium* as a whole is its comparative difficulty in performance. The work is heard quite frequently in Western Europe and the U.S.A. today, yet those very parts (One to Three) which are most frequently performed are especially difficult in ensemble, in interpretation and in technical respects for both singers and instrumentalists. Very frequently the result is catastrophic, and the author has spent more moments during this work wondering about the abilities of Bach's own performers than he has during any other. In Part One the opening movement is difficult in ensemble, and has awkward string figures in combination with pronuncia- tion challenges for the choir. The aria for trumpet and bass is among Bach's most difficult pieces for trumpet, and that for alto demands subtle and sensitive accentuation from the whole ensemble. The chorale commentary also demands nice precision in timing and accentuation, and the solo vocal materials all place heavy demands on good performers. In Part Two the beautiful pastoral Sinfonia presents multiple problems of ensemble for the woodwind, problems of tempo in varied acoustical contexts and the usual problems associated with the duration and articulation of dotted notes—but to an unusual degree and over an extended period. The "Gloria in excelsis" chorus can easily sound aggressive rather than festive, especially when the soprano line is uncontrolled and of poor intonation—alas, a fault all-too-frequently encountered in choirs containing too many female sopranos. The two arias both demand excellent breath-control and require extended con- centration and sympathy of both the singers and the players of the wind

---

* Walther himself describes "recitative" as sung declamation—a definition that well suits the recitative texts of Salomo Franck of Weimar, with which he would be familiar. The recitative of much oratorio is narration rather than commentary, hence is not declamatory; the term "Gesprächen," used here in the context of a "representation IN MUSIC," might well refer here to recitatives which recount.

obbligati; and in the great lullaby-aria ("Schlafe, mein liebster") there were already problems of blending between the five woodwinds and the voice before they were made more acute by Nineteenth-century developments in oboe and flute construction. The extremely effective *alternatim* treatment of the final chorale is often spoilt by imprecision, poor disposition of the performing ensemble and imbalances of volume between the choral and the woodwind consorts. In Part Three the opening and closing chorus is very hard to sing effectively: lyricism is often lost if the many repeated notes are too emphatically detached, yet too little articulation from the choir often leads to ridiculous anomalies between it and the orchestral accompaniment; the presence of the brass and percussion is too often to be associated with poor intonation and balance—faults which are particularly exposed in this rather homophonic, even dance-like, style of fugato. The poised and sensuous beauty of the duet aria, "Herr, dein Mitlied, dein Erbarmen," calls again for well-maintained precision from all concerned; most performances seem to have been ill-prepared from the very point-of-view that is most essential for success. The Marian alto aria, "Schliesse, mein Herze," has a solo violin obbligato that is pitched at just the level where modern violin tone, techniques, and even modern linear interpretation of phrasing, sound most remote from that of the Baroque: as a result, we customarily hear performances that are, quite frankly, inappropriate to Bach's intentions. Even good modern violinists admit that Bach is none too easy to play at all, let alone well; an affected, over-emotional string interpretation is all too frequently the prelude to an even less dignified and subtly expressive one from the alto.*

Only a few of the above difficulties will have been any the easier for Bach's original performers. In fact, the oratorio as a whole gives further strong testimony to Bach's ability as a trainer and director of ensemble pieces. The death of the veteran trumpeter Gottfried Reiche —after an actual performance of Cantata No. 215 in October 1734—

---

* The recorded performances include (rare luxury!) two which claim to employ authentic *timbres* and interpretative features. The Concentus Musicus Vienna performance has some curious rhythmic and tonal unevennesses, especially in Parts One to Four, some poor trumpet-playing, some curious balances and a variable standard of solo singing. The Collegium Aureum/Tölzer choir reading produces a slightly more orthdox sense of rhythm and balance (although the trumpets and drums sound distant), but the soloists and instrumentalists smack of modern, rather than Eighteenth-century, thinking. The Tölzer *ripieno* trebles are, however, especially excellent. The Richter/Munich performance with Gundula Janowitz, etc., somehow lacks the choral precision of their older B minor Mass--a pity, since competition in that department is desirable; better in general is another Munich interpretation under Jochum, which has good controlled speeds and balance within the limitations imposed by modern instrumentation and an inappropriate harpsichord continuo. Münchinger's Stuttgart performance is predictably rather heavy and lacking in grace, the Leipzig Thomanerchor and Gewandhaus reading none too ingratiating tonally—especially on the instrumental side.

would have resulted in the loss of a distinguished soloist, yet here we encounter some of Bach's most difficult clarino parts, presumably composed expressly to show off Reiche's virtuoso abilities. The varied styles and considerable rhythmic life expected from the chorus through-out the six parts of the work also demonstrate that the *Erste Kantorei* (the official title of the Thomasschule's First Choir) was musically well-trained, though the school's current *Rektor* was known not to favour church music. The solo arias are precisely conceived, with notation especially clear, the textures mainly on the lighter side, and always most attractively devised as sensuous sound. To those who argue that Bach composed unrealistically, that he knew that his performers would not realise his intentions, this work provides a special answer: if this were the case, why did the composer choose to re-use such demand-ing material from secular pieces? Had he planned performances before the king (whose honorary *Capellmeister* he was currently applying to become) in the expectation that they would have a poor effect? Is there, indeed, any record that indicates that Bach was anything but sensitive with regard to performance?

Finally, two *Kirchenstücke* from the year 1731 must not be excluded from brief discussion here. The Ratswahl (Civic Election) piece, CANTATA NO. 29, *Wir danken dir, Gott* (We thank thee, Lord), is espe-cially impressive in a light-footed festive style not altogether dissimilar from that of the later *Weihnachts-Oratorium*. However, the first chorus is in a very different style. This is the magnificent *alla breve* movement that was later used twice in significant positions in the B minor Mass. The Sinfonia that precedes this is an arrangement for organ and orchestra of the *Preludio* of the unaccompanied Third Violin Partita in E (here transposed to D). It was probably designed to display the performing talents of one of Bach's organ-students (Wilhelm Friedemann Bach?); the attractive Italianate hues of the orchestra-tion—especially towards the conclusion of the movement—lead most effectively into the chorus that is to follow. The remaining movements are by no means without charm (especially the delightful ensemble "Amen"), continuity, and musical interest (the form of the *Siciliano* aria for soprano, as well as the *motifs* and bass-line, is closely modelled on the characteristics of the dance), and the whole has a pleasant compactness.

The second work referred to above is the well-known CANTATA NO. 140, *Wachet auf!* (Wake ye!). This is Bach's only *Kirchenstück* for Trinity + 27—a Sunday that occurs rarely in the calendar, and for which the Gospel recounts the parable of the unprepared wedding-maidens. The two solo recitatives with duet arias are sensuously evocative settings of texts based on biblical compilations; despite Schering's and Dürr's assertions that these movements could well have come from an actual wedding-cantata, their sensuous and even uninhibited expression might well have made them inappropriate for such earthly occasions in the Leipzig Bach knew so well. The opening chorus, with its gently dramatic emphasis of the dominant seventh chord in accented root position—not a common effect in Bach—conveys the spirit of Nicolai's poetry effectively; this treatment of the chord gives impetus to the almost Corellian solo-figures that punctuate and accompany the separated choral lines. The final chorale (verse 3 of Nicolai's poem; the melody is also his) has a rather Seventeenth-century musical manner, and may have been taken over by Bach from a setting known to him; it certainly produces a sturdy and highly Protestant effect. The most familiar movement of this work is, of course, the hypnotic setting of Stanza 2, which was later published for organ as the first of Schübler's *Sechs Choräle von verschiedener Art* around 1748. The accompaniment, for unison upper strings with continuo, has that special intimate but expansive freedom that we have observed in the aria in the *Matthäuspassion*, together with a similarly economical and refined bass. Here, however, there are added qualities. First, the chorale itself is presented as a tenor (*ripieno?*) *cantus firmus*, in separated lines; the accompanying materials remain more or less constant, as in the setting which terminates either half of "Die Elenden sollen essen" (Cantata No. 75). Second, the accompanying figures are treated in contrapuntal and harmonic permutations that are essentially motivic and concentrated. The three main ideas

This occurs ten times and is harmonised in six different ways.

This occurs eight times: there are five differing harmonisations, and the indicated bowing varies.

This is heard fifteen times, in such changing forms that it seems to grow throughout the movement.

form the basis of nearly all of the material, and the results are at times far from orthodox

and sometimes barely capable of analysis. Yet the sense of vigilant watching, of exposed expectancy and of the most acute anticipation of the rapture that is to come deflects our attention from the detailed mysteries of the art that produces them. One can guess that Bach was aware of this very aspect, and that he included the work in the later publication because the *art* which is involved here is barely explicable and is also, no doubt, the product of no little divine contemplation.

7: Leipzig: The Art of the Last Years

The dominating aspect of Bach's last ten years of creative work—from around 1739 to his undatable incapacity through illness—is a constantly recurring desire to assemble collections. This had been evident to some degree throughout the composer's working life: the grouped keyboard sets (inventions, sinfonias, suites, preludes and fugues, partitas, chorale settings, sonatas for organ), chamber-music sets (sonatas, unaccompanied sonatas, partitas and suites), ensemble sets (Brandenburg Concerti, harpsichord concerti, violin concerti, *Ouverturen*), and even certain groups of *Kirchenstücke* conceived in series, had shown a strong tendency to demonstrate diversity within common limits. From now on, however, it is more pronounced. Throughout the late instrumental collections flows a common feature: within each, Bach seems to have sought less to provide examples of the glorious Art (in all senses) of the past than to have striven for a maximum variety within the apparently wide limits of his own artistic tastes and personality.

There are no really late *Kirchenstücke*: a neatly concise and highly effective Whitsun piece, CANTATA NO. 34, *O ewiges Feuer* (O eternal fire) is actually derived from a wedding-cantata of early 1726

(No. 34a, with the same title, but longer and in two parts). The fifth movement's great cry of rejoicing at Israel's peace may have been directly linked to the hopes of Saxony (hence Leipzig) in the Second Silesian War, May 1744 or 1745; these would, in either case, have proved ill-founded. The gentle aria for alto, strings and subtly doubling flutes is among Bach's most restful songs of pastoral contentment. The opening chorus's fire-imagery might well remind us of the organ-prelude on *Komm Heiliger Geist, Herre Gott* (BWV 651)—also, significantly, for Whitsuntide and associated occasions. The final Allegro, a binary movement with chorus added for the repeats, is festive and assertive (neat trumpet punctuations in the second half), but also tightly organised and none the less dramatic as a result.

The "Bauernkantate" of 1742 has already been mentioned above (see Chapter Six). Bach's last great effort in choral music was not in the realm of the ordinary *Kirchenstück*: such a type of music could hardly be on such a monumental scale as to be representative, except in the form of an extended series or *Jahrgang*, and Bach had already composed examples of those. Neither was it a Passion, although it does appear that the last performance of the *Johannespassion* was organised for a larger choir and string section than the previous ones, and that because of this a bassono grosso was added—whatever kind of bassoon that may actually have been—to selected movements. It was not a piece of Funeral Music (we should remember that Bach's admired elder cousin Johann Ludwig had composed particularly successfully in that *genre*). Neither was it a liturgically acceptable Mass setting. However, a Mass it was—the B MINOR MASS (BWV 232)—and although very little of the actual musical material originated towards the end of Bach's career (the "Kyrie" and "Gloria" having been taken to Dresden already complete in 1733), its totality, its refinement and its special relevance as an act of Christian witness all belong alongside the other representative works from the close of Bach's remarkable career.

There are other Mass settings by Bach, including attractive short settings in G major, G minor and A, and a rather different one in F (BWV 236, 235, 234 and 233 respectively). All of these involve adaptations from *Kirchenstücke*, and possibly others from lost Bach sources. Their purpose is still somewhat obscure, although the Bohemian court of Graf Sporck has been suggested as a plausible context for their commission or performance. However, these "short Masses" lack the grand rhetoric that characterises the equivalent portions of that short *Missa* which Bach took to Dresden in 1733. They are probably all assemblies made as some kind of preliminary study towards compiling the late sections of the B minor Mass; they probably date from the 1740s.

There are various special aspects of the *Mass*. First, the "Kyrie" seems to have been loosely composed on a model from Dresden—the

Mass in F by Johann Hugo von Wilderer (1670–1724). Second, the opening soprano *motif* is clearly derived from Luther's *German Mass 1525* (published in 1526):

This *motif* (simply a rising scale) is heard at the start of Bach's work in various transformations:

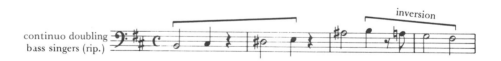

Such elaboration abounds throughout the work. Third, the great Mass seems to have been composed with a certain degree of historical awareness—very probably after study of other works in similar *genres*. This may well have applied to the original *Missa* no less than the completed whole, but, as Christoph Wolff has made clear, many of Bach's copies of music by composers employing, for example, the *stile antico* come from the later years: this activity may well have been inspired by Lorenz Mitzler's German edition of Fux's "Gradus ad Parnassum," issued in Leipzig in 1742. However, there is a remarkable common *motif* which the second "Kyrie" shares with Vivaldi's double-chorus "Kyrie" in G minor (RV 587); the "Qui tollis" contains thematic resemblances to that composer's "Et misericordia" (*Magnificat*, RV 610/3); the bass-line of the great "Crucifixus" has the universally understood poignancy of the lament, and the same kind of emotional expression as the above. Fourth, the whole work relates in a specially interesting way to Bach's own Magnificat settings, where once again a concise Latin text dictates lack of recitative and hence greater involvement of chorus and ensemble, and last—but most significantly—a special relationship between the meaning of the text and its illustration in musical gestures. The B minor Mass requires a choir capable of sustaining freshness of tone, freshness of interpretation, technical authority and rhythmic sensitivity over an extended period.* Also like the Magnificat, it calls for a minimum of five soloists SSATB, and those conductors who try to manage with four only emphasise their own insensitivity to Bach's music; Bach writes with economy: to starve him of his requirements results in losses that are far more serious than the begrudging of a soloist's fee.†

---

* Chorally, the best recordings are those under Richter, Klemperer and Harnoncourt. Klemperer's choir is large, his conception traditional in that it focuses attention on emotional interpretation; his chorus has been far better trained than either Münchinger's or Karajan's. Richter's Munich Bach Choir was plausibly at its best in this work: the sense of balanced warmth is infinitely more satisfying than that conveyed under Rilling. Rilling also starts the whole work very slowly and heavily. Harnoncourt has the advantage of boy-soprano and -alto *ripieni*; there are, nevertheless, moments when both technique and stamina are under strain. Unfortunately the B minor Mass is one of Telefunken's least satisfactory recordings of Bach from a technical point-of-view.

† The best accounts of the solo and ensemble numbers on records are in the performances directed by Harnoncourt and Rilling. Each has a superb "Agnus Dei," each includes excellent instrumental touches. The superiority of Harnoncourt's choral conception and execution should not blind specialist collectors to the virtues of Rilling's soloists; this is one of those cases where the ideal solution is to know two interpretations.

The old point about the music being "more in D major than it is in B minor" is insignificant, since for Bach B minor is a key of profound joy also. To Bach and his generation the word "mode" was used more widely and richly than it usually is today: the organ *Prelude* (BWV 544) and the harpsichord *Ouverture* (BWV 831) share the festive character we encounter here.

The "Credo" somehow involves the community musically: its performance is ours even as we listen, whereas all that has gone before has been sung and played on our behalf. In internal distribution, Bach handles the Creed text extremely sensitively: its grouped clauses balance in music as they do in speech, its proportioned manner and its balanced structure have been reinforced musically, but not clumsily exaggerated. In a sense, the great "Crucifixus" lies at the core: yet the famous *lamentoso* chorus is itself not a static unit for contemplation, but a prelude to the fine Resurrection chorus that follows. The "Sanctus," first conceived for a festive Christmas service, resembles the Magnificats in its sense of contrast within a framework of tightly-proportioned relationships. It recalls the "Gloria patri" of the Magnificat (especially rhythmically), and it shares with that movement a wide diversity of interpretations in our own time: both are among the most challenging with which a choral conductor is likely to be confronted from the standard repertoire. In the "Sanctus," the "Pleni" is a highly spirited fugue, slightly less compactly organised than the "Omnes generationes" of the Magnificat, but similar in its vivid portrayal of confident collective praise. This section is all the more striking since it resembles the later "Osanna" in manner. It may well be that neither of these movements was originally planned in association with its Mass text: however, there is no obvious earlier context for the music other than the "Sanctus" for Christmas 1724.

The last section of the work, with its five movements (chorus A—solo a—chorus A—solo b—chorus B) is remarkable among the many great Mass settings of history for its active and celebratory musical character: the "Credo" clearly has to be positive, the "Sanctus" either festive or rarified. The unified "Agnus Dei" (which for some reason Bach has split into two movements and prefaced with the end of the true text of the "Sanctus") is usually set with restrained and pure beauty, so that the musical conclusion is peaceful and spiritually uplifting. Bach, on the other hand, seizes on the elements of ritual dialogue structure within the Ordinary, starting at the latter portion of the "Sanctus" proper:

Osanna in excelsis
Benedictus qui venit in nomine Domini
Osanna in excelsis

and continuing to the end:

Agnus Dei qui tollis peccata mundi miserere nobis
                                  miserere nobis
                                  dona nobis pacem

In order to achieve a thoroughly positive (and as he would have thought, an evangelical) effect, Bach adopts the following strategy.

The "Osanna" is given to full double-chorus and orchestra. Its *concertante* echoes and its symbolic unisons are homophonic and rhythmic, yet the effect is as diversified and full of textural contrast as many a movement which appears to be more contrapuntal on paper. These strong contrasts make it stand out effectively even in modern performances, and although it follows the exciting "Pleni sunt coeli."

The "Benedictus" is very gentle and clear, a much more "modern" kind of movement than its companions, but an example of Bach's own special blend of the new styles of the 1730s and 1740s. Within the Mass itself it is probably closest to the "Domine Deus"; outside, it recalls the closing "Schübler" chorale, which is itself derived from Cantata No. 137 of 1725, also performed in the 1740s. All three of these movements call for subtle rhythmic flexibility in interpretation, yet the "Benedictus" is usually very inadequately performed today.

The "Agnus Dei" is probably the best-known and the best-loved solo from the whole work. Again a "Schübler" prelude arrangement is recalled, this time the opening one *(Wachet auf)*; the two movements share a completely novel approach to the relationship between melody and harmony, a telling manipulation of the tonal character of the various ingredients and an almost hypnotic regularity of bass-rhythm that is closely associated with *ostinato*-types like the chaconne and passacaglia. The material is economically delivered, but there is subtlety in the manner of its repetition, its development and its relationship with the text. Both the "Benedictus" and "Agnus Dei" are essentially character trios: the artistic refinements of the trio-sonata tradition are blended with the fluidity of vocal lines and associations both biblical and theological. This emphasis of *character in context* is essential to the end of the Mass and is a part of the structural purpose of its last section.

The "Dona nobis pacem" returns to the music used earlier for the "Gratias agimus tibi." If Bach did envisage wholesale performances—a *Ganze Messe*—it was a neat touch to follow the recapitulation of the recent "Osanna" with that of a movement from way back in the "Gloria." The texts (of thanksgiving for God's magnificence and of the universal prayer for peace in Christendom and among mankind) are theologically distinct, but not wholly unrelated to one another: the music underlines the positive, even evangelical, aspect of both, the focusing of attention away from selfish considerations.* In this final chorus, a feeling of inspired unfulfilled intention for good is created through the music; this had almost created imbalance when, in 1731, it had first served as the opening chorus of an election cantata. The fugal style is rather traditional—stylistically reminiscent of the Sixteenth as well as the Seventeenth century. Its rising entries generally succeed one another closely, creating a strong sense of growth from start to finish. The accompaniment is also cumulative: especially notable is the reservation of the full trumpet ensemble until the last third of the piece. The fugue subject is essentially square and solid, as traditional and universal in Western music as the opening of the Finale of Mozart's "Jupiter" Symphony—the sense of power forwards, of elevation upwards, that the music conveys on behalf of the text. The counterpoints which grow from and around it are emphatic and regenerative because they contrast with it without lowering the sense of either grandeur or progress. Less remarkable music of both the Seventeenth and Eighteenth centuries is full of magnificent thematic gestures that rest unfulfilled, or even seem comical, because of their surroundings. In striving to achieve a greater sense of purpose, of following triumphant adoration, both communal and individual, with something more powerful than he has already expressed, the master of multiple contexts in music had set himself a problem.† Only he, perhaps, would have dared to resort to the repetition of an earlier movement, serving a different purpose, from the same work. Only he, perhaps, could have foreseen its complete appropriateness in this, its final context.

Bach's great Mass ends purposefully and, in a sense, unconcluded spiritually. So do nearly all of the books of the New Testament. So, to Christians of widely differing outlooks, does the Ordinary of the Mass itself. The celebration is of a God who lives: God with us. The two Passions end on an inconclusive but optimistic note, with their moving lullaby-choruses anticipating the joyful Easter tidings. Bach excels in optimistic conclusions: the chorales which conclude nearly all of his preserved choral compositions for church use have the high tenor-lines, the dignified restraint and the harmonic vigour that mark the final movement of the B minor Mass. The Christian Mass is a Sacrament because it is expressive—an expression of heartfelt truth. It is *celebrated* because its expression is positive; it is positive because it is associated with Christ. Whatever emotion Bach depicts, his music is always of uplifting beauty; in his church music, and especially in his Mass, this

---

* This might seem strange to persons unacquainted with the Christian concept of "our Peace," which is, of course, with God and oneself, as well as with one's fellows.
† The "Osanna" was itself certainly based on a (lost) celebratory cantata for double-chorus and double orchestra with two trumpet-choirs—the largest forces Bach had ever directed.

beauty conveys a positive, visionary spirituality. However, it is because of his special relish in producing an assertive *oeuvre* that Bach's music has appealed to such a wide range of different kinds of people in different contexts—historically, philosophically, artistically and politically. Only where it is misunderstood does it usually fail to delight.

Appendix

Recommended Books

There is no up-to-date and reliable book in English on Bach's choral music, nor, for that matter, on any section of it. The most extended summary that is aware and awake is contained within Irene and Karl Geiringer's "J. S. Bach: The Culmination of an Era" (London/New York, 1966), but space limits adequate treatment. This volume is also the best general English book on Bach, although it is none too authoritative where details of Baroque instrumental *timbres* and balance are concerned; particularly disappointing is the portion on the organ music, which is rapidly becoming outdated. Those who can read German should own Alfred Dürr's "Die Kantaten von J. S. Bach" (Kassel, 2. Auflage 1975, here referred to as Dürr1971), which treats each of the cantatas separately with consistent relevance, scholarship and stylistic grace. Werner Neumann's "Handbuch der Kantaten J. S. Bachs" (Leipzig, 4. Auflage, 1971), a catalogue with analytical listings, is more than it might at first appear: bibliography, tonal analysis, *tessitura* analysis, structural analysis, chronology, bibliography, all under one cover. It takes very little practice for English readers to use it readily, and until the expected "new Schmieder" Bach-Werke-Verzeichnis is published—and possibly after—it contains our best cantata list: here it is referred to as Neumann1971. Neither Dürr1971 nor Neumann1971 deal with non-cantatas apart from the oratorios (no passions or motets). However, all of Bach's choral output with preserved libretto is listed in Neumann's collected book of texts: "Sämtliche von J. S. Bach vertonte Texte" (Leipzig, 1974) (here, Neumann1974). Any self-respecting public library with a music section ought to own this, since it makes available the layout, print-styles and titling that are so helpful to our appreciation.

All documents referring to Bach himself (or signed by him) which come from the Eighteenth century or earlier are included in the Leipzig Bach-Archiv's magnificent volumes of "Bach-Dokumente"—three expensive volumes to date, but essential tools for serious Bach research: the editors are Werner Neumann and Hans-Joachim Schulze, and appendices appear in Volume 3 to add items and comments to 1 and 2. Bärenreiter also publish a concentrated categorised selection in paperback: "J. S. Bach. Leben und Werk in Dokumenten" (ed. Schulze, 1975). The English reader has a rough equivalent in David and Mendel's "The Bach Reader" (New York and London, rev. 2nd edn. 1966): there is a wealth of stimulating material here, also, but translations are rather casual and at times even misleading. This volume's special value is contained in those portions of the book devoted to the late Eighteenth and early Nineteenth centuries.

For information regarding Bach's social and cultural background, W. H. Bruford's "Germany in the Eighteenth Century: A Background to the Literary Revival" (Cambridge, England, 5th reprint 1965) forms a fascinating introduction. Neumann's illustrated biography ("Bach. Eine Bildbiographie," rev. 1960, München, variously translated and briefly available with two differing titles in English) is of sound orthodox scholarship. Pictorial backgrounds are afforded by Neumann ("Auf den Lebenswegen J. S. Bachs," Berlin DDR, 1953), Schwendowius and Dömling ("J. S. Bach: Zeit, Leben, Wirken," Kassel, 1976), in preparation in an English-language version (1977) and, expected, in the fourth volume of the Bach-Archiv's "Dokumente" series. The most significant current journal is the Bach-Jahrbuch, published under the auspices of the Neue Bach-Gesellschaft: recent volumes have included short abstracts in various languages including English. The Riemenschneider Bach Institute, Berea, Ohio, publishes a quarterly journal "Bach," the contents of which are of more variable quality. Both of these journals are obtainable at very reasonable prices by subscription: to read them is to keep oneself up-to-date with the most recent advances or excursions of international Bach scholarship.

The relevant Commentary volumes of the NBA give many kinds of invaluable information concerning the documentary evidence behind each published work. Performers are all-too-frequently shown to neglect these commentaries to their cost, just as many foolishly disregard the Urtext and facsimile editions which have been produced with much toil and expense for their use as well as for scholars'. Ignorance can be no defence in the world of the re-creative arts.

Editions and Scores

The first and third series (Cantatas and Passions) of the current New Bach Edition (NBA, Neue Ausgabe sämtlicher Werke, hrsg. vom

J.-S.-Bach-Institut Göttingen und vom Bach-Archiv Leipzig, Kassel &c und Leipzig, 1954ff—proceeding) can be recommended with only very minor reservations. The most important of these involve historical comments in the commentaries on volumes issued before later discoveries were made—for example, Frederick Hudson's fascinating volume of Wedding-Cantatas (1/33), issued with impressive scholarship in 1958, already requires revision in certain respects by 1977, and will probably require more by the time that Series I is completed. Any large-scale publishing venture of this kind is bound to involve apparent anachronisms to the wholesale purchaser at its completion: no doubt corrected appendices are envisaged by the editors. The edition is extremely handsome, and is a credit to all concerned. Furthermore, derived miniature scores and performing materials are quite plentifully produced by the publishers, so that its stated aim to be a practical, as well as a scholarly, edition is given more than token substance.

The volumes issued so far in Series II are also excellent, with the exception of II/1 (dated 1956), which presents the B minor Mass (there, *Höhe Messe*) in Friedrich Smend's edition. This was seriously criticised by Georg von Dadelsen on its first appearance, and the verdict of time must be that these criticisms were justifiable: preferable is Volbach's old Eulenburg miniature score, based on the Bach-Gesellschaft Edition, and instead of Smend's commentary the reader is recommended to Walter Blankenburg's booklet "Einführung in Bachs h-moll-Messe" (3. Auflage, Kassel &c., 1974).

Generally, the old collected edition of the Bach-Gesellschaft (here BG) was remarkably accurate regarding the notes of Bach's choral works; however, the edition lacked tight supervision, and its results are disparate from volume to volume. This is especially true with regard to details of phrasing and interpretation (dynamics, bowing, spellings of obsolete words, etc.)—details which can reveal or disguise significant points like stress, the possibility for rhythmic inequalities and authentic pronunciation. The scholarly commentaries of the BG formed its prefaces: some of these were excellent, others very poor; they were decidedly uneven and disorganised by the standards of the NBA. The BG edition is still available for sale both in reprint and in reduced pocket-score format (complete, but without the commentaries, and re-organised in distribution to some extent). This latter edition, produced by Kalmus, is our only source for cantatas not republished in the Twentieth century: the Telefunken record series started by enclosing this edition within its packages, but by Volume 9 had begun to include NBA scores—some in unique reduction—in answer to critical protest: where the NBA has not yet covered subsequent music in the Telefunken project, various editions have been substituted.

Among non-collected editions, the work of Edition Hänssler must be singled out. The work of Hans Grischkat in revising and freshly editing a wide range of Bach's music has been dedicated and consistently reliable; Edition Hänssler is, indeed, too little known outside Germany. The more recent Eulenburg pocket scores of cantatas twin with the Hänssler full scores and parts, but much of Eulenburg's series had been prepared under Arnold Schering's supervision before 1950, and that is based on the BG without significant improvement apart from Schering's prefaces, which are generally fairly reliable. Grischkat's scores for Eulenburg are their best Bach publications.

The larger German firms—especially Breitkopf of Wiesbaden and Peters of Frankfurt—have produced large quantities of material, and some specialist publications (facsimiles, etc.); Novello of Britain are more significant as agents for Hänssler than they are as publishers of Bach's choral music. The choral conductor searching for an edition of any Bach choral work (with the exception of the B minor Mass—see above) would do best to search out the following catalogues, in the following order: NBA/Hänssler/New Breitkopf/Eulenberg/Old Breitkopf (=pre-1940)/BG (via Kalmus). There are obvious exceptions, but that is a good rule. Those belonging to a record library holding the Telefunken series might well refer to their enclosed scores for cantatas above No. 30: Harnoncourt's textual notes (where he directs) contain much of that magic which turns dots on paper into melodious and appropriate sounds—more than any book on conducting that this writer has so far seen.

Musical Resources of Bach's Time

We know very little positive about choral training before the Nineteenth century, and earlier reports that a particular soloist had unusual beauty of tone, clarity of enunciation, dexterity or even power must thus be interpreted with caution. Information is very limited in Bach's case. The known ages of his Weimar sopranos and altos indicate that their voices were unchanged (treble) and changing or about to change (boy alto) rather than falsettists. The theory that counter-tenor soloists sang as falsetto-sopranos and -altos in Leipzig in Bach's day is built on slim evidence: it was first argued by Arnold Schering in 1936, but his evidence was incompletely researched and partly derived from contexts irrelevant to Bach. Financial, artistic and sectarian influences probably favoured the most natural manner of expression in Leipzig's churches, and we might do well to conclude, without certainty, that the direct

BALANCE
bdf = balance detracts from . . .
bf = balance favours . . .

CONTINUO
ch = continuo harpsichord
co = continuo organ
ctps = continuo too prominent or showy, hence
chtps = continuo harpsichord too prominent or showy
crd = continuo detached in recitatives
crs = continuo sustained in recitatives
crv = continuo treatment within *secco* recitatives varies

DOCUMENTATION (1 = good; 2 = adequate; 3 = poor)
d = documentation in general (critical notes)
dt = documentation including translation into English (or as specified)
ds = study score provided (ds = BG indicates that a study-score in the
     Bach-Gesellschaft edition is included)

EDITION
eNBA = New Bach Edition (Bärenreiter/Deutscher Verlag) apparently
     used
eBG = Bach-Gesellschaft Edition apparently used
eBR = Breitkopf Edition apparently used
(other editions are indicated by their full names, e.g. eHänssler, and
     where doubt exists, a question-mark (?) is added)

Not all the records are necessarily still available, and those that are
sometimes form single items in boxed sets; the catalogue numbers make
this clear to those familiar with the national catalogues. The most
up-to-date number is given unless records are available in small and large
issues simultaneously: in that event, the smaller purchase is indicated.
Bach couplings on the same record or in paired sets are indicated in
parentheses.

Cantatas

No. 1: Wie schön leuchtet der Morgenstern
Harnoncourt—Vienna Boy Soprano/Equiluz/Van Egmond/Vienna Boys with
Chorus Viennensis/Concentus Musicus Vienna.
     (2–4) Telefunken EX6 35027; US: Telefunken 2635027.
aa afss ai ap co crd d dt3 ds = BG eBr?
Richter?Mathis/Haefliger3Fischer-Dieskau/Munich Bach Choir/Munich Bach
Orchestra.
     (111) DG Archiv 2722 018.
so crs d3 dt eBG.

No. 2 : Ach Gott, vom Himmel sieh darein
Harnoncourt—Vienna Boy Soprano/Esswood/Equiluz/Van Egmond/Vienna
Boys with Chorus Viennensis/Concentus Musicus Vienna.
    (1, 3, 4) Telefunken EX6 35027; US: Telefunken 2635027.
aa ai ap co crd d dt3 ds=BG eBR?

No. 3 : Ach Gott, wie manches Herzeleid (I)
Harnoncourt—Vienna Boy Soprano/Esswood/Equiluz/Van Egmond/Vienna
Boys with Chorus Viennensis/Concentus Musicus Vienna.
    (1, 2, 4) Telefunken EX6 35027; US: Telefunken 2635027.

No. 4 : Christ lag in Todes Banden
Harnoncourt—Vienna Boy Soprano/Esswood/Equiluz/Van Egmond/Vienna
Boys with Chorus Viennensis/Concentus Musicus Vienna.
    (1, 2, 3) Telefunken EX6 35027; US: (1, 2, 3) Telefunken 2635027.
aa afss ai ap co d/2 ds=BG dt2/3 eBr?
Ehmann—Wehrung/Haasemann/Hoefflin/Pommerein/Westfalische Kantorei/
Westfalische Orchestra.
    (182) Peerless-Oryx BACH 1113; US: (182) Vanguard S-225.
*choral—aa afcs slight—brf co d3 (wrong date) dt2 e? This performance
includes the trombone choir added by Bach for a Leipzig performance; it does
not therefore represent the Weimar or pre-Weimar first working. Neither of
the recommended recordings involves the ripieno singing of movements of
solo or duet character. Earlier readings directed by Werner (Erato) and
Prohaska (Vanguard Bach Guild) did treat the work in this way quite
defensibly.*

No. 5 : Wo soll ich fliehen hin
Harnoncourt—Vienna Boy Soprano/Esswood/Equiluz/Van Egmond/Vienna
Boys with Chorus Viennensis/Concentus Musicus Vienna.
    (6, 7, 8) Telefunken EX6 35028; US: (6, 7, 8) Telefunken 2635028.
aa afss ai ap co crd d/2 ds=BG eBr?

No. 6 : Bleib bei uns, denn es will Abend werden
Harnoncourt—Vienna Boy Soprano/Esswood/Equiluz/Van Egmond/Vienna
Boys with Chorus Viennensis/Concentus Musicus Vienna.
    (5, 7, 8) Telefunken EX6 35028; US: (5, 7, 8) Telefunken 2635028.
aa afss ai ap co crd d/2 ds=BG dt2/3 eNBA?
Richter—Reynolds/Schreier/Fischer-Dieskau/Munich Bach Choir/Munich

Bach Orchestra.

    (158, 67, etc.) DG Archiv 2722 018.

bbt orch. & soloists; some brf co crs d3 eNBA. Richter uses the full ripieno for the commentary "Ach bleib bei uns"; Harnoncourt gives the chorale line to a soloist, and regrettably does not seem inclined to adopt the ripieno disposition of such movements; Richter's named cellist plays a modern (probably full-size) instrument far too heavily, however.

No. 7: Christ unser Herr zum Jordan kam

Leonhardt—Esswood/Equiluz/Van Egmond/Regensburg Dom Boys and King's College Cambridge Men/aug. Leonhardt Consort.

    (5, 6, 8) Telefunken EEX6 35028; US: (5, 6, 8) Telefunken 2635028.

aa ai afss ap co crd/crv d/2 ds=BG dt2 eNBA?

No. 8: Liebster Gott, wann werd ich sterben?

Leonhardt—Kiefer/Esswood/Van Egmond/Regensburg Dom Boys and King's College Cambridge Men/aug. Leonhardt Consort.

    (5, 6, 7) Telefunken EX6 35028; US: (5, 6, 7) Telefunken 2635028.

aa afss ai ap co crd/crv d/2 ds=BG dt2 eBr?

No. 9: Es ist das Heil

Leonhardt—Esswood/Equiluz/Van Egmond/Regensburg Dom Boys and King's College Cambridge Men/aug. Leonhardt Consort.

    (10, 11) Telefunken EX6 35029; US: (10, 11) Telefunken 2635029.

aa afss ai ap co crd/crv d/2 ds=BG dt2 eBr?

No. 10: Mein Seel erhebt den Herren

Leonhardt—Esswood/Equiluz/Van Egmond/Regensburg Dom Boys and King's College Cambridge Men/aug. Leonhardt Consort.

    (9, 11) Telefunken EX6 35029; US: (9, 11) Telefunken 2635029.

aa afss ai ap co crd/crv d/2 ds=BG dts eBR?

Münchinger—Ameling/Watts/Krenn/Rentzler/Vienna Academiech./Stuttgart Chamber Orchestra.

    (243) Decca EXL 6400; US: (243) Lon 26103.

so crs stps d3 dt2 eBR?

Steinitz (?)—Le Sage/Minty/Rogers/Howlett/London Bach Society/English Chamber Orchestra.

    (47,241) Peerless-Oryx BACH 1101; US: (47,241) Lyr 7175.

co crs ds dt2 e? The musical forces have been so arranged as to produce a

strong imbalance in favour of the choral and solo voices in this recording.
Richter—Mathis/Reynolds/Schreier/Fischer-Dieskau/Munich Bach Choir/
Munich Bach Orchestra.
    (24,135) DG Archiv 2533 329.
co crs d2 dt eBG.

No. 11 : Lobet Gott in seinen Reichen
Harnoncourt—Vienna Boy Soprano/Esswood/Equiluz/Van Egmond/Vienna
Boys with Chorus Viennensis/Concentus Musicus Vienna.
    (9, 10) Telefunken EX6 35029; US: (9, 10) Telefunken 2635029.
aa afss ai ap co crd d/2 ds=eBG dt2/3 eBr with modifications?
Richter—Mathis/Reynolds/Schreier/Fischer-Dieskau/Munich Bach Choir/
Munich Bach Orchestra.
    (44) DG Archiv 2722 025.
co crs d3 dt eBG.
Somary—Palmer/Watts/Tear/Rippon/Amor Artis Chorale/English Chamber
Orchestra.
    US: (80) Van 71193.

No. 12 : Weinen, Klagen, Sorgen, Zagen
Leonhardt—Esswood/Equiluz/Van Altena/Van Egmond/Regensburg Dom
Boys with King's College Cambridge Men/augmented Leonhardt Consort.
    (13–16) Telefunken EX6 35030; US: (13–16) Telefunken 2635030.
as ai ap co crd d/2 ds=BG dt2 eBr?
Wöldike—Rössl-Majdan/Dermota/Berry/Wiener Kammerchor/ Wiener
Staatsopera-Orchester.
    (29) Philips AL 3541; US: Bach 5036.
brf co d3 dt2 eBr?

No. 13 : Meine Seufzer, meine Tränen
Leonhardt—Esswood/Equiluz/Van Altena/Van Egmond/Regensburg Dom
Boys with King's College Cambridge Men/augmented Leonhardt Consort.
    (12, 14, 16) Telefunken EX6 35030; US: Telefunken 2635030
aa afss ai ap co mainly-crd d ds=BG dt2 eBr?
Richter—Mathis/Reynolds/Schreier/Adam/Munich Bach Choir/Munich Bach
Orchestra.
    (111) DG Archiv 2722 005.
co crs d2 dt eBG.

No. 14 : Wär Gott nicht mit uns diese Zeit
Leonhardt—Gampert/Equiluz/Van Egmond/Regensburg Dom Boys with

King's College Cambridge Men.
(12, 1, 16) Telefunken EX6 35030; US: Telefunken 2635030.
aa afss ai ap co mainly-crd dl ds=BG dt3 eBr?

No. 16: Herr Gott, dich loben wir
Leonhardt—Esswood/Equiluz/Van Altena/Van Egmond/Regensburg Dom Boys with King's College Cambridge Men/augmented Leonhardt Consort.
(12–14) Telefunken EX6 35030; US: Telefunken 2635030.
aa afss ai ap co mainly-crd d ds=BG dt3 eBr?

No. 17: Wer Dank opfert, der preiset mich
Harnoncourt—Vienna Boy Soprano/Esswood/Equiluz/Van Egmond/Vienna Boys with Chorus Viennensis/Concentus Musicus Vienna.
(18–20) Telefunken EX6 35031; US: Telefunken 2632031.
aa ai ap co crd d ds=BG dt3 eBG—but with specified modifications.

No. 18: Gleich wie der Regen und Schnee vom Himmel fällt
Harnoncourt—Vienna Boy Soprano/Esswood/Equiluz/Van Egmond/Vienna Boys with Chorus Viennensis/Concentus Musicus Vienna.
(17, 19, 20) Telefunken EX6 33031; US: Telefunken 2635031.
Weimar instrumentation without recorders: aa afss ai ap co crd d ds=BG —including recorders (!) dt3 eBr—modified
Leonhardt—Giebel/Van t'Hoff/Villisech/Hamburg Montiverdichor/ ensemble led Schroeder.
(122) Telefunken SAWT 94 42B; US: Telefunken 641059.
Includes baroque recorders (Leipzig version): aa ai co crs d2 eBr?

No. 19: Es erhub sich ein Streit
Harnoncourt—Vienna Boy Soprano/Esswood/Equiluz/Van Egmond/Vienna Boys with Chorus Viennensis/Concentus Musicus Vienna.
(20, 17, 18) Telefunken EX6 35031; US: Telefunken 2635031.
aa afss ai ap co crd d ds=BG dt3 eBG—revised after NBA (Helms).
Rilling—Rondelli/Kraus/Nimsgern/Gächinger Kantorei/Bach-Collegium Stuttgart.
(191) Erato STU 70702–5.
brf—slightly ch+co crs chtpe dl/2—but in French only dt—into French eNBA?

No. 20 : O Ewigkeit, du Donnerwort (I)
Harnoncourt—Vienna Boy Soprano/Esswood/Equiluz/Van Egmond/Vienna
Boys with Chorus Viennensis/Concentus Musicus Vienna.
    (19, 17, 18) Telefunken EX6 35031; US: 26350331.
aa ai ap co crd dl ds=BG dt3 eBG—revised Harnoncourt.
Rilling—Kessler & Gohl/Altmeyer & Kraus/Schöne/Frankfurt Kantorei/
Bach-Collegium Stuttgart.
    (168) Erato STU 70703.
brf—slight ch+co crs chtps dl/2—only in French dt2—into French eBr?

No. 21 : Ich hatte viel Bekümmernis
Harnoncourt—Vienna Boy Soprano/Esswood/Equiluz/Van Egmond/ Vienna
Boys with Chorus Viennensis/Concentus Musicus Vienna.
    (22, 23) Telefunken EX6 35032; US: 2635032.
*aa afss ai ap co crd dl! ds=BG dt3 eBG—with modifications after projected
NBA (Brainard) and by Harnoncourt; performed in low D minor (correct for
Leipzig) but without the trombone choir involved in at least one performance
there.*
Richter—Mathis/Haefliger/Fischer-Dieskau/Munich Bach Choir/Munich Bach
Orchestra.
    DG Archiv 2722 019; US: DG Archiv 2533049.
Rilling—Burns/Marova/Melzer/Reich/Gächinger Kantorei/Bach-Collegium
Stuttgart.
    Supraphon 112 0792; W. Germany: Musicaphon SDG 610 101.
The Leipzig-added trombone choir is included in the ninth movement.

No. 22 : Jesus nahm zu sich die Zwölfe
Leonhardt—Esswood/Equiluz/Van Egmond/Tölz Boys with King's College
Cambridge Men/augmented Leonhardt Consort.
    (21,23) Telefunken EX6 35032; US: 2635032.
*aa afcs ai ap co crd dl dsBG dt3 eBG—with specified disposition of fourth
movement.*

No. 23 : Du wahrer Gott und Davids Sohn
Leonhardt—Gambert/Esswood/Van Altena/Tölz Boys with King's College
Cambridge Men/Concentus Musicus Vienna.
    (21,22) Telefunken EX6 35032; US: 2635032.
aa afcs ai ap co crd dl dsBG dt3 eBr?

No. 24 : Ein ungefärbt Gemüte
Harnoncourt—Vienna Boy Soprano/Esswood/Equiluz/Van Egmond/Vienna

Boys with Chorus Viennensis/Concentus Musicus Vienna.
     (25, 26, 27) Telefunken EX6 35033; US: Telefunken 2635033.
*aa afcs ai ap co crd d2 ds=BG dt3 eBG—with specified modifications, includ-
ing the solo soprano treatment in the third movement.*
Richter—Reynolds/Schreier/Fischer-Dieskau/Munich Bach Choir/Munich
Bach Orchestra.
     (10,135) DG Archiv 2533 329.
co crs d2 dtl eBG.

No. 25: Es ist nichts Gesundes an meinem Leibe
Harnoncourt—Vienna Boy Soprano/Esswood/Equiluz/Van Egmond/Vienna
Boys with Chorus Viennensis/Concentus Musicus Vienna.
     (24, 26, 27) Telefunken EX6 35033; US: Telefunken 2635033.
aa afss afcs ai ap co crd dl ds=BG dt3 eBG—with indicated modifications.

No. 26: Ach wie flüchtig, ach wie nichtig
Harnoncourt—Vienna Boy Soprano/Esswood/Equiluz/Van Egmond/Vienna
Boys with Chorus Viennensis/Concentus Musicus Vienna.
     (24, 25, 27) Telefunken EX6 35033; US: Telefunken 2635033.
aa ai ap co crd dl ds=BG dt3 eBG—with stated adjustments.

No. 27: Wer weiss, wie nahe mir mein Ende?
Harnoncourt—Vienna Boy Soprano/Esswood/Equiluz/Van Egmond/Vienna
Boys with Chorus Viennensis/Concentus Musicus Vienna.
     (24, 25, 26) Telefunken EX6 35033; US: Telefunken 2635033.
*aa afcs—in first movement ai ap co crd dl ds=BG dt3 eBG—modified as
stated.*
Schroeder—Hansmann/Watts/Equiluz/Van Egmond/Hamburg Montever-
dichor/Concerto Amsterdam.
     (59, 118, 158) Telefunken AS6 41070.
*aa partly-ai co crd d2 eBr?; as always in Schroeder's performances, the lyrical
aspect is beautifully stressed.*

No. 28: Gottlob! nun geht das Jahr zu Ende
Harnoncourt—Vienna Boy Soprano/Esswood/Equiluz/Nimsgern/Vienna Boys
with Chorus Viennensis/Concentus Musicus Vienna.
     (29, 30) Telefunken EX6 35033; US: Telefunken 2635033.
aa ai ap co crd dl ds=BG dt3 eBG—with oboe parts disposed as specified.
Richter—Mathis/Töpper/Schreier/Fischer—Dieskau/Munich Bach Choir/

Munich Bach Orchestra.
  (64, 151) DG Archiv 2722 005.
co crs ctps d3 dtl eBG.

No. 29 : Wir danken dir, Gott, wir danken dir
Harnoncourt—Vienna Boy Soprano/Esswood/Equiluz/Van Egmond/Tachezi
(obbl. organ, first movement)/Vienna Boys with Chorus Viennensis/
Concentus Musicus Vienna.
  (28, 30) Telefunken EX6 35033; US: Telefunken 2635033.
aa ai ap bdf—concertante *organ, slightly co crd dl!*—*interesting facsimiles
ds=BG*—*erroneous* Presto *shouldn't have passed without comment at opening
dt3 eBG*—*with oboe disposed as specified.*
Wöldike—Davrath/Rössl-Majden/Dermota/Berry/Kammerchor Wien/
Vienna Staatsopera-Orchester.
  (12) Philips AL 3514; US: Bach 5036.
bdf—concertante *organ (slight) co crs ctps d2 dtl eBr?*
Gönnewein—Wehrung/Lisken/Hoeffln/Stämpfli/Suddeutsches Madrigalchor
Stuttgart/Deutsche Bachsolisten.
  (135) Bärenreiter-Musicaphon SDG 610 112.

No. 30 : Freue dich, erlöste Schar
Harnoncourt—Vienna Boy Soprano/Esswood/Equiluz/Van Egmond/Vienna
Boys with Chorus Viennensis/Concentus Musicus Vienna.
  (28, 29) Telefunken EX6 35034; US: Telefunken 2635033.
aa ai ap co crd dl! ds=BG—*includes unoriginal parts for trumpets and drums,
but the documentation clarifies this dt3 eBG*—*with modifications, some of
which are specified.*
Richter—Mathis/Reynolds/Schreier/Fischer-Dieskau/Munich Bach Choir/
Munich Bach Orchestra.
  DG Archiv 2533 30.

No. 31 : Der Himmel lacht, die Erde jubilieret
Harnoncourt—Vienna Boy Soprano & Alto Soloists (*ripieni*)/Equiluz/Nims-
gern/Vienna Boys with Chorus Viennensis/Concentus Musicus Vienna.
  (32, 33, 31) Telefunken EX6 35035; US: Telefunken 2635035.
aa afss ai ap co crd dl ds=Br? dt3 eBr?—*with instrumental and choral
dispositions as specified. The variable tempi in the first movement have given
rise to comment, but their motivic treatment is perfectly defensible; the
Sinfonia only may be heard in a steadier rather solid reading under Ansermet
on Decca ECS 754 (US: London 6243).*

No. 32 : Liebster Jesu, mein verlangen
Leonhardt—Gampert/Van Egmond/Hannover Boys' Choir/augmented Leonhardt Consort.
    (31, 33, 34) Telefunken EX6 35035; US: Telefunken 2635035.
aa afss afcs ai ap co most-crd dl ds=NBA—ed. Helms dt3 eNBA—with adjustments as specified. The leading violinist here is Sigiswald Kuijken.

No. 33 : Allein zu dir, Herr Jesu Christ
Leonhardt—Jacobs/Van Altena/Van Egmond/Hannover Boys' Choir/augmented Leonhardt Consort.
    (31, 32, 34) Telefunken EX6 35035; US: Telefunken 2635035.
aa afcs ai ap co crd dl ds=NBE—ed. Neumann dt3 eNBA. Sigiswald Kuijken leads.

No. 34 : O ewiges Feuer, o Ursprung der Liebe
Harnoncourt—Esswood/Equiluz/Nimsgern/Vienna Boys with Chorus Viennensis/Concentus Musicus Vienna.
    (31, 32, 33) Telefunken EX6 35035; US: Telefunken 2635035.
aa ai ap co crd dl ds=Br? dt3 eBr? Oboe da caccia used—continuo disposed as specified.
Richter—Reynolds/Schreier/Fischer-Dieskau/Munich Bach Choir/Munich Bach Orchestra.
    (68,175) DG Archiv 2533 306.
co crs d2 dtl eBG.

No. 35 : Geist und Seele wird verwirret
Harnoncourt—Vienna Boy Soprano/Esswood/Equiluz/Van der Meer/Vienna
    (36, 37, 38) Telefunken EX6 35036; US: Telefunken 2635/36.
aa ai ap co crd dl ds=Br? dt3 eBr? Oboe da caccia used—continuo disposed as specified.

No. 36 : Schwingt freudig euch empor
Harnoncourt—Vienna Boy Soprano/Esswood/Equiluz/Van der Meer/Vienna Boys with Chorus Viennensis/Concentus Musicus Vienna.
    (35, 37, 38) Telefunken EX6 3506; US: Telefunken 2635036.
aa ai ap co dl ds=NBAed. Dürr & Neumann dt3 eNBA—with editorial adjustments regarding distribution and articulations.

No. 37: Wer da gläubet und getauft wird
Harnoncourt—Vienna Boy Soprano/Esswood/Equiluz/Van der Meer/Vienna Boys with Chorus Viennensis/Concentus Musicus Vienna.
    (35, 36, 38) Telefunken EX6 35036; US: Telefunken 2635036.
aa ai ap co crd dl ds=NBA—ed. Dürr dt3 eNBA—but see booklet regarding articulation, especially of the tenor aria No. 2.

No. 38: Aus tiefer Not schrei ich zu dir
Harnoncourt—Vienna Boy Soprano/Esswood/Equiluz/Van der Meer/Vienna Boys with Chorus Viennensis/Concentus Musicus Vienna.
    (35, 36, 37) Telefunken EX6 35036; US: Telefunken 2635036.
aa ai ap co crd dl ds=Br? dt3 eBr.

No. 39: Brich dem Hungrigen dein Brot
Leonhardt—Hannover Boy Soprano/Jacobs/Van Egmond/Hannover Boys' Choir/augmented Leonhardt Consort.
    (40, 41, 424) Telefunken EX6 35269; US: Telefunken 2635269.
aa afct ai ap co crd dl ds=NBA—ed. Dürr, Freeman & Webster dt3 eNBA.
Richter—Mathis/Reynolds/Fischer-Dieskau/Munich Bach Choir/Munich Bach Orchestra.
    (129) DG Archiv 2722 019.
co crs d2 dtl eBG—although recorded in 1974–5.

No. 40: Dazu ist erschienen der Sohn Gottes
Leonhardt—Jacobs/Van Altena/Van Egmond/Hannover Boys' Choir/augmented Leonhardt Consort.
    (39, 41, 42) Telefunken EX6 35269; US: Telefunken 2635269.
aa afcs ai ap co crd dl ds=Br? dt3 eBr?
Rilling—Gohl/Kraus/Nimsgern/Figuralchor des Gedachtniskirche Stuttgart/Bach-Collegium Stuttgart.
    (70) Erato STU 70704.
co-&-ch crhs chtps-whereas-bdfco(!) d2—very full but of variable authority; many musical quotations dt2—from German into French only eBG?

No. 41: Jesu, nun sei gepreiset
Harnoncourt—Vienna Boy Soprano/Esswood/Equiluz/Van der Meer/Vienna Boys with Chorus Viennensis/Concentus Musicus Vienna.
    (39, 40, 42) Telefunken EX6 35269; US: 2635269.

aa ai ap co crd dl ds=NBA—ed. Neumann dt3 eNBA—with specified detailed interpretations.

No. 42 : Am Abend aber desselbigen Sabbats
Harnoncourt—Vienna Boy Soprano/Esswood/Equiluz/Van der Meer/Vienna Boys with Chorus Viennensis/Concentus Musicus Vienna.
(39, 40, 41) Telefunken EX6 35269; US: Telefunken 2635269.
aa ai co crd dl ds=Br? dt3 eBr?—but see Harnoncourt's notes regarding the continuo part of the fourth movemnet.

No. 43 : Gott fähret auf mit Jauchzen
Harnoncourt—Jelosits/Esswood/Equiluz/Van der Meer/Vienna Boys with Chorus Viennensis/Concentus Musicus Vienna.
(44, 45, 46) Telefunken EX6 352833; US: Telefunken 2635283.
aa ai ap co crd dl ds=NBA—ed Dürr dt3 eNBA—with minor specified adjustments.

No. 44 : Sie werden euch in den Bann tun (I)
Harnoncourt—Jelosits/Esswood/Equiluz/Van der Meer/Vienna Boys with Chorus Viennensis/Concentus Musicus Vienna.
(43, 45, 46) Telefunken EX6 35283; US: 2635283.
Richter—Mathis/Reynolds/Fischer-Dieskau/Munich Bach Choir/Munich Bach Orchestra.
(11) DG Archiv 2722 018.
co crs d2/3 dtl eNBA.
Harbison—Brydon/Fortunato/Sorensen/Baker/Cantata Singers/ens.?
US: (101) Advent Corp 1015.

No. 45 : Es ist dir gesagt, Mensch, was gut ist
Leonhardt—Jacobs/Equiluz/Kunz/Hamburg Boys' Choir/augmented Leonhardt Consort.
(43, 44, 46) Telefunken EX6 35283; US: Telefunken 2635283.
aa afcs ai ap co crd dl ds=NBA—ed. Dürr & Treitler dt3 eNBA.
Ansermet—Watts/Partridge/Krause/Chorus of the Suisse Romande/Orchestra of the Suisse Romande.
(105) Decca SDD 384.
bdf—instruments ch crs d2 dt2 e?

No. 46: Schauet doch und sehet, ob irgendein Schmerz sei
Leonhardt—Jacobs/Equiluz/Kunz/Hamburg Boys' Choir/augmented Leonhardt Consort.
    (43, 44, 45) Telefunken EX6 35283; US: Telefunken 2635283.
aa afcs ai ap co crd dl ds=Eulenberg? dt3 eBr?
Kahlhöfer—Wolf-Matthaus/Jelden/Stämpfli/Barmen-Gemarke Choir/Barmen-Gemarke Orchestra.
    (65) Bach Recordings BACH 103; US: Vanguard S-226.
ai—recorders and narrow-bore trumpet virtuosity from Walter Holy, mostly outstanding co crs dl—in the English version the original Tromba da Tirarsi part was depicted on the cover dt2 e?

No. 47: Wer sich selbst erhöhet, der soll erniedriget werden
Harnoncourt—Jelosits/Van der Meer/Vienna Boys with Chorus Viennensis/Concentus Musicus Vienna.
    (48, 49, 50) Telefunken EX6 35284; US: Telefunken 2635284.
aa afss ai ap co crd dl e?—Hänssler? dt3 e?

No. 48: Ich elender Mensch, wer wird mich erlösen
Harnoncourt/Esswood/Equiluz/Vienna Boys with Chorus Viennensis/Concentus Musicus Vienna.
    (47, 49, 50) Telefunken EX6 35284; US: Telefunken 2635284.
aa ai ap co crd dl ds=Eulenberg? dt3 eBr? Harnoncourt's note regarding the divergent references to the brass instrument in the sources is significant.

No. 49: Ich geh und suche mit Verlangen (Dialogus)
Harnoncourt—Jelosits/Van der Meer/Concentus Musicus Vienna.
    (47, 48, 50) Telefunken EX6 35284; US: Telefunken 2635284.
aa afss ai ap co crd dl ds=Eulenberg? dt3 e?
Ehmann—Giebel/Stämpfli/Westfälisches-ensemble.
    (84) Bärenreiter Musicaphon SDG 610 110; US: Nonesuch 71273.

No. 50: Nun ist das Heil und die Kraft
Harnoncourt—Vienna Boys with Chorus Viennensis/Concentus Musicus Vienna.
    (47, 48, 49) Telefunken EX6 35284; US: Telefunken 2635284.
aa ai ap dl ds=Eulenberg? dt2 eBr? (recorded in 1967, and none the worse for that).

No. 51 : Jauchzet Gott in allen Landen
Leonhardt—Kweksilber/Smithers (tp.)/augmented Leonhardt Consort.
    (52–56) Telefunken EX6 35304; US: Telefunken 2635304.
aa ai ap co dl ds=Eulenberg? dt3 eBr? It was most striking that the Telefunken series should introduce a female soprano—although she sings with style and spirit, there is no historical justification for the use of such a voice (the part is, however, of great difficulty).
Schroeder—Giebel/Concerto Amsterdam with Maurice André (tp.).
    (202) Telefunken AS6 41077; US: Telefunken 641077.
aa co crv dl dt3 eBr? A lyrical reading of sympathy and stylistic integrity (yet not really ai or ap); especially outstanding after the opening movement.
Winschermann—Ameling/Deutsche Bachsolisten with Maurice André.
    (199) Philips 6500 014; US: Philips 6500 014.
co-&-ch dl dlt eBr?

No. 52 : Falsche Welt, dir trau ich nicht
Leonhardt—Kronwitter/Hannover Boys' Choir/Leonhardt Consort.
    (51, 54–56) Telefunken EX6 35304; US: Telefunken 2635304.
aa ai ap co crd dl ds=? dt3 eBr?
Göttsche—Van der Spek/Mannheim Bach Choir/Heidelberg Chamber Orchestra.
    (209) Peerless-Oryx BACH 1116.
ch crs-too prominently by the bassoonist! oc-inaudible, although mentioned on record-cover d3 dtl eBr? The life and unanimity of the woodwinds in the fifth movement redeem an otherwise routine reading.

No. 54 : Widerstehe doch der Sünde
Leonhardt—Deller/Leonhardt-Barockensemble.
    (170, "Agnus Dei" fr. 232) Austrian Vanguard Amadeo AVRS 6045.
aa ai ap co crd dl—in German only eBr? The ensemble includes Nikolaus and Alice Harnoncourt, Gustiv and Marie Leonhardt, Michel Piguet, Eduard Melkus and Karl Theiner. The recording (mono) must date from the late Fifties, and sounds too resonant an tinny for modern tastes; yet the performance is both beautiful and extremely interesting historically.
Leonhardt—Esswood/Leonhardt Consrot.
    (51, 52, 55, 56) Telefunken EX6 35304; US: Telefunken 2635304.
aa ai ap co crd dl ds=NBA—ed. Dürr dt3 eNBA.
Dart—Watts/Philomusica Orchestra.
    ("53" [unauth.] 200) Decca SOL 60003; US: Oiseau-Lyre 60003.

No. 55 : Ich armer Mensch, ich Sünderknecht
Leonhardt/Equiluz/Hannover Boys' Choir/Leonhardt Consort.
    (51, 52, 54, 56) Telefunken EX6 35304; US: Telefunken 2635304.
aa ai ap co crd dl ds=Br? dt3 eBr?

No. 56 : Ich will den Kreutzstab gerne tragen
Leonhardt—Schopper/Hannover Boys' Choir/Leonhardt Consort.
(51, 52, 54, 56) Telefunken EX6 35304; US: Telefunken 2635304.
aa ai ap co crd dl ds=Br? dt3 eBr?
Richter—Fischer-Dieskau/Munich Bach Choir/Munich Bach Orchestra.
(82) DG Archiv 198477; US: DG Archiv 198477.
ch ctps—at times d2 dtl eBr.
Marriner—Shirley Quirk/St. Anthony Singers/Academy of St. Martin-in-the-Fields, London.
(82) Oiseau-Lyre SOL 280; US: Oiseau-Lyre S-280.
afss-a stylish and youthful soloist co crs ctps d3 dt2 eBr?
Ristenpart—Stämpfli/Saar Chamber Choir/Saar Chamber Orchestra.
US: (169—unauthentic) Nonesuch 71142.
Thomas—Prey/Leipzig Thomanerchor/Gewandhaus-Orchester ensemble.
(82) Classics for Pleasure CFP 40038.

No. 57 : Selig ist der Mann (Dialogus)
Harnoncourt—Jelosits/Van der Meer/Tölz Chamber Choir/Concentus Musicus Vienna.
(58–60) Telefunken EX6 35305; US: Telefunken 2635305.
aa afcs afss ai ap co crd dl ds=ePeters? dt3 eNBA
Winschermann—Ameling/Prey/Deutsche Bachsolistne.
(32) Philips 6500 080.
Ristenpart—Buckel/Stämpfli/Saar Chamber Choir/Saar Chamber Orchestra.
US: (140) Nonesuch 71029.

No. 58 : Ach Gott, wie manches Herzeleid (II) (Dialogus)
Harnoncourt—Kronwitter/Van der Meer/Concentus Musicus Vienna.
(57, 59, 60) Telefunken EX6 35305; US: Telefunken 2635305.
aa afcs afss ai ap co crd dl ds=NBA—ed. Dürr dt3 eNBA.
Rilling—Reichelt/Schöne/Bach-Cellegium Stuttgart.
(72) Erato STU 70745–9.
co crs ctps d2 dtl eBG. This performance has the added oboes of the 1733/34 performance, upon which it claims to be based.

No. 59 : Wer mich liebet, der wird mein Wort halten (I)
Harnoncourt—Gelosits/Van der Meer/Tölz Boys' Choir/Concentus Musicus Vienna.
(57, 58, 60) Telefunken EX6 35305; US: Telefunken 2635305.
aa afcs afss ai ap co crd dl ds=NBA--ed. Dürr dt3 eNBA.
Schroeder—Hansmann/Van Egmond/Hamburg Monteverdichor/Concerto Amsterdam.
(27, 118, 158) Telefunken AS6 41070; US: Telefunken S-9498.
aa some-ai co crd d2 eBr?

No. 60: O Ewigkeit, du Donnerwort (II) (Dialogus)
Harnoncourt—Esswood/Equiluz/Van der Meer/Tölz Boys' Choir/Concentus Musicus Vienna.
(57–59) Telefunken EX6 35305; US: Telefunken 2635305.
aa afcs ai ap co crd dl ds=NBA—ed. Dürr dt3 eNBA.
Richter—Töpper/Haefliger/Engen/Munich Bach Choir/Munich Bach Orchestra.
(147) DG Archiv 19831; US: DGG GArchiv 1983331.
ch stps d2 dtl eBG.

No. 61: Nun komm, der Heiden Heiland (I)
Harnoncourt—Kronwitter/Equiluz/Van der Meer/Tölz Boys' Choir/Concentus Musicus Vienna.
(62–64) Telefunken EX6 35306; US: Telefunken 2635306.
aa afcs afss ai ap co crd dl ds=NBA—ed. Neumann dt3 eNBA.
Richter—Mathis/Schreier/Fischer-Dieskau/Munich Bach Choir/Munich Bach Orchestra.
(243) DG Archiv 2.722 018.
brf co crs d3 dtl eNBA.

No. 62: Nun komm, der Heiden Heiland (II)
Harnoncourt—Jelosits/Esswood/Equiluz/Van der Meer/Tölz Boys' Choir/Concentus Musicus Vianna.
(61, 63, 64) Telefunken EX6 35306; US: Telefunken 2635306.
aa afcs ai ap co crd dl ds=NBA—ed. Neumann dt3 eNBA.
Göttsche—Kruse/Kirchner/Melzer/Illerhaus/Mannheim Bach Choir/Heidelberg Chamber Orchestra.
(142—which is not Bach; possibly Kuhnau) Peerless-Oryx BACH 1112.
ch crs stps d3—note incorrect numbering on spine of cover dtl eNBA?

No. 63: Christen, ätzet diesen Tag
Harnoncourt—Jelosits/Esswood/Van der Meer/Tölz Boys' Choir/Concentus Musicus Vienna.
(61, 62, 64) Telefunken EX6 35306; US: Telefunken 2635306.
aa afcs ai ap co crd dl ds=NBA—ed. Dürr dt3 eNBA.
Rilling—Friesenhausen & Schwartz/Laurich/Kraus/Schöne/Frankfurt Kantorei/Bach-Collegium Stuttgart.
(151) Erato STU 70745–9; West Germany. Claudius-Verlag 71905.
ch-&-co crs chtps dl/2—questionable assumptions mar an otherwise absorbing study no-dt—from either Erato's French or Claudius's German eNBA?

No. 64 : Sehet, welch eine Liebe hat uns der Vater erzeiget
Harnoncourt/Jelosits/Esswood/Van der Meer/Tölz Boys' Choir/Concentus Musicus Vienna.
(61–63) Telefunken EX6 35306; US: Telefunken 2635306.
aa afcs ai ap co crd dl ds=ePeters? dt3 eBr?
Richter—Mathis/Reynolds/Fischer-Dieskau/Munich Bach Choir/Munich Bach Orchestra.
(121) DG Archiv 2722 018.
co crs d3 dtl eBG.

No. 65 : Sie werden aus Saba alle kommen
Harnoncourt—Equiluz/Van der Meer/Tölz Boys' Choir/Concentus Musicus Vienna.
(66, 67, 68) Telefunken EX6 35307; US: Telefunken 2635307.
aa ai ap co crd dl ds=NBA—ed. Dürr dt3 eNBA.
Richter—Haefliger/Adam/Munich Bach Choir/Munich Bach Orchestra.
(58,124) DG Archiv 2722 005.
co crs d2—by von Dadelsen, but brief dtl eBG.
Kahlhöfer—Jelden/Stämpfli/Barmen-Gemarke Choir/Barmen-Gemarke Orchestra.
(46) Bach Recordings BACH 103; US: Vanguard S-226.
coc rs dl—by Dürr, trans Emery dt2 eBr?

No. 66 : Erfreut euch, ihr Herzen (Dialogus)
Leonhardt—Esswood/Equiluz/Hannover Boys with Collegium Vocale, Ghent/ augmented Leonhardt Consort.
(65, 67, 68) Telefunken EX6 35307; US: Telefunken 2635307.
aa ai ap crv dl ds=NBA—ed. Dürr dt3 eNBA.
Rilling—Kraus/Schöne/Gächinger Kantorei/Bach-Collegium Stuttgart.
West Germany: (77) Claudius Verlag CL V 71912.

No. 67 : Halt in Gedächtnis Jesum Christ
Leonhardt—Esswood/Equiluz/Van der Meer/Hannover Boys with Collegium Vocale, Ghent/augmented Leonhardt Consort.
(65, 66, 68) Telefunken EX6 35307; US: Telefunken 2635307.
aa ai ap crv dl ds=ePeters? dt3 e
Richter—Reynolds/Schreier/Fischer-Dieskau/Munich Bach Choir/Munich Bach Orchestra.
(6,158) DG Archiv 2722 018.
co crs d3 dtl eBG.
Ansermet—Watts/Krenn/Krause/Lausanne Choir/Lausanne Chamber Orchestra.
(130, 101—first mvt. only) Decca ECS 790; US: London 26098.
A large-scaled account of characteristic warm sensitivity.

No. 68: Also hat Gott die Welt geliebt
Harnoncourt—Jelosits/Van der Meer/Tölz Boys' Choir/Concentus Musicus Vienna.
   (65–67) Telefunken EX6 35307; US: Telefunken 2635307.
aa afcs afss ai ap co crd dl ds=NBA—ed. Dürr dt3 eNBA.
Richter—Mathis/Adam/Munich Bach Choir/Munich Bach Orchestra.
   (34,175) DG Archiv 2722 019—also (coupling?) 2722 025.
co crs ctps d3/l—in 025 sest dtl eBG.
Ziegler—Buckel/Stämpfli/Vokalensemble Kassel/Deutsche Bachsolisten.
   (172) Bärenreiter-Musicaphon SDG 610; US: Nonesuch 71256.

No. 69a: Lobe den Herrn, meine Seele (I)
Harnoncourt—Wiedl/Esswood/Equiluz/Van der Meer/Tölz Boys' Choir/
Concentus Musicus Vienna.
   (70, 71, 72, 69 Telefunken EX6 35340; US: Telefunken 2635340.
aa afcs afss ai ap co crd dl dt3 ds=ePeters? eBr?

No. 69: Lobe den Herrn, meine Seele (I) (reworked portions)
Harnoncourt—Wiedl/Esswood/Equiluz/Tölz Boys' Choir/Concentus Musicus
   (69a, 70–72) Telefunken EX6 35340; US: Telefunken 2635340.

No. 70: Wachet! betet! wachet!
Harnoncourt—Wiedl/Esswood/Equiluz/Van der Meer/Tölz Boys' Choir/
Concentus Musicus Vienna.
   (69a, 71, 72, 69 exc.) Telefunken EX6 35340; US: Telefunken
2635340.
aa afcs ai ap co crd dt dt3 ds=NBA—ed. Dürr eNBA.
Rilling—Gohl/Kraus/Nimsgern/Figuralchor, Gedächtniskirche Stuttgart/
Bach-Collegium Stuttgart.
   (40) Erato STU 70704; West Germany: Claudius Verlag CLV 71903.
*ch-&-co crs chtps dl/3—in French for Erato, partly speculative dt2—into
French for Erato eNBA?*

No. 71: Gott ist mein König
Harnoncourt—Wiedl/Esswood/Equiluz/Visser/Tölz Boys' Choir/Concentus
Musicus Vienna.
   (69a, 70, 72, 69 evc.) Telefunken Ex6 35340; UE: Telefunken 2635340.
aa afcs ai ap co dt dt3 ds=eBr? eBr?
Rilling—Graf/Schwarz & Gardow/Kraus & Senger & Baldin-Tüller &
Schöne/Gachinger Kantorei/Bach-Collegium Stuttgart.

US: (14) Musical Heritage Society MHS 3451 (formerly on West German Claudius Verlag label).
ch-&-co recording rather remote in effect d3 dt2 eBr?
Thomas—Giebel/Höffgen/Roitsch/Adam/Leipzig Thomanerchor/Leipzig Gewandhausorchester-einsemble.
(52) EMI CSD 3528 (mono).
afcs—although St. Thomas's Choir is today too large, the tonal quality of the boy sopranos and altos is excellent co crs d3 dt2 eBr? Recorded in the early Sixties.

No. 72 : Alles nur nach Gottes Willen
Harnoncourt—Wiedl/Esswood/Van der Meer/Tölz Boys' Choir/Concentus Musicus Vienna.
(69a, 70, 71, 69 exc.) Telefunken EX6 35340; US: Telefunken 2635340.
aa afcs ai ap co crd dl dt3 ds=eBR?
Rilling—Friesenhausen/Laurich/Kunz/Figuralchor, Gedächtniskirche Stuttgart/Bach-Collegium Stuttgart.
(58) Erato STU 70745–9; West Germany: Claudius Verlag CLV 71914.
ch-&-co crs d/3—it requires some ingenuity and knowledge to distinguish fact from speculation here—and only in French for Erato dt2—into French, Erato only.

No. 73 : Herr, wie du willt, so schick's mit mir
Leonhardt—Erler/Equiluz/Van Egmond/Hannover Boys with Collegium Vocale Ghent/augmented Leonhardt Consort.
(74, 75) Telefunken EX6 35341; US: Telefunken 2635341.
aa afss ai ap co crv dl/2 ds=Hänssler?? dt3 e?
Rilling—Reichelt & Gohl/Kraus/Kunz/Frankfurt Kantorei/Bach-Collegium Stuttgart.
(178) West Germany: Claudius Verlag CLV 71914.

No. 74 : Wer mich liebet, der wird mein Wort halten (II)
Leonhardt—Erler/Esswood/Equiluz/Van Egmond/Hannover Boys with Collegium Vocale Ghent/augmented Leonhardt Consort.
(73, 75) Telefunken EX6 353411; US: Telefunken 2635341.
aa ai ap co crv dl/2 ds=NBA—ed. Kilian dt3 eNBA.
Winschermann—Cotrubas/Hamari/Equiluz/Reimer/Netherlands Vocal Ensemble/Deutsche Bach-Solisten.
(147) Philips 6500 386; US: Philips 6500 386.
ch-&-co crs d2 dtl eNBA?

No. 75 : Die Elenden sollen essen
Leonhardt—Klein/Esswood/Kraus/Van Egmond/Hannover Boys with
Collegium Vocale Ghent/augmented Leonhardt Consort.
    (73, 74) Telefunken EX6 35341; US: Telefunken 2635341.
aa ai ap co crv dl/2 ds=NBA—ed. Dürr, Freeman & Webster dt3 eNBA.
Rilling—Reichelt/Gohl/Kraus/Kunz/Frankfurter Kantorei/Bach-Collegium
Stuttgart.
    Erato STU 7072; West Germany: Claudius Verlag CLV 71901.
*ch-&-co crs chtps d2—unreliable because uncautious, but full and stimulating
—in French for Erato, German for Claudius dt2—into French only, for Erato
eNBA?*

No. 76 : Die Himmel erzählen die Ehre Gottes
Richter—Mathis/Reynolds/Schreier/Moll/Munich Bach Choir/Munich Bach
Orchestra.
    DG Ardchiv 2722 025.
co crs ctps d2 dtl eBG.
Ehmann—Van der Speek/Haasemann/Hoefflin/Pommerien/Westfalische
Kantorei/Deutsche Bachsolisten.
    (37) Peerless-Oryx BACH 1114; West Germany: (225) Musicaphon
Cantate 656 004.
co crs d3 dt2 eBr?

No. 77 : Du sollt, Gott, deinem Herren, lieben
Rilling—Donath/Watts/Kraus/Schöne/Gächinger Kantorei/Bach-Collegium
Stuttgart.
    West Germany: (66) Claudius Verlag CLV 71912.

No. 78 : Jesu, der du meine Seele
Prohaska—Stich-Randall/Hermann/Dermota/Braun/Bach Guild Choir,
Vienna/Bach Guild Orchestra.
    (106) Pye Bach Guild HM21.
*co crs dr—even for 1960 out of date chronologically dt2 eBG—revised
Prohaska. Recorded c. 1959.*
Richter—Buckel/Topper/Van Kesteren/Engen/Munich Bach Choir/Munich
Bach Orchtestra.
    (243) DG Archiv 178197; US: DG Archiv 178197.

No. 79 : Gott der Herr ist Sonn und Schild
Ramin—Schwichert/Lutze/Hauptmann/Leipzig Thomanerchor/Stadt— und

Gewandhausorchester Leipzig.
  (137) Bärenreiter-Musicaphon Cantate 657 605.
*afcs afss—boy alto co-&-ch d2—German language only eBG? The performance
dates from the early-Fifties, when both Ramin and Karl Richter (continuo)
were still available in Leipzig.*
Gönnenwein—Ameling/Baker/Sotin/Süddeutsche Madrigalchor/Consortium
Musicum.
  (148, 149) HMV ASD 2396; US: Serenus S-60248.
*As in most of Gonnenwein's Bach recordings, the effect is warm and lyrical,
but somewhat at the expense of rhythm and detailed shaping; some good
solo singing.*

No. 80: Ein feste Burg ist unser Gott
Mauersberger—Giebel/Töpper/Schreier/Adam/Leipzig Thomanerchor/Leipzig
Gewandhausorchester Ensemble.
  (140) DG Archiv 198407; US: DG Archiv 198407.
*afcs co ars dl!—by Werner Neumann dtl eBG—rev. Neumann? No other
performance on disc omits the trumpet choir added by a later hand (W. F.
Bach) after Sebastian's death.*

No. 81: Jesus schläft, was soll ich hoffen?
Rilling—Lerer & Schwarz/Melzer/Nimsgern/Gächinger Kantorei/Bach-
Collegium Stuttgart.
  (187) Erato STU 70749; West Germany: Claudius Verlag CLV 71909.
*ch-&-cor crs d2-full, but should be approached cautiously; from German
language translated into French only dt2—into French eBG?*
Richter—Reynolds/Schreier/Adam/Munich Bach Choir/Munich Bach
Orchestra.
  (82) DG Archiv 2722 005.
*co crs ctps-n.b. mismanagement in recitative of concluding cadence to line
d2 dtl eBG.*

No. 82: Ich habe genung
Richter—Fischer-Dieskau/Munich Bach Orchestra Ensemble.
  (56) DG Archiv 198477; US: DG Archiv 198477.
*co crs d2 dtl eBG The organ continuo playing is here notably discreet and
rhythmically positive.*
Thomas—Prey/Leipzig Gewandhausorchester Ensemble.
  (56) Classics for Pleasure CFP 40038.
Marriner—Shirley-Quirk/Academy of St. Martin-in-the-Fields, London.
  (56) Oiseau-lyre SCL 280; US: Oiseau-lyre S-280.
*afss—sensible mature singing by a soloist of youthful timbre co crs d3
dt2 eBr?*

No. 82b: Ich habe genung
Menuhin—Baker/Bath Festival Ensemble.
   (169) EMI ASD 2302; US: Angel S-36419.

No. 82a, Aria 3: Schlummert ein, ihr matten Augen
(?) Leonhardt—Ameling/Collegium Aurem.
   West German Harmonia Mundi 30183 L.
ai ap ch crd d2 eNBA? For a short time available in England c. 1975
Redel—Giebel/Munich Pro Antiqua.
   Erato STU 70692.

No. 83: Erfreute Zeit im neuen Bunde
Harnoncourt—Vienna Boy alto/Equiluz/Van Egmond/augmented Vienna
Boys' Choir/Concentus Musicus Vienna.
   (50,197) Telefunken AS6 41100; US: Telefunken 641100.
*aa afss ai ap co crv dl dt3 eBr? The boy alto is impressive throughout this
record, and we may well be led to question the wisdom of Harnoncourt,
Leonhardt and others who have later advocated the employment of counter-
tenor and haute-contre timbres for Bach's alto lines: maybe their main motives
were expediency and impatience—two aspects apparently absent from the
best traditions of the Thomanerchor, Leipzig.*

No. 84: Ich bin vergnügt mit meinem Glücke
Ehmann—Giebel/Westfälische Kantorei/Westfälische Orchestra.
   (49) Bärenreiter-Musicaphon SDG 610 110; US: Nonesuch 71273.

No. 87: Bisher habt ihr nichts gebeten in meinem Namen
Richter—Reynolds/Schreier/Fischer-Dieskau/Munich Bach Choir/Munich
Bach Orchestra.
   (23) DG Archiv 2533 313.

No. 88: Siehe, ich will viel Fischer aussenden
Rilling—Reichlet/Gohl/Kraus/Schöne/Figuralchor, Gedächtniskirche Stutt-
gart/Bach-Collegium Stuttgart.
   (150) Erato STU 70705; West Germany: Claudius Verlag CLV 71904.

*ch-&-co crs chtps d2—full, but misleadingly subjective: in French for Erato
dt2—into French for Erato eBr?*

No. 89 : Was soll ich aus dir machen, Ephraim?
Schroeder—Armstrong/Watts/Van Egmond/Monteverdichor Hamburg/
Concerto Amsterdam.
 (90, 161) Telefunken AS6 41102; US: Telefunken 641102.
aa partly-ai co crd dl dt2 eBr?

No. 90 : Es reisset euch ein schrecklich Ende
Schroeder—Watts/Equiluz/Van Egmond/Monteverdichor Hamburg/Concerto
Amsterdam.
 (89, 161) Telefunken AS6 41102; US: Telefunken 641102.
aa partly-ai co crd dl dt2 eBr?

No. 91 : Gelobet seist du, Jesu Christ
Rilling—Donath/Watts/Kraus/Schöne/Frankfurt Kantorei/Bach-Collegium
Stuttgart.
West Germany: (122) Claudius Verlag CLV 71913.

No. 92 : Ich hab in Gottes Herz und Sinn
Richter—Mathis/Munich Bach Choir Alto/Schreier/Fischer-Dieskau/Munich
Bach Choir/Munich Bach Orchestra.
 (126) DG Archiv 2533 312; US: DG Archiv 2533 312.
co crs ctps d2 dtl eNBA.

No. 93 : Wer nur den lieben Gott lässt walten
Richter—Mathis/Reynolds/Schreier/Fischer-Dieskau/Munich Bach Choir/
Munich Bach Orchestra.
 (51) DG Archiv 2722 025.
co crs ctps d2 dtl eBG.
Doormann—Reichlet/Wolf–Matthäus/Feyerabend/Hudemann/Göttinger
Stadtkantorei/Frankfurt Orchestral Ensemble.
 (117) Bärenreiter-Musicaphon SDG 610 102; US: Vanguard S-241.

No. 95 : Christus, der ist mein Leben
Heintze—Bernat-Klein/Bornemann/Jelden/Kunz/Bremer Domchor/Bremen
Orchestral Ensemble.
(33) Barenreiter Musicaphon SDG 610 104; US: Vanguard S-243.

No. 100 : Was Gott tut, das ist wohlgetan (III)
Wunderlich—Schwarzweller/Wolf-Matthäus/Rotsche/Müller/Kantorei Sancti
Jacobi Hamburg/Hamburg Chamber Orchestra.
(175) Bärenreiter-Musicaphon SDG 610 107; US: Vanguard S-230.

No. 101 : Nimm von uns, Herr, du treuer Gott
??—Bryden/Fortunato/Sorensen/Harbison/Cantata Singers/?Ensemble.
US: (44) Advent Corporation 1015.

No. 101, Chorus 1 : Nimm von uns, Herr
Ansermet—Lausanne Choir/Lausanne Orchestra.
(67,130) Decca ECS 790.
A warm, well-proportioned, traditional reading.

No. 102 : Herr, deine Augen sehen nach dem Glauben?
Werner—Scherler/Altmeyer/Chorale Heinrich Schütz Heilbronn/Heilbronn
Chamber Orchestra.
(137) Erato STU 70672.
co crs d2 dtl eBr?
Rilling—Randova/Equiluz/Schöne/Gächinger Kantorei/Bach-Collegium
Stuttgart.
West Germany: (12) Claudius Verlag CLV 71911.

No. 103 : Ihr werdet weinen und heulen
Graulich—Waldbauer/Gilvan/Motettenchor Stuttgart/Heidelberg Chamber
Orchestra.
(25) Peerless-Oryx BACH 1107; West Germany: Da Camera 94010.
bbt—solo singers co crs d3 eBr?

No. 104 : Du Hirte Isreal, höre
Richter—Schreier/Fischer-Dieskau/Munich Bach Choir/Munich Bach Orchestra.
    (12) DG Archiv 2722 022.
co crs d3 dtl eBG.

No. 105 : Herr, gehe nicht ins Gericht mit deinem Knecht
Ansermet—Giebel/Watts/Partridge/Krause/augmented Choir of the Suisse Romande/Orchestra of the Suisse Romande.
    (45) Decca SDD 384.
bdf—instruments ch crs d2 dt2 eBr?

No. 106 : Gottes Zeit ist der allerbeste Zeit (Actus Tragicus)
Leonhardt—Falk/Villisech/Monteverdichor Hamburg/Leonhardt Consort.
    (182) Telefunken AS6 41060; US: Telefunken 641060.
aa ai ap co crd dl eBr?
Göttsche—Kirchner/Müller/Mannheim Bach Choir/Mannheim Back Orchestra.
    (151) Peerless-Oryx BACH 1102; West Germany: Da Camera CH 94002.
ch-&-co d2 dt2 eBr?
Öhrwall—Rödin/Hagegård/Adolf Fredriks Bachkör Stockholm/Stockholm Ensemble.
    (140) CRD—Swedish Proprius 7713; Meridian E 77016.
co d2—in Swedish only dt2?—German/Swedish parallel texts only eBr?

No. 108 : Es ist euch gut, dass ich hingehe
Richter—Töpper/Haefliger/Adam/Munich Bach Choir/Munich Bach Orchestra.
    West Germany: (65, 124) DG Archiv 198416.

No. 109 : Ich glaube, lieber Herr. hilf meinem unglauben!
Rilling—Laurich/Equilùz/Gächinger Kantorei/Bach-Collegium Stuttgart.
    (155) Erato STU 70745–9; West Germany: Claudius Verlag 71906.
ch-&-co crs chtps d2—but interpretations should be treated cautionsly: in French only for Erato dt2—into French for Erato eBr?

No. 110 : Unser Mund sei voll Lachens
??—Gampert/Stein/Altmeyer/Nimsgern/Tölz Boys' Choir/Collegium Aurem.

US: (143) BASF 21584 (marketed briefly in the UK c. 1975).
afcs afss partly-ai ap co crd d2 eNBA?
Werner—Sailer/Hellmann/Krebs/Wenk/Chorale Heinrich Schütz Heilbronn/
Pforzheim Chamber Orchestra.
(8) Erato STA 50086.
*bdf—instruments in chamber-scaled numbers co crs d2—in French only dt2
—into French only eNBA? A sound modern reading distinguished by some
excellent woodwind obbligati and solo singing.*
Thamm—Wehrung/Lisken/Jelden/Stampfli/Windsbach Boys' Choir/
ᴾforzheim Chamber Orchestra.
(17) Bärenreiter-Musicaphon SDG 610 108.

No. 111: Was mein Gott will, das g'scheh allzeit
Richter—Mathis/Reynolds/Schreier/Adam/Munch Bach Choir/Munich Bach
Orchestra.
(13) DG Archiv 2722 005.
co xrs d2 dtl eBG.

No. 117: Sei Lob und Ehr dem höchsten Gut
Doormann—Wolf-Matthäus/Feyerabend/Hudemann/Göttinger Stadtkantorei/
Frankfurter Kantatenorchester.
(93) Bärenreiter-Musicaphon SDG 610 102; US: Vanguard S-241.

No. 118: see below under Motets

No. 119: Preise, Jerusalem, den Herrn
Hellmann—Buckel/Conrad/Krebs/Müller/Mainz Bach Choir/Mainz Bach
Orchestra.
(129) Peerless-Oryx BACH 1118; West Germany: Da Camera 94019.
*co crs d3 dt2 eHänssler—ed. Hellmann, incorporating a new revised text
—adapted from that set by Bach by Albrecht Goes. The recording lacks
immediacy and definition—a great pity in a work of this character.*
Werner—Friesenhausen/Lisken/Jelden/McDaniel/Chorale Heinrich Schütz
Heilbronn/Pforzheim Chamber Orchestra.
(28) Erato STE 50285.
*ch-&-co crs d2—in French only dt2—into French e? The text corresponds
with that of edition BG (i.e. roughly with the original). The editing of the
recording has been mismanaged.*

No. 120: Gott, man lobet dich in der Stille
Dickinson—Kelley/Hardin/Brown/Epley/Choir of Louisville Bach Society/
Louisville Bach Society Orchestra.
  US: (69) Rivergate 1002.

No. 121: Christum wir sollen loben schon
Richter—Mathis/Reynolds/Schreier/Fischer-Dieskau/Munich Bach Choir/
Munich Bach Orchestra.
  (63) DG Archiv 2722 005.
co crs d2 dtl eBG.

No. 122: Das neugeborne Kindelein
Rilling—Donath/Watts/Kraus/Tüller/Frankfurt Kantorei/Bach-Collegium
Stuttgart.
  (91) West Germany: Claudius Verlag CLV 71913.

No. 124: Meinem Jesum lass ich nicht
Richter—Schädle/Töpper/Haefliger/Adam/Munich Bach Choir/Munich Bach
Orchestra.
  (58, 65) DG Archiv 2722 005.
coc rs d2 dtl eBG.

No. 126: Erhalt uns, Herr, bei deinem Wort
Richter—Reynolds/Schreier/Adam/Munich Bach Choir/Munich Bach
Orchestra.
  (92) DG Archiv 2533 312.
co crs dl dtl eNBA.

No. 127: Herr Jesu Christ, wahr' Mensch und Gott
Gönnenwein—Wehrung/Lisken/Jelden/Stämpfli/Süddeutscher Madrigalchor/
Südwestdeutsches Chamber Orchestra Pforzheim.
  (171) Bärenreiter-Musicaphon SDG 610 109.
co crs—no audible continuo in choruses, but ctpsy in solos d3 eNBA—pre-
publication. Wehrung's voice suits Bach and her aria is well done; the whole
ensemble strives manfully with the very demanding bass and trumpet solo.

No. 128: Auf Christi Himmelfahrt allein
Winschermann—Hamari/Equiluz/Prey/Kantorei Barmen-Gemarke/Deutsche Bachsolisten.
(134) West German Philips 6747 006.

No. 129: Gelobet sei der Herr, mein Gott
Richter—Mathis/Reynolds/Fischer-Dieskau/Munich Bach Choir/Munich Bach Orchestra.
(39) DG Archiv 2722 025.
coc rs ctps d3 dt1 eHänssler.

No. 130: Herr Gott, dich loben alle wir
Ansermet—Ameling/Watts/Krenn/Krause/Lausanne Choir/Lausanne Orchestral Ensemble.
(67, 101—first chorus) Decca ECS 790; US: London 26098.

No. 131: Aus der Tiefen rufe ich, Herr, zu dir
Steinitz—Eathorne/Esswood/Jenkins/Noble/London Bach Society Chorus/Steinitz Bach Players.
Nonesuch H 71294; US: Nonesuch 71294.
co d2 dtl eHänssler?

No. 132: Bereitet die Wege, bereitet die Bahn!
Richter—Mathis/Reynolds/Schreier/Adam/Munich Bach Choir/Munich Bach Orchestra.
(61) DG Archiv 2722 005.
co crs ctps d2 dtl eNBA.

No. 135: Ach Herr, mich armen Sünder
Richter—Reynolds/Schreier/Fischer-Dieskau/Munich Bach Choir/Munich Bach Orchestra.
(10, 24) DG Archiv 2533 329.
coc rs dl dtl eBG.

No. 137: Lobe den Herren, den mächtigen Konig der Ehren
Werner—Reichelt/Scherler/Melzer/Abel/Chorale Heinrich Schütz Heilbronn/

Heilbronn Chamber Orchestra.

(102) Erato STU 70672.

co crs d2 dtl e? Generally the strongest of several available recordings; the rushed speeds spoiled Ramin's old Leipzig recording (Bärenreiter-Musicaphon Cantate 657 605), which had a good boy alto and fine ripieno work from the Thomanerchor.

No. 138: Warum betrübst du dich, mein Herz

Ramin—Lutze/Oettel/Leipzig Thomanarchor/Leipzig Gewandhausorchester Ensemble.

(72) Oryx BACH 108.

No. 140: Wachet auf, ruft uns die Stimme

Mauersberger—Schreier/Adam/Leipzig Thomanerchor/Leipzig Gewandhausorchester Ensemble.

(80) DG Archiv 198407; US: DG Archiv 198407.

afcs afss co crs dl!—Neumann dtl eBG—revised Neumann?

Öhrwall—Björkegren/Hagegård/Adolf Fredriks Bachkör Stockholm/ Stockholm Ensemble.

(106) CRD Swedish Proprius 7713; Meridian E 77016.

co crd d2—in Swedish dt2—from German to Swedish eNBA.

No. 144: Nimm, was dein ist, und gehe hin

Ramin—Burkhardt/Wolf-Mätthaus/Lutze/Leipzig Thomanerchor/Gewandhausorchester Ensemble.

(92) Oryx BACH 110.

No. 147: Herz und Mund und Tat und Leben

Willcocks—Ameling/Baker/Partridge/Shirley Quirk/King's College Choir Cambridge/Academy of St. Martin-in-the-Fields, London.

(226, 228, 230) EMI HQS 1254; US: Angel S-36804.

co crs d2 dt2 eBr?

Winschermann—Cotrubaş/Hamari/Equiluz/Reimer/Netherlands Vocal Ensemble/Deutsche Bachsolisten.

(74) Philips 6500 386.

ch-&-ch crs dl dtl eBr? This record is banded in separate movements, which makes possible the omission of the movements added at Leipzig to Cantata No. 147a.

No. 148 : Bringet dem Herrn Ehre seines Namens
Gönnenwein—Baker/Altmeyer/Süddeutscher Madrigalchor/Consortium Musicum.
    (79, 149) EMI ASD 2396; West Germany: Electrola (140) 1 C 063–19012.

No. 149 : Man singet mit Freuden vom Sieg in den Hütten der Gerechten
Gönnenwein—Baker/Altmeyer/Süddeutscher Madrigalchor/Consortium Musicum.
    (79,148) EMI ASD 2396; West Germany: Electrola (126) 1 C 063–28490.

No. 150 : Nach dir, Herr, verlanget mich
Rilling—Schreiber/Jetter/Maus/Kunz/Gächinger Kantorei/Bach-Collegium Stuttgart.
    (88) Erato STU 70705; West Germany: Claudius Verlag CLV 71904.
co-&lch crs d3—unusually subjective—in French only for Erato dt2—into French (Erato) eBr?

No. 151 : Süsser Trost, mein Jesu kömmt
Rilling—Yamamoto/Laurich/Kraus/Kunz/Frankfurt Kantorei/Bach-Collegium Stuttgart.
    (63) Erato STU 70745/9; West Germany: Claudius Vrelag CLV 71905.
ch-&-co crs ds—full, but variable, in French for Erato, German for Claudius dt2—into French only for Erato e?

No. 152 : Tritt auf die Glabensbahn
Leonhardt—Giebel/Villisech/Amsterdam Ensemble.
    (18) Telefunken SAWT 9442; US: Telefunken 641059.
aa partly-ai co crs d2 eBr?

No. 155 : Mein Gott, wie lang, ach lange?
Rilling—Reichelt/Lerer/Melzer/Kunz/Gächinger Kantorei/Bach-Collegium Stuttgart.
    (109) Erato STU 70745/9; West Germany: Claudius Verlag CLV 71905.
ch-&-co crs d2—speculative but absorbing—in French for Erato dt2—into French for Erato e?

Hamburg/Hamburg Chamber Orchestra.
 (100) Barenreiter Musicaphon SDG 610 107; US: Vanguard S-230.

No. 178: Wo Gott der Herr nicht bei uns hält
Rilling—Watts & Laurich/Equiluz & Wilhelm/Nimsgern/Figuarchor,
Gedächtniskirche Stuttgart/Bach-Collegium Stuttgart.
 (73) West Germany: Claudius Verlag CLV 71914.

No. 179: Siehe du, dass deine Gottesfurcht nicht Heuchelei sei
Ramin—Meinel-Ashahar/Rotsch/Oettel/Leipzig Thomanerchor/Leipzig
Gewandhausorchester Ensemble.
 (41) Oryx BACH 106.

No. 182: Himmelskönig, sei willkommen
Leonhardt—Falk/Van t'Hoff/Villisech/Monteverdichor Hamburg/Leonhardt
Consort.
 (106) Telefunken AS6 41060; US: Telefunken 641060.
*aa ai co crv d2 eBr? An elegant recording featuring a stylish female alto
soloist.*
Ehmann—Haasemann/Hoefflin/Pommerien/Westfälische Kantorei/Deutsche
Bachsolisten.
 (4) Peerless-Oryx BACH 1113; US: Vanguard S-225; also Bärenreiter
 Musicaphon SDG 610 116 (available internationally).
*co crs d3 dt2 eBr? Pitched around modern G major—hence closer to original
pitch than the low-G pitching of Leonhardt: the Bach performances sounded
at our low B flat major.*

No. 187: Es wartet alles auf dich
Rilling—Friesenhausen/Laurich/Schöne/Gächinger Kantorei/Bach-Collegium
Stuttgart.
 (81) Erato STU 70745/9; West Germany: Claudius Verlag CLV 71909.
*ch-&-co crs chtps d2—lacks caution but stimulating; in French only for Erato
dt2—into French only for Erato eNBA?*

No. 190: Singet dem Herrn ein neues Lied!
Thamm/Russ/Schreier/Crass/Windbach Kantorei/Consortium Musicum.
 West Germany: (137) Electrola 1 C 063–28997.

No. 191 : Gloria in excelsis deo
Rilling—Gamo & Yamamoto/Kraus/Gächinger Kantorei/Bach-Collegium Stuttgart.
    (19) Erato STU 70745/9; West Germany: Claudius Verlag CLV 71907.
ch--&-co crs chtps d2—only in French for Erato; variable but stimulating dt2—into French only for Erato eNBA?

No. 192 : Nun danket alle Gott
Achenbach—Wehrung/Achenbach(!)/Tübinger Kantatenchor/Suddeutscher Jugendsynfonie-orch.
    (172) Peerless-Oryz BACH 1111; West Germany: Da Camera 94012.
co d3 dt2 eHänssler?

No. 197 : Gott ist unsre Zuversicht
Harnoncourt—Vienna Boy Alto/Equiluz/Van Egmond/Vienna Boys' Choir (augmented)/ Concentus Musicus Vienna.
    (50, 83) Telefunken AS6 41100; US: Telefunken 641100.
aa afss—good boy alto ai ap co crv dl dt3 eNBA?

No. 198 : Lass, Fürstin, lass noch einen Strahl (Trauer-Ode)
Schroeder—Hansmann/Watts/Equiluz/Van Egmond/Hamburg Monteverdi-chor/Concerto Amsterdam.
    Telefunken AW6 41215; US: Telefunken 641215.
aa co crv—mostly—crd dl! (Ludwig Finscher, but only in untranslated German in my copy) no-dt in sample eBr/NBA? Curious that there is no audible harpsichord in this cantata, of all; possibly there was room also for more distinctive characterisation of each movement. The final chorus, however, is excellent—full of Schroeder's characteristic lyricism.

No. 199 : Mein Herze schwimmt im Blut
Winschermann—Ameling/Deutsche Bachsolisten.
    (51) Philips 6500 014; US: Philips 6500 014.
coc rs d2 dt2 eNeue Bach Gesellschaft?

No. 200 : Bekennen will ich seinen Namen
Hellmann—Conrad/Maind Bach Orchestra.
    (Pergolesi/Bach: Psalm 51) Peerless-Oryx BACH 1120.
co d2 dt2 eNeue Bach Gesellschaft?

Dart—Watts/London Philomusica.
　　(54, 53—the latter not by Bach) Oiseau-Lyre 60003; US: Oiseau-Lyre 60003.

No. 201 : Geschwinde, ihr wirbeinden Winde
Rilling—Mathis/Russ/Jachims & Schreier/Wenk & Stämpfli/Figuralchor, Gedächtniskirche Stuttgart/Bach-Collegium Stuttgart.
　　Barenreiter-Musicaphon 1352.
Thomas—Stolte/Fleisher/Rotsch & Apreck/Leib & Adam/Leipzig Thomanerchor/Leipzig Gewandhausorchester.
　　DG Archiv 2722 019.
ch crs d3 dtl eBr Rather a dry reading from 1960.

No. 202 : Weichet nur, betrübte Schatten
Schroeder—Giebel/Concerto Amsterdam.
　　(51) Telefunken AS6 41077; US: Telefunken 641077.
aa ch crv dl dt3 eNBA? Excellent, especially in the instrumental characterisation of the final aria.
Peters—Ameling/Collegium Aurem.
　　(209, 211, 212) Harmonia Mundi HM 2252/3; US: BASF 20330.
aa partly-ai ch crs d2/3 no-dt eNBA? Good singing from Ameling, but overall slightly inferior to the above.

No. 203 : Amore traditore
Villisech—Leonhardt.
　　(209) Telefunken SAWT 9465; US: Telefunken 641067.
An expressive account that somehow fails to reach the peaks one might expect.

No. 204 : Ich bin in mir vergnügt
Ewehard—Speiser/Württemberg Chamber Orchestra Heilbronn.
　　(209) Turnabout TV 341275; US: Turnabout 34127.

No. 205 : Zerreisset, zersprenget, zertrümmert die Gruft
Koch—Speiser/Springer/Schreier/Lorenz/Solistenvereinigung Berlin/ Berlin Chamber Orchestra.

DG Archiv 2722 019.
ch crs d3 dtl eBr-DDR.
Rilling—Speiser/Bence/Van Kesteren/Stämpfli/Figuralchor, Gedächtniskirche Stuttgart/Bach-Collegium Stuttgart.
Bärenreiter Musicaphon 1353.

No. 206 : Schleicht, spielende Wellen, und murmelt gelinde
Rieu—Jacobeit/Matthès/Brand/Villisech/Hamburg Monteverdichor/Amsterdam Chamber Orchestra.
Telefunken SAWT 9425; US: Telefunken 641047.
ch crv dl no-dt- eBr?
Koch—Speiser/Springer/Schreier/Adam/Solistenvereiningung Berlin/Berlin Chamber Orchestra.
DG Archiv 2722 019.
ch crs d3 dtl eBr--DDR.

No. 207a : Auf, schmetternde Töne der muntern Trompeten
Kahlhöfer—Reichelt/Lisken/Jelden/Wollitz/Barmen-Gemarke Choir/Barmen-Gemarke Chamber Orchestra.
US: (214) Vanguard S-231.

No. 208 : Was mir behagt, ist nur die muntre Jagd!
Rieu—Spoorenberg & Jacobeit/Brand/Villisech/Hamburg Monteverdichor/Amsterdam Chamber Orchestra.
Telefunken AS6 41050; US: Telefunken 641050.
some-aa partly-ai ch crv dl no-dt eNBA?
Rilling—Donath & Speiser/Jochims/Stämpfli/Figuralchor, Gedächtniskirche Stuttgart/Bach-Collegium Stuttgart.
Barenreiter Musicaphon 1352; US: Nonesuch 71147.

No. 209 : Non sa che sia dolore
Leonhardt—Giebel/Leonhardt Consort.
(203) Telefunken SAWT 9465; US: Telefunken 641067.
aa ai ch crv d3 no-dt? eBr?
Leonhardt—Ameling/Collegium Aureum.
(202, 211, 212) BASF Harmonia Mundi HM 2252; US: BASF 20330.
aa partly-ai ch crv d3 no-dt? eBr?

No. 211 : Schweigt stille, plaudert nicht (Cantate Burlesque)
Harnoncourt—Hansmann/Equiluz/Van Egmond/Concentus Musicus Vienna.

(212) Telefunken SAWT 9515; US: Telefunken 61079.
aa afss ai ap ch crv d2 dt eBr?
Maier—Ameling/English/Nimsgern/Collegium Aureum.
(212, 209, 202) BASF Harmonia Munidi HM 2252/3; US: BASF 20330.
partly-ai ch crv d3 no-dt? eBr?

No. 212 : Mer hahn en neue Oberkeet (Cantate Burlesque)
Harnoncourt—Hansmann/Van Egmond/augmented Vienna Boys' Choir/
Concentus Musicus Vienna.
(211) Telefunken SAWT 9515; US: Telefunken 61079.
aa afss ai ap ch crv d2 dt3 ePeters?
Maier—Ameling/Nimsgern/Tölz Boys' Choir/Collegium Aureum.
(211, 209, 202) BASF Harmonia Mundi HM2252; US: BASF 20330.
afss partly-ai ch crv d3 no-dt eBr?

No. 213 : Lasst uns sorgen, lasst uns wachen (Hercules auf dem
Scheidewege)
Rilling—Armstrong/Töpper/Altmeyer/Stämpfli/Figuralchor, Gedächniskirche
Stuttgart/Bach-Collegium Stuttgart.
Bärenreiter Musicaphon 1356; US: Nonesuch 71226.
ch crv dl-Dürr—in German only for Musicaphon eNBA.

No. 214 : Tonet, ihr Pauken! Erschallet, Trompeten!
Kahlhöfer—Reichelt/Lisken/Jelden/Wollitz/Barmen-Gemarke Choir/
Barmen-Gemarke Chamber Orchestra.
US: (207a) Vanguard S-231.

No. 215 : Preise dein Glucke, gesegnetes Sachsen
Rilling—Spoorenberg/Krenn/Wenk/Gächinger Kantorei/Bach-Collegium
Stuttgart.
Bärenreiter Musicaphon 1355; US: Nonesuch 71206.
*ch crv dl-Dürr—in Germany only for Musicaphon no-dt—for Musicaphon
eNBA.*

No. 249a : Entfliehet, verschwindet, entweichet, ihr Sorgen (Schäferkantate)
Rilling—Mathis/Plümacher/Altmeyer/Stämpfli/augmented Figuralchor,

Gedächtniskirche Stuttgart/Bach-Collegium Stuttgart.
   Bärenreiter Musicaphon 1357; US: Nonesuch 71243.
ch dl—in German only (Dürr) no-dt eNBA.

Motets

The six usually collected into record sets are: 225—Singet dem Herrn ein neues Lied; 226—Der Geist hilft unser Schwachheit auf; 227—Jesu, meine Freude; 228—Fürchte dich nicht; 229—Komm, Jesu, komm; 230—Lobet den Herrn, alle Heiden. To these may be added: 118—O Jesus Christ, meins Lebens Licht (I); 118a—O Jesu Christ, meins Lebens Licht (II); 231—Sei Lob und Preis mit Ehren; Anh. 159—Ich lasse dich nicht (by Johann Christoph Bach, d. 1703).

Schneidt—Regensburg Domspatzen/Capella Academica Vienna.
   (231, Anh. 159) DG Archiv 2708 031.
afcs partly-ai ap discreet instrumental doubling throughout dl dtl eNBA/ Hänssler (Anh. 159 only).
Forbes—Aeolian Singers/Ensemble.
   (118, 11) Decca ECS 598/9; US: London STS-15186/7.
Discreet instrumental doublings; oboes play for Litui in 118 d3 no-dt? eNBA?
Halsey—Louis Halsey Singers/Lumsden org.).
   (131) Oiseau-Lyre SOL 340/1.
Very faint organ doubling and continuo support; a less coloured and rich reading than Schneidt's, despite the mixed choir. The performance by the Hamburg Monteverdichor of BWV 118a alone (27, 59, 158—all Cantatas) should also be mentioned (Telefunken AS6 41070; US: Telefunken 641070— at some-ai co d2 eNBA?).

Oratorios

No. 248: Weihnachts-Oratorium

Harnoncourt—Vienna Boy Soprano/Esswood/Equiluz/Nimsgern/Vienna Boys with Chorus Viennensis/Concentus Musicus Vienna.
   Telefunken FK6 35022; US: Telefunken 3635022.
ai ap co crd dl ds=Peters—ed. Seiffert dt2 eNBA/Peters?

Schmidt-Gaden—Buchhier/Stein/Altmeyer/McDaniel/Tölz Boys' Choir/
Collegium Aureum.
> BASF Harmonia Mundi HM 59 21749–.
aa afss partly-ai ap co crd d3 no-dt? eNBA?
Jochum—Ameling/Fassbender/Laubenthal/Prey/Munich Radio Choir/
Munich Radio Orchestra.
> Philipps 6703037; US: Philips 6703037.
*ch-&-co crv—mostly crs d2 dt2 eNBA? This reading earns preference here
over the comparable ones of Münchinger, Richter and Thomas because of its
positive musical and rhythmic character.*
Ledger—Ameling/Baker/Tear/Fischer-Dieskau/Choir of King's College
Cambridge/Academy of St. Martin-in-the-Fields, London.
> EMI SLS 5098.
*co crv d2 dt2 eNBA? Despite defects in many details of the performance, it is
included here because of its excellent reproduction of modern orchestral
timbres.*

No. 249 : Oster-Oratorium
Münchinger—Ameling/Watts/Krenn/Kraus/Vienna Academiechor/Stuttgart
Chamber Orchestra.
> Decca SET 389; US: London 26100.
co crs d2 dt2 eBr? One of Münchinger's best records.
Gönnenwein—Zylis-Gara/Johnson/Altmeyer/Fischer-Dieskau/Südwestdeut-
scher Chorus/Südwestdeutscher Chamber Orchestra.
> EMI ASD 626 (also World Record Club ST95); US: Angel S-26322.

Passion Music

No. 244 : Matthäuspassion
Harnoncourt—Vienna Boy Soprano/Esswood & Sutcliffe & Bowman/Equiluz
& Rogers/Ridderbusch & Van Egmond & Schopper/Vienna Boys with Chorus
Viennensis & Regensburg Dom Boys with King's College Cambridge men/
augmented Concentus Musicus Vienna.
> Telefunken HF6 35047; US: Telefunken 4635047.
*aa afss--boy sopranos ai ap co-x2 crv-mostly-crd dl no-ds dt2 eBr-revised.
Attention is reported to have been given to appropriate word-enunciation in
this recording, but many traces of recent and local accents—Viennese, North
German and even English—remain. Generally the performance is lyrical,
dignified and clear, but there are also a great many moments where the same
performers could have done so much better—for example the bass-line of the
opening chorus hinders rather than helps, coordination is variable, etc. Still
the best representation on record of Bach's original conception, though.*

Klemperer—Schwarzkopf/Ludwig/Pears/Fischer-Dieskau & others/Boys Choir of Hamstead Parish Church London/Philharmonica Chorus/Philharmonia Orchestra.
    EMI SMS 1013; US: Angel S-3599.
co crs d2 dt2 eBr? The most moving and the best proportioned of the traditional, symphonic readings.
Münchinger—Ameling/Hoffgen/Pears/Wunderlich & others/Stuttgart Vokal-Ensemble/Stuttgart Chamber Orchestra.
    Decca SET 288–291; US: 4-London 1431.
A warmer and less monumental treatment from the mid-Sixties, with some excellent solo singing.
Mauersberger—Stolte/Burmeister/Schreier/Adam & others/Leipzig
Thomanerchor erchor & Dresdener Kreuzchor/Leipzig Gewandhausorchester.
    RCA LRL 4 5098; West Germany: Electrola Eurodisc 80613 from East German Eterna originals.
afcs bdf—instrumental and orchestral contributions crv-mostly-crs d?—by author for RCA dt2 eBr—with revisions by Leipzig specialists? This much-criticised reading is included because of its musical vocal qualities, and because this account presents a valid interpertation of apparent integrity and commitment.

No. 245: Johannespassion

Harnoncourt—Vienna Boy Soprano/Vienna Boy Alto/Equiluz/Van Egmond and others/Vienna Boys with Chorus Viennensis/Concentus Musicus Vienna.
    Telefunken FK6 35018; US: 3-Telefunken 3635018.
aa afss ai ap co crv-mostly-crd d2 no-ds eBr-revised?
Richter—Lear/Töpper/Haefliger/Prey & Engen & others/Munich Bach Choir/ Munich Bach Orchestra.
    DG Archiv 6703 004; US: 3-DG Archiv 27 10002.
co crs d2 dt2 eBG Although the account is not as strong in character as the earlier Matthäuspassion, it remains an integrated interpretation, with Haefliger a persuasive lyrical Evangelist.
Corboz—Palmer/Finnilä/Equiluz & Krenn/Van der Meer & Huttenlocher/ Ensemble Vocal de Lausanne/Lausanne Chamber Orchestra.
    Erato STU 71151.
co crv—mainly sustained dl dt2 eNBA? A warmly evocative account in which the solo work and the choruses are particularly fine, but the chorales are also striking of their kind. The opening chorus is perhaps too drastically contrasted, the turbae are too slow to match Equiluz's business-like Gospel narrative.

Latin Church Music

Nos. 233–236: Missae

Rilling-Stuttgart Ensemble.
    Nonesuch HC 73020; UE: Nonesuch 73020.

Nos. 235 & 236 only
Winschermann—Ameling/Finnilä/Altmeyer/Reimer/Westfalische Kantorei/
Deutsche Bachsolisten.
    Philips 6500 031.

No. 232 : Messe H-Moll (B minor Mass)
Harnoncourt—Hansmann & Liyama / Watts / Equiluz / Van Egmond / Vienna
Boys with Chorus Viennensis / Concentus Musicus Vienna.
    Telefunken FK6 35019; US: Telefunken 3635019.
*aa ai ap co d2 dtl no-ds eBr-revised? Although there are many weaknesses,
specially vocally and of ensemble, some of the solo passages are outstandingly
beautiful; also, textures are extremely clear throughout.*
Richter—Stader/Töpper/Haefliger/Fischer-Dieskau & Engen/Munich Bach
Choir/Munich Bach Orchestra.
    DG Archiv 2710 001; US: 3-DG Archiv 2710001.
*co d2 dt2 eBr? Fine choral discipline in timing from the large choir, but poor
instrumental work in sime of the solos.*
Münchinger—Ameling & Minton/Watts/Krenn/Kraus/Vienna Singakademie
Choir/Stuttgart Chamber Orchestra.
    Decca SET 477–8; US: 2-London 1287.
Marriner—Marshall/Baker/Tear/Ramey/Chorus of St. Martin-in-the-Fields,
London/Academy of St. Martin-in-the-Fields, London.
    Philips 9500 413.
*A modern performance especially notable for its good choral discipline;
however, in detail and interpretation, no more consistent than the Vienna
performance, if better than the Munich one; clear recording, if acoustically
short of character.*

No. 243 : Magnificat in D
??—Gampert/Stein/Altmeyer/Nimsgern/Tölz Boys' Choir/Collegium Aureum.
    (110) US: BASF 21584 (also marketed briefly c. 1975 in UK).
afcs afss partly-ai ap co d3 no-dt eNBA?
Münchinger—Ameling & Van Bork/Watts/Krenn/Krause/Vienna Academie-
chor/Stuttgart Chamber Orchestra.
    (10 Decca SXL 6400; US: London 26103.
co d3 dt2 eNBA? Good, balanced modern interpretation.
Jones—Wolf/Watts/Lewis/Hemsley/Geraint Jones Singers London/Geraint
Jones Orchestra London.
    HMV CLP 1128 (mono only).
*ch-'-co d2 no-dt e? A vigorous and colourful account from the Fifties, in
which the restricted sound quality and occasional orchestral indiscretions
failed to spoil a spirited and positive traditional performance.*

No. 243a : Magnificat in E flat with Christmas Interpolations
Rilling—Gundermann/Rütgers/Equiluz/Wenk/Figuralchor, Gedächtniskirche

Stuttgart/Bach-Collegium Stuttgart.
 Turnabout TV 34173-S; US: Turnabout 4173.
ch-&-co none dt2 eBärenreiter—in modern D major throughout. See below.
Gönnenwein—Donath & Bernat-Klein/Finnilä/Schreier/McDaniel/Süddeutscher Madrigalchor/Deutsche Bachsolisten.
 Peerless-Oryx BACH 1183 also Bärenreiter-Musicaphon SDG 610 903; US: CMS/Oryx 1183.
co dl-Dürr dt2 eBärenreiter—in modern D major throughout. Both of the above performances follow the Bärenreiter compromise score, in which the D major version forms the basis of all instrumentation and structure besides the four Interludes; an English ensemble is understood to be preparing an account of the real E flat Magnificat at original pitch with original instruments and structure, following the text of the NBA full score and Bärenreiter study score.

Chronology of Known Performances of Bach's Choral Works

Date	No.	Purpose	Title/Text
PRE-WEIMAR			
c.1707	131	unspecified	*Aus der Tiefen rufe ich*
c.1707	4	Easter Day?	*Christ lag in Todes Banden*
c.1707	524	secular wedding	Hochzeits-Quodlibet (frag.)
c.1707	106	memorial service	*Gottes Zeit*
4. 2.1708	71	Mühlhausen election	*Gott ist mein König*
5. 6.1708	196	wedding	*Der Herr denket an uns*
c.1708	XIX	unspecified	*Meine Seele soll Gott loben* (frag.)
WEIMAR			
1708/9	150	unspecified	*Nach dir, Herr, verlanget mich*
4. 2.1709	XXIV	Mühlhausen election	not reliably preserved
23. 2.1713	208	birthday homage-cantata	*Was mir behagt*

Date	No.	Purpose	Title/Text
c.12.12.1713	?	Halle*	?
1. 1.1707/14	143	New Year's Day	Lobe den Herrn, meine Seele
?	63	Christmas Day	Christen, ätzet diesen Tag
?	21a	?	Ich hatte viel Bekümmernis
?	21b	?	Dass Lamm, das erwürget ist
4. 3.1714	54	Oculi	Widerstehe doch der Sünde
25. 3.1714	182	Palm Sunday	Himmelskönig, sei willkommen
22. 4.1714	12	Jubilate	Weinen, Klagen, Sorgen, Zagen
20. 5.1714	172	Whitsunday	Erschallet, ihr Lieder
17. 6.1714	21	Trinity + 3	Ich hatte viel Bekümmernis
15. 7.1714	?	?	?
12. 8.1714	199	Trinity + 11	Mein Herze schwimmt im Blut
Sept. 1714	?	?	?
Oct. 1714	?	?	?
Nov. 1714	?	?	?
2.12.1714	61	1st Advent	Nun komm, der Heiden Heiland
30.12.1714	152	Christmas + 1	Tritt auf die Glaubensbahn
Jan. 1715?	?	?	?
by 24.2.1715	18	Sexagesima	Gleichwie der Regen
24. 3.1715	80a	Oculi	Alles, was von Gott geboren
21. 4.1715	31	Easter Day	Der Himmel lacht!
19. 5.1715?	?	Cantate	Leb ich oder leb ich nicht
16. 6.1715	165	Trinity Sunday	O heilges Geist- und Wasserbad
14. 7.1715	185	Trinity + 4	Barmherziges Herze
Aug. 1715	?	?	?
Sept. 1715	?	?	?
6.10.1715	161	Trinity + 16	Komm, du süsse Todesstunde
3.11.1715	162	Trinity + 20	Ach! ich sehe
24.11.1715	163	Trinity + 23	Nur jedem das Seine
22.12.1715	132	4th Advent	Bereitet die Wege
19. 1.1716	155	Epiphany + 2	Mein Gott, wie lang, ach lange
Feb. 1716	?	?	?
Mar. 1716	?	?	?
Apr. 1716	?	?	?
May 1716	?	?	?
Jun. 1716	?	?	?
Jul. 1716	?	?	?
Aug. 1716	?	?	?
Sept. 1716	?	?	?
Oct. 1716	?	?	?
Nov. 1716	?	?	?

---

* Bach was "obliged to compose and perform a particular piece" in Halle.

Date	No.	Purpose	Title/Text
6.12.1716	70a	2nd Advent	*Wachet! betet! betet! wachet!*
13.12.1716	186a	3rd Advent	*Ärgre dich, o Seele, nicht*
20.12.1716	147a	4th Advent	*Herz und Mund und Tat und Leben*
25.12.1716?	63*	Christmas Day	*Christen, ätzet diesen Tag*

The following pieces performed later in Leipzig may have origins in lost Weimar compositions: Nos. 72, 154, 164?, 158, 168, Mvt. 181/5?, Mvt. 23/4. Pre-23, 4.

CÖTHEN

Date	No.	Purpose	Title/Text
10.12.1717	?	birthday homage	?
1. 1.1718	?	New Year	?
10.12.1718	66a	birthday homage	*Der Himmel dacht'*
10.12.1718	XIII	as above in Jakobikirche	*Loben den Herrn alle*
1. 1.1719	134a	New Year	*Die Zeit, die Tag und Jahre macht*
10.12.1719	?	birthday homage	*So bringt, Durchlauchtigster*
1. 1.1720	IX	New Year	*Dich loben die lieblichen Strahlen der Sonne*
10.12.1720	XII	birthday homage	*Heut ist gewiss ein guter Tag*
1. 1.1721	?	New Year	?
			?
?. 8.1721	?	homage-cantata	?
10.12.1721	?	birthday homage	?
Dec. 1721/ Jan. 1722	?	wedding	
9. 8.1722	XXII	birthday homage	?
10.12.1722	?	birthday homage	?
1. 1.1723	XXIII	New Year	?

The following cantatas or sections of cantatas have certain or possible origins in the Cöthen period: Nos. 202?, XVIII?, 173a, 184a, 194a, 32, 145/1 & 3, 181/5.

LEIPZIG

Date	No.	Purpose	Title/Text
7. 2.1723	22	Estomihi/Probestück	*Jesus nahm zu sich die Zwölfe*

---

* A second performance, but possibly the first that was very close to the version we know today.

Date	No.	Purpose	Title/Text
7. 2.1723	23, 1–3	after sermon?	Du wahrer Gott und Davids Sohn
16. 5.1723	59	Whitsunday	Wer mich liebet, der wird mein Wort halten
16. 5.1723	237?	festive Sanctus	Sanctus in C
23. 5.1723?	237	Trinity Sunday	Sanctus in C

JAHRGANG I

Date	No.	Purpose	Title/Text
30. 5.1723	75	Trinity + 1	Die Elenden sollen essen
6. 6.1723	76	Trinity + 2	Die Himmel erzählen die Ehre Gottes
9. 6.1723?	XXVI	University tribute	Murmelt nur, ihr heiten Bäche
13. 6.1723	21	Trinity + 3	Ich hatte viel Bekümmernis
20. 6.1723	24	Trinity + 4	Ein ungefärbt Gemüte
20. 6.1723	185	after sermon?	Barmherziges Herze der ewigen Liebe
24. 6.1723	185	St. John Baptist	Ihr Menschen, rühmet Gottes Liebe
27. 6.1723	?	Trinity + 5	?
2. 7.1723	147	Feast of the Visitation	Herz und Mund und Tat und Leben
4. 7.1723	?	Trinity + 6	?
11. 7.1723	186	Trinity + 7	Ärgre dich, o Seele, nicht
18. 7.1723	136	Trinity + 8	Erforsche mich, Gott, und erfahre mein Herz
18. 7.1723	227	memorial service	Motet: Jesu, meine Freude
25. 7.1723	105	Trinity + 9	Herr, gehe nicht ins Gericht
1. 8.1723	46	Trinity + 10	Schauet doch und sehet
8. 8.1723	179	Trinity + 11	Siehe zu, dass deine Gottesfurcht
8. 8.1723	199	after sermon?	Mein Herze schwimmt im Blut
9. 8.1723	Anh. 20	University homage ode	Lateinische Ode (lost)
15. 8.1723	69a	Trinity + 12	Lobe den Herrn, meine Seele
22. 8.1723	77	Trinity + 13	Du sollt Gott, deinen Herren lieben
29. 8.1723	25	Trinity + 14	Es ist nichts Gesundes
30. 8.1723	119	civic election	Preise, Jerusalem, den Herrn
5. 9.1723	138	Trinity + 15	Warum betrübst du dich, mein Herz
12. 9.1723	95	Trinity + 16	Christus, der ist mein Leben
19. 9.1723	148?	Trinity + 17	Bringet dem Herrn Ehre seines Namens
26. 9.1723	?	Trinity + 18	?
29. 9.1723	?	Feast of St. Michael	?
3.10.1723	48	Trinity + 19	Ich elender Mensch, wer wird mich erlösen
10.10.1723	162	Trinity + 20	Ach! ich sehe

Date	No.	Purpose	Title/Text
17.10.1723	109	Trinity + 21	*Ich glaube, lieber Herr*
24.10.1723	89	Trinity + 22	*Was soll ich aus dir machen, Ephraim?*
31.10.1723	163?	Trinity + 23/Reformation commemoration	*Nur jedem das Seine(?)*
31.10.1723	?	University Reformation commemoration	?
2.11.1723	194	Dedication of Church and Organ in Störmthal	*Hochsterwünschtes Freudenfest*
7.11.1723	60	Trinity + 24	*Dialogus: O Ewigkeit, du Donnerwort*
14.11.1723	90	Trinity + 25	*Es reisset euch ein schrecklich Ende*
21.11.1723	70	Trinity + 26	*Wachet! betet!*
28.11.1723	61	Advent 1	*Nun komm der Heiden Heiland*
25.12.1723	63	Christmas Day	*Christen, ätzet diesen Tag.*
25.12.1723	238*	festive Sanctus	*Sanctus in D*
25.12.1723	?	University observance	?
25.12.1723	243a	*Abendmahl* (Lutheran Vespers)	*Magnificat*
26.12.1723	40	2nd Day Christmas/Feast of St. John	*Dazu ist erschienen der Sohn Gottes*
27.12.1723	64	2nd Day Christmas/Feast of St. John	*Sehet, welch eine Liebe*
1. 1.1724	190	New Year	*Singet dem Herrn ein neues Lied*
2. 1.1724	153	Sunday after New Year	*Schau, lieber Gott, wie meine Feind*
6. 1.1724	65	Epiphany	*Sie werden aus Saba alle kommen*
9. 1.1724	154	Epiphany + 1	*Mein liebster Jesu ist verloren*
16. 1.1724	155	Epiphany + 2	*Mein Gott, wie lang, ach lange?*
23. 1.1724	73	Epiphany + 3	*Herr, wie du willt, so schicks mit mir*
30. 1.1724	81	Epiphany + 4	*Jesus schläft, was soll ich hoffen?*
2. 2.1724	83	Feast of the Purification	*Erfreute Zeit in neuen Bunde*
6. 2.1724	144	Septuagesima	*Nimm, was dein ist, und gehe hin*
13. 2.1724	181	Sexagesima	*Leichtgesinnte Flattergeister*
20. 2.1724	22	Estomihi	*Jesus nahm zu sich die Zwölfe*
25. 3.1724	uncl. 1*	Feast of the Annunciation	*Siehe, ein Jungfrau ist schwanger*
7. 4.1724	245	Good Friday Passion Music	*Johannespassion*

* = unclassified item.

Date	No.	Purpose	Title/Text
9. 4.1724	31	Easter Day	Der Himmel lacht, die Erde jubilieret
9. 4.1724	4	University Easter Service	Christ lag in Todes Banden (excerpts?)
10. 4.1724	66	2nd Day Easter	Erfreut euch, ihr Herzen
11. 4.1724	134	3rd Day Easter	Ein Herz, das seinen Jesum lebend weiss
16. 4.1724	67	Quasimodogeniti	Halt in Gedächtnis Jesum Christ
23. 4.1724	104	Misericordias domini	Du Hirte Israel, höre
30. 4.1724	12	Jubilate	Weinen, Klagen, Sorgen, Zagen
7. 5.1724	166	Cantate	Wo gehest du hin?
14. 5.1724	86	Rogate	Wahrlich, wahrlich, ich sage euch
18. 5.1724	37	Ascension Day	Wer da gläubet und getauft wird
21. 5.1724	44	Exaudi	Sie werden euch in den Bann tun (first setting)
28. 5.1724	59	Whitsunday	Erschallet, ihr Lieder
28. 5.1724	59	University Whitsun Service	Wer mich liebet, der wird mein Wort halten
29. 5.1724	173	2nd Day Whitsun	Erhöhtes Fleisch und Blut
30. 5.1724	?	3rd Day Whitsun	Erwünschtes Freudenlicht
4. 6.1724	194	Trinity Sunday	Höchsterwünschtes Freudenfest
4. 6.1724	165?	University service?	O heilges Geist
?	Pez 1 (=BWV Anh. 24)	c. Whitsun 1724	Johann Christoph Pez: Missa in A minor*

JAHRGANG II

Date	No.	Purpose	Title/Text
11. 6.1724	20	Trinity +1	O Ewigkeit, du Donnerwort (second setting)
18. 6.1724	2	Trinity +2	Ach Gott, vom Himmel sieh darein
24. 6.1724	7	St. John Baptist	Christ unser Herr zum Jordan kam
25. 6.1724	135	Trinity +3	Ach Herr, mich armen Sünder
2. 7.1724	10	Feast of the Visitation/ Trinity +4	Meine Seel erhebt den Herren
9. 7.1724	93	Trinity +5	Wer nur den lieben Gott lässt walten
16. 7.1724	?	Trinity +6	?

---

* Information kindly supplied by Dr. Alfred Dürr in a private communication to the author (of 1969); reproduced here with many thanks. Such works—by other composers but re-copied by Bach (see main text)—have been included in this chronology since Bach clearly considered them as adoptive works.

Date	No.	Purpose	Title/Text
23. 7.1724	107	Trinity+7	*Was willst du dich betrüben*
30. 7.1724	178	Trinity+8	*Wo Gott der Herr nicht bei uns hält*
6. 8.1724	94	Trinity+9	*Was frag ich nach der Welt*
13. 8.1724	101	Trinity+10	*Nimm von uns, Herr, du treuer Gott*
20. 8.1724	113	Trinity+11	*Herr Jesu Christ, du höchstes Gut*
27. 8.1724	?	Trinity+12	?
28. 8.1724	?	civic election	?
3. 9.1724	33	Trinity+13	*Allein zu dir, Herr Jesu Christ*
10. 9.1724	78	Trinity+14	*Jesu, der du meine Seele*
17. 9.1724	99	Trinity+15	*Was Gott tut, das ist wohlgetan*
24. 9.1724	8	Trinity+16	*Liebster Gott, wenn werd ich sterben*
29. 9.1724	130	St. Michael	*Herr Gott, dich loben alle wir*
1.10.1724	114	Trinity+17	*Ach, lieben Christen, seid getrost*
8.10.1724	96	Trinity+18	*Herr Christ, der einge Gottessohn*
15.10.1724	5	Trinity+19	*Wo soll ich fliehen hin*
22.10.1724	180	Trinity+20	*Schmücke dich, o liebe Seele*
29.10.1724	38	Trinity+21	*Aus tiefer Not schrei ich zu dir*
31.10.1724	80?	Reformation commemoration	*Ein feste Burg ist unser Gott*
31.10.1724	76, Pt.II	University Reformation commemoration	*Gott segne noch die treue Schar*
5.11.1724	115	Trinity+22	*Mache dich, mein Geist, bereit*
12.11.1724	139	Trinity+23	*Wohl dem, der sich auf seinen Gott*
19.11.1724	26	Trinity+24	*Ach wie flüchtig, ach wie nichtig*
26.11.1724	116	Trinity+25	*Du Friedefürst, Herr Jesu Christ*
3.12.1724	62	1st Advent	*Nun komm der Heiden Heiland* (second setting)
25.12.1724	91	Christmas Day	*Gelobet seist du, Jesu Christ*
25.12.1724	232^III	Festive Sanctus	*Sanctus in D*
25.12.1724	?	University Christmas Service	?
26.12.1724	121	2nd Day Christmas/ Feast of St. Stephen	*Christum wir sollen loben schon*
27.12.1724	133	3rd Day Christmas/ Feast of St. John	*Ich freue mich in dir*
31.12.1724	122	Sunday after Christmas	*Das neugeborne Kindelein*
1. 1.1725	41	New Year	*Jesu, nun sei gepreiset*

Date	No.	Purpose	Title/Text
6. 1.1725	123	Epiphany	Liebster Immanuel, Herzog der Frommen
7. 1.1725	124	Epiphany + 1	Meinem Jesum lass ich nicht
14. 1.1725	3	Epiphany + 2	Ach Gott, wie manches Herzeleid
21. 1.1725	111	Epiphany + 3	Was mein Gott will, das g'scheh allzeit
28. 1.1725	92	Septuagesima	Ich hab in Gottes Herz und Sinn
2. 2.1725	125	Feast of the Purification	Mit Fried und Freud ich fahr dahin
4. 2.1725	126	Sexagesima	Erhalt uns, Herr, bei deinem Wort
11. 2.1725	127	Estomihi	Herr Jesu Christ, wahr' Mensch und Gott
12. 2.1725	XIV	wedding	Sein Segen fliesst daher wie ein Strom
23. 2.1725	249a	birthday homage	Entfliehet, verschwindet, entweichet, ihr Sorgen
25. 3.1725	1	Palm Sunday/Feast of the Annunciation	Wie schön leuchtet der Morgenstern
30. 3.1725	245	Good Friday Passion Music	Johannespassion
1. 4.1725	249	Easter Day University Easter	Oster-Oratorium
1. 4.1725	?	Service	?
2. 4.1725	6	2nd Day Easter	Bleib bei uns, denn es will Abend werden
3. 4.1725	4?	3rd Day Easter	Christ lag in Todes Banden(?)
8. 4.1725	42	Quasimodogeniti	Am Abend der desselbigen Sabbats
15. 4.1725	85	Misericordias domini	Ich bin ein guter Hirt
22. 4.1725	103	Jubilate	Ihr werdet weinen und heulen
29. 4.1725	108	Cantate	Es ist euch gut, dass ich hingehe
6. 5.1725	87	Rogate	Bisher habt ihr nichts gebeten in meinem Namen
10. 5.1725	128	Ascension Day	Auf Christi Himmelfahrt allein
13. 5.1725	183	Exaudi	Sie werden euch in den Bann tun (second setting)
20. 5.1725	74	Whitsunday	Wer mich liebet, der wird mein Wort halten
20. 5.1725	?	University Whitsun Service	?
21. 5.1725	68	2nd Day Whitsun	Also hat Gott die Welt geliebt
22. 5.1725	175	3rd Day Whitsun	Er rufet seinen Schafen mit Namen

Date	No.	Purpose	Title/Text
27. 5.1725	176	Trinity Sunday	*Es ist ein trotzig verzagt Ding*
Apr./May 1725?	36c	birthday	*Schwingt freudig euch empor*

Jahrgang II properly ends here. For the period of June–November 1725 (i.e. before the start of Jahrgang III) Bach apparently composed to texts which he had received, but not set, earlier in his career.

Date	No.	Purpose	Title/Text
3. 6.1725	?	Trinity +1	?
10. 6.1725	76, Part II?	Trinity +2	*Gott segne noch die treue Schar*
17. 6.1725	177?	Trinity +3	*Ich ruf zu dir, Herr Jesu Christ*
24. 6.1725	uncl. 2	St. John Baptist/ Trinity +4	*Gelobet sey der Herr, der Gott Israel*
1. 7.1725	uncl. 3	Trinity +5	*Der Seegen des Herrn machet reich ohne Mühe*
2. 6.1725	uncl. 4	Feast of the Visitation	*Meine Seele erhebt den Herrn* [Neumeister]
8. 7.1725	uncl. 5	Trinity +6	*Wer sich rächet, am dem wird*
15. 7.1725	?	Trinity +7	?
22. 7.1725	?	Trinity +8	?
29. 7.1725	168	Trinity +9	*Tue Rechnung! Donnerwort*
3. 8.1725	205	University homage (dramma per musica)	*Zereisset, zersprenget, zertrümmert die Gruft*
5. 8.1725	?	Trinity +10	?
12. 8.1725	?	Trinity +11	?
19. 8.1725	137	Trinity +12	*Lobe den Herren, den mächtigen König der Ehren*
26. 8.1725	164	Trinity +13	*Ihr, die ihr euch von Christo nennet*
27. 8.1725	?	civic election	?
2. 9.1725	?	Trinity +14	?
9. 9.1725	?	Trinity +15	?
16. 9.1725	?	Trinity +16	?
23. 9.1725	?	Trinity +17	?
29. 9.1725	?	St. Michael	?
30. 9.1725	?	Trinity +18	?
7.10.1725	?	Trinity +19	?
14.10.1725	?	Trinity +20	?
21.10.1725	?	Trinity +21	?
28.10.1725	?	Trinity +22	?
31.10.1725	79	Reformation Commemoration	*Gott der Herr ist Sonn und Schild*
4.11.1725	?	Trinity +23	?
11.11.1725	?	Trinity +24	?

Date	No.	Purpose	Title/Text
18.11.1725	?	Trinity + 25	?
25.11.1725	?	Trinity + 26	?
27.11.1725	34a	Nuptial Mass	O ewiges Feuer, O Ursprung der Liebe

JAHRGANG III

Date	No.	Purpose	Title/Text
2.12.1725	?	1st Advent	?
25.12.1725	110	Christmas Day	Unser Mund sei voll Lachens
25.12.1725	?	festive Sanctus	?
25.12.1725	?	University Service	?
26.12.1725	57	2nd Day Christmas/ St. Stephen	Dialogus: Selig ist der Mann
27.12.1725	151	3rd Day Christmas/ St. John	Süsser Trost, mein Jesus kömmt
30.12.1725	28	Sunday after Christmas	Gottlob! nun geht das Jahr zu Ende
1. 1.1726	16	New Year	Herr Gott, dich loben wir
6. 1.1726	uncl. 6 or uncl. 7?	Epiphany	either Ich freue mich in Herren or Hier ist mein Herz, geliebter Jesu?
13. 1.1726	32	Epiphany + 1	Dialogus: Liebster Jesu, mein Verlangen
20. 1.1726	13	Epiphany + 2	Meine Seufzer, meine Tränen
27. 1.1726	72	Epiphany + 3	Alles nur nach Gottes Willen
3. 3.1726	JLB	Feast of the Purification	Mache dich auff, wered Licht
3. 2.1726	JLB 1	Epiphany + 4	Gott ist unsere Zuversicht
10. 2.1726	JLB 2	Epiphany + 5	Der Gottlösen Arbeit wird fehlen
17. 2.1726	JLB 3	Septuagesima	Darum will ich auch erwehlen
24. 2.1726	JLB 4	Sexagesima	Darum säet euch Gerechtig-keit
3. 3.1726	JLB 5	Estomihi	Ja, mir hastu Arbeit gemacht
6. 3.1726	I	wedding	Auf! süss entzückende Gewalt
19. 4.1726	–	Good Friday Passion Music	Reinhard Keiser: Markus-passion
21. 4.1726	15	Easter Day	Johann Ludwig Bach: Denn du wirst meine Seele nicht in der Hölle lassen
22. 4.1726	JLB 10	2nd Day Easter	Er ist aus der Angst
23. 4.1726	JLB 11	3rd Day Easter	Er machet uns legendig
28. 4.1726	JLB 6	Quasimodogeniti	Wie lieblich sind aus den Berg
5. 5.1726	JLB 12	Misericordias domini	Und ich will . . . erwecken
12. 5.1726	146(?)	Jubilate	Wir müssen durch . . . eingehen
19. 5.1726	JLB 14	Cantate	Die Weissheit kommt

Date	No.	Purpose	Title/Text
26. 5.1726	?	Rogate	?
30. 5.1726	43	Ascension Day	*Gott fähret auf mit Jauchzen*
2. 6.1726	?	Exaudi	?
9. 6.1726	?	Whitsunday	?
9. 6.1726	?	other music	?
10. 6.1726	?	2nd Day Whitsun	?
11. 6.1726	?	3rd Day Whitsun	?
16. 6.1726	129 and/or 194	Trinity Sunday	*Gelobet sei der Herr, mein Gott/Höchsterwünschtes Freudenfest*
23. 6.1726	39	Trinity+1	*Brich dem Hungrigen dein Brot*
24. 6.1726	JLB 17	St. John Baptist	*Siehe, ich will meinen Engel senden*
30. 6.1726	?	Trinity+2	?
2. 7.1726	JLB 13	Feast of the Visitation	*Der Herr wird . . . erschaffen*
7. 7.1726	?	Trinity+3	?
14. 7.1726	?	Trinity+4	?
21. 7.1726	88	Trinity+5	*Siehe, ich will viel Fischer aussenden*
28. 7.1726	170	Trinity+6	*Vergnügte Ruh, beliebte Seelenlust*
28. 7.1726	JLB 7	Trinity+6	*Ich will meinen Geist in euch geben*
4. 8.1726	187	Trinity+7	*Es wartet alles auf dich*
11. 8.1726	45	Trinity+8	*Es ist dir gesagt, Mensch, was gut ist*
18. 8.1726	?	Trinity+9	?
25. 8.1726	102	Trinity+10	*Herr, deine Augen sehen nach dem Glauben!*
25. 8.1726	249b	birthday homage	*Verjaget, zerstreuet, zerrüttet, ihr Sterne*
26. 8.1726	193?	civic election celebrations	*Ihr Tore (Pforten) zu Zion*
1. 9.1726	JLB 15	Trinity+11	*Durch sein Erkändtniss*
8. 9.1726	35	Trinity+12	*Geist und Seele wird verwirret*
15. 9.1726	JLB 16	Trinity+13	*Ich aber ging für dir über*
22. 9.1726	17	Trinity+14	*Wer Dank opfert, der preiset mich*
29. 9.1726	19	St. Michael/Trinity+15	*Es erhub sich ein Streit*
6.10.1726	27	Trinity+16	*Wer weiss, wie nahe mir mein Ende*
13.10.1726	47	Trinity+17	*Wer sich selbst erhöhet, der soll erniedriget werden*
20.10.1726	169	Trinity+18	*Gott soll allein mein Herze haben*
27.10.1726	56	Trinity+19	*Ich will den Kreuzstab gerne tragen*
31.10.1726	?	Reformation Commemoration	?

Date	No.	Purpose	Title/Text
3.11.1726	49	Trinity + 20	Dialogus: *Ich geh und suche mit Verlangen*
10.11.1726	98	Trinity + 21	*Was Gott tut, das ist wohlgetan* (second setting)
17.11.1726	55	Trinity + 22	*Ich armer Mensch, ich Sündenknecht*
24.11.1726	52	Trinity + 23	*Falsche Welt, dir trau ich nicht*
30.11.1726	36a	birthday homage	*Steigt freudig in die Luft*

LEIPZIG MIDDLE YEARS

Date	No.	Purpose	Title/Text
11.12.1726	207	gratulatory cantata	Dramma per musica: *Vereinigte Zwietracht der wechs'nden Saitel*
1. 1.1727?	225	New Year	Motet: *Singet dem Herrn ein neues Lied*
5. 1.1727	58	Sunday after New Year	Dialogus: *Ach Gott, wie manches Herzeleid*
2. 2.1727	82	Feast of Purification	*Ich habe genung*
2. 2.1727	83	as above	*Erfreute Zeit im neuen Bunde*
6. 2.1727	157	Funeral Service	*Ich lasse dich nicht, du segnest mich denn!*
9. 2.1727	84	Septuagesima	*Ich bin vergnügt mit meinem Glucke*
11. 4.1727	Pre-244, 65	Good Friday Passion Music	*Mache dich, mein Herze, rein, &c.*
12. 5.1727	X	birthday homage	*Entfernet euch, ihr heitern Sterne*
12. 5.1727?	225	birthday homage	Motet: *Singet dem Herrn ein neues Lied*
3. 8.1727	193a	nameday homage	Dramma per musica: *Ihr Häuser des Himmels*
25. 8.1727	XVIa	civic election	*Wünschet Jerusalem Glück*
31. 8.1727	69a	Trinity + 12	*Lobe den Herrn, meine Seele*
17.10.1727	198*	Ode of Mourning	Trauer-Ode: *Lass, Furstin, lass noch einen Strahl*
1726/27	204	unknown festive purpose	*Ich bin in mir vergnügt*
5. 2.1728	216	wedding	*Vergnügte Pleissenstadt*
c.1728	182	Feast of the Annunciation	*Himmelskönig, sei willkommen*
c.1728	173	2nd Day Whitsun	*Erhöhtes Fleisch und Blut*
c.1728	188	Trinity + 21	*Ich habe meine Zuversicht*
c.1728	197a	Christmas Day	*Ehre sei Gott in der Höhe*
1. 1.1729?	171	New Year	*Gott, wie dein Name, so ist auch dein Ruhm*

---

* From September 7, 1727 (Trinity + 13) until Christmas, Leipzig was affected by the official period of mourning at the death of Queen Christine Ebernardine. This was the only work performed during the period.

Date	No.	Purpose	Title/Text
c.1729	155?	Epiphany +1	*Mein Gott, wie lang, ach lange*
c.1729	156	Epiphany +3	*Ich steh mit einem Fuss im Grabe*
c.1729	159	Estomihi	*Sehet! wir gehn hinauf gen Jerusalem*
24. 3.1729	244a	music of mourning	*Klagt, Kinder, klagt es aller Welt*
15. 4.1729?	244*	Good Friday Passion Music	*Matthäuspassion*
18. 4.1729	VI	2nd Day Easter	*Ich bin ein Pilgrim auf der Welt*
19. 4.1729	145	3rd Day Easter	*Ich lebe, mein Herze, zu deinem Ergötzen*
c.1728	174	2nd Day Whitsun	*Ich liebe den Höchsten von ganzem Gemüte*
1728/29	120	council election	*Gott, man lobet dich in der Stille*
1728/29	149	Feast of St. Michael (29.9)	*Man singet mit Freuden*
25.12.1729?	63	Christmas Day	*Christen, ätzet diesen Tag*
1729	120a	wedding	*Herr Gott, Beherrscher aller Dinge*
1729	250	wedding	*Was Gott tut, das ist*
1729	251	wedding	*Sei Lob und Ehr'*
1729	252	wedding	*Nun danket alle Gott*
after Easter	201	concert performance?	Dramma per musica: *Der Streit zwischen Phoebus*
after Easter	209	concert performance?	*Non sa che sia dolore*
7. 4.1730?	"246"†	Good Friday Passion Music	*Lucaspassion* (not by Bach)
23. 5.1730?	175	3rd Day Whitsun	*Er rufet seinen Schafen mit Namen*
25. 6.1730	190a	Augsburg Confession Anniversary	*Singet dem Herrn ein neues Lied*
26. 6.1730	120b	Anniversary Festival 2nd Day	*Gott, man lobet dich in der Stille*
27. 6.1730	XVIb	Anniversary Festival 3rd Day	*Wünschet Jerusalem Glück*
25. 8.1730	XI	civic election	*Gott, gib dein Gerichte dem Könige*
31.10.1730	80?	Reformation Commemoration	*Ein feste Burg ist unser Gott*
31.10.1730	192?	Reformation Commemoration	*Nun danket alle Gott*

* The first version of the work, with differences from the version usually heard today.
† The possibility that this work may have been that performed—with Bach's permission—in the Leipzig Neukirche on Good Friday, 1729, under Christoph Gottlieb Fröber, and that it was, in fact, by Fröber, has yet to be adequately investigated.

Date	No.	Purpose	Title/Text
c.1730	51	?	Jauchzet Gott in allen Landen!
2. 2.1731?*	82	Feast of the Purification	Ich habe genung
23. 3.1731	247	Good Friday Passion Music	Markuspassion
25. 3.1731	31	Easter Day	Der Himmel lacht!
26. 3.1731	66	2nd Day Easter	Dialogus: Erfreut euch ihr Herzen
27. 3.1731	134	3rd Day Easter	Ein Herz, das seinen Jesum lebend weiss
1. 4.1731	42	Quasimodogeniti	Am Abend aber desselbigen Sabbats
8. 4.1731	112†	Misericordias domini	Der Herr ist mein getreuer Hirt
15. 4.1731	103	Jubilate	Ihr werdet weinen und heulen
3. 5.1731	37	Ascension Day	Wer da gläubet und getauft wird
13. 5.17331	172	Whitsunday	Erschallet, ihr Lieder
14. 5.1731	173	2nd Day Whitsun	Erhöhte Fleisch und Blut
15. 5.1731	184	3rd Day Whitsun	Erwünschtes Freudenlicht
20. 5.1731	194	Trinity Sunday	Hochsterwünschtes Freudenfest
25. 8.1731	VII	1st Advent	Schwingt freudich euch empor
27. 8.1731	29	Trinity+27	Wachet auf, ruft uns die Stimme
18.11.1731	70	Trinity+26	Wachet! betet! betet! wachet!
25.11.1731	140	civic election	Wir danken dir, Gott
2.12.1731	36	birthday homage	So kämpfet nur, ihr muntern Töne
1728/31	117	for general use	Sei Lob und Ehr dem höchsten Gut
1728/31	158	probably 3rd Day Easter?	Der Friede sei mit dir
5. 6.1732	III	dedication of Thomas-schule building	Froher Tag, verlangte Stunden
6. 7.1732	177	Trinity+4	Ich ruf zu dir, Herr Jesu Christ
3. 8.1732	II	nameday homage	Es lebe der König, der Vater im Lande
21. 4.1732(?)	232,1	Service of Allegiance	Missa: Kyrie and Gloria (only)
1732/3	93	Trinity+5	Wer nur den lieben Gott
3. 8.1733	IV	nameday homage	Frohes Volk, vergnügte Sachsen
5. 9.1733	213	birthday homage	Hercules auf dem Scheidewege

---

* Or possibly 1730. Perhaps performed on both years, or heard as domestic sacred music in Bach's home.

† Possibly performed earlier in 1729 or in both years.

Date	No.	Purpose	Title/Text
8.12.1733	214	birthday homage	Dramma per musica: *Tönet, ihr Pauken! Erschallet, Trompeten*
1733/4	58	Sunday after New Year	Dialogus: *Ach Gott, wie manches Herzeleid*
19. 2.1734	205a	coronation*	Dramma per musica: *Blast Lärmen, ihr Feinde! verstärket die Macht*
5.10.174	215	homage music	Dramma per musica: *Preise dein Glücke, gesegnetes Sachsen*
24.10.1734?	96	Trinity + 18	*Herr Christ, der einge Gottessohn*
21.11.1734	VIII	celebratory music	*Thomana sass annoch betrübt*
by Advent 1734†	97	unspecified	*In allen meinen Taten*
28.11.1734	GPTI§	1st Sunday in Advent	Telemann: *Machet die Tore weit*
25.12.1734	248I	Christmas Day	*Weihnachts-Oratorium, I: Jauchzet, frohlocket, auf, preiset der Tage*
26.12.1734	248II	Feast of St. Stephen/ 2nd Day of Christmas	*Weihnachts–Oratorium II: Und es waren Hirten in derselben Gegend*
27.12.1734	248III	Feast of St. John/ 3rd Day of Christmas	*Weihnachts–Oratorium III: Herrscher des Himmels, erhöre das Lallen*
1. 1.1735	248IV	Feast of the Circumcision/ New Year	*Weihnachts–Oratorium IV: Fallt mit Danken, fallt mit Loben*
2. 1.1735	248V	Sunday after New Year	*Weihnachts–Oratorium V: Ehre sei dir, Gott, gesungen*
6. 1.1735	248VI	Epiphany Sunday	*Weihnachts-Oratorium VI: Herr, wenn die stolzen Feinde schnauben*
by 6.1.1735	248a	sacred piece	*?*
30. 1.1735	14	Epiphany + 4	*Wär Gott nicht mit uns diese Zeit*
2. 2.1735	82a	Feast of the Purification	*Ich habe genung* (E minor version)
11. 4.1735?	66	2nd Day Easter	Dialogus: *Erfreut euch, ihr Herzen*
19. 5.1735	11	Ascension Day	*Himmelfahrts-Oratorium: Lobet Gott in seinen Reichen*

---

*The coronation occurred on January 17, but Bach's homage music was not performed until over a month later.

†The autograph is dated "1734," but parts, at least, of the cantata may be older.

§ =Georg Phillipp Telemann, work cited in Index of Works under his name no. 1.

Date	No.	Purpose	Title/Text
3. 8.1735	207a	nameday homage	Dramma per musica: *Auf, schmetternde Töne der muntern Trompeten*

THE LATE YEARS

Date	No.	Purpose	Title/Text
30. 3.1736?	244	Good Friday Passion Music	*Matthäuspassion*
7.10.1736	206	birthday	*Schleicht, spielende Wellen*
2.12.1736?	62	Advent 1	*Nun kom* (II)
28. 9.1737	30a	homage performance	*Angenehmes Wiederau*
28. 4.1738	XV	homage serenade	*Willkommen! Ihr herrschenden Götter der Erden!*
31. 8.1739	29	council election	*Wir danken dir, Gott, wir danken dir*
3. 8.1740	208a or 206	nameday homage	*Was mir behagt, ist nur die muntre Jagd/Schleicht, spielende Wellen*
29. 8.1740	V	council election	*Herrscher des Himmels*
28. 8.1741	XVIa	council election celebrations	*Wünschet Jerusalem Glück*
3. 4.1742	210?	Marriage: Graff/Bose	*O holder Tag*
3. 8.1742	208a or 206	nameday homage	*Was mir behagt/Schleicht, spielende Wellen*
30. 8.1742	212	homage performance	*Mer hahn en neue Oberkeet*
25. 8.1749	29	council election	*Wir danken dir, Gott, wir danken dir*

During the years between about 1735 and 1750, a number of Bach performances took place which are less exactly datable than those listed above, yet roughly attributable to specified periods. They are possibly best grouped in two collections.

1. Works performed between about 1735 and about 1745:

early 1740s	200	Feast of the Purification (2.2.)?	*Bekennen will ich* (fragment)
first half of 1740s	34	Whitsunday	*O ewiges Feuer*
c. 1738–c. 1742	30	St. John Baptist (24.6)	*Freue dich, erlöste Schar*
first half of 1740s	191	Christmas Day (25.12)	*Gloria in excelsis Deo*
c. 1736/37	154	Epiphany + 1	*Mein liebster Jesus ist verloten*
c. 1736/37	118	funeral	*O Jesus Christ, meins Lebens Licht* (I)
by c. 1742	197	wedding	*Gott ist unsre Zuversicht*

Date	No.	Purpose	Title/Text
there seem to have been three revisions between c. 1738 and c. 1741	210	wedding	*O holder Tag*
early in period	240	Sanctus (festive)	Sanctus in G

2. Works performed between about 1742 + and about 1749 :

in Bach's last years (say after 1746/47)	245	Good Friday Passion Music	*Johannespassion IV*
in Bach's last years	118	funeral/burial	*O Jesu Christ . . .* II
in Bach's last years	210	wedding	*O holder Tag*
of vague date, and possibly earlier than 1742, but the second was revised by Bach in his last years		uncertain	Mass (Missa) in G
	234	uncertain	Mass (Missa) in A
c. 1742?	1045	?	Textless fragment
in Bach's last years	232[II-IV]	?	Final portions of the B Minor Mass

Rather more slender evidence indicates that the following works were performed after about 1735 but within Bach's lifetime :

	91	Christmas Day	*Gelobet seist du*
	64	3rd Day Christmas	*Singet dem Herrn*
later (after c. 1744	190	New Year	*Sehet, welch eine Liebe*
from 1740s?	16	New Year	*Herr Gott, dich loben*
after 1738, by c. 1741	82	Feast of Purification	*Ich habe genung*
	181	Sexagesima	*Leichtgesinnte Flattergeister*
late?	246	Good Friday Passion Music	*Lukaspassion*
late	249	Easter Day	*Oster-Oratorium: Kommt, eilet*
	42	Quasimodogeniti	*Am abend, aber*
	175	3rd Day Whitsun	*Er rufet seinen Schafen*

Date	No.	Purpose	Title/Text
late	129	Trinity Sunday	*Gelobet sei der Herr*
late	10	Feast of Visitation	*Mein Seel erhebt*
	177	Trinity +4	*Ich ruf zu dir*
late?	170	Trinity +6	*Vergnügte Ruh*
late	187	Trinity +7	*Es wartet alles*
	94	Trinity +9	*Was frag ich*
	101	Trinity +10	*Nimm von uns, Herr*
	102	Trinity +10	*Herr, deine Augen sehen*
mid-1740s?	8 in D	Trinity +16	*Liebster Gott, wenn*
(with organ obbl.)	27	Trinity +16	*Wer weiss, wie nahe mir*
	47	Trinity +17	*Wer sich selbst*
mid-1740s?	96	Trinity +18	*Herr Christ, der einge*
mid-1740s	139	Trinity +23	*Wohl dem*
by c. 1742?	97	various	*In allen meinen Taten*
after c. 1742?	97	various	*In allen meinen Taten*
latish?	100	various	*Was Gott tut*
from Bach's last years	69	council election	*Lobe den Herrn*

During the last ten years or so of his activities, Bach carried out a number of revisions of earlier works which were apparently not always performed before his death: the third version of the *Johannespassion*, consisting of adjustments to the best score which were never transferred to the parts, is an example. It is possible, therefore, that even source "evidence" from the late period may not indicate an actual performance; the whole of the B minor Mass was probably never performed under Bach's direction, despite its completion well before his eventual infirmity and death. Also, the quantity of music by other composers (including the *Lukaspassion*) which Bach copied during this last portion of his life need not be taken to represent certain evidence that those works —especially the ones preserved in score only—were performed by him.

The chronology above owes its existence to the work of German scholars, especially Dr. Alfred Dürr, Professor Georg von Dadelsen, Dr. Werner Neumann and his assistant and successor Hans-Joachim Schulze.

Index of Bach's Works
Cantatas

Italics denotes a main reference

Motets

Latin Church Music

Other Choral Works

Instrumental Works